The
Discipline
of Hope

Learning from
a Lifetime
of Teaching

Herbert Kohl

Simon & Schuster

SIMON & SCHUSTER
Rockefeller Center
1230 Avenue of the Americas
New York, NY 10020

SIMON & SCHUSTER and colophon are registered trademarks
of Simon & Schuster Inc.

Designed by Levavi & Levavi

Manufactured in the United States of America

1   3   5   7   9   10   8   6   4   2

Library of Congress Cataloging-in-Publication Data

Kohl, Herbert R.
The discipline of hope : learning from a lifetime of teaching / Herbert Kohl.
p.   cm.
1. Kohl, Herbert R.   2. Teachers—United States—Biography.
3. Effective teaching—United States.   4. Teacher-student
relationships—United States.   5. Socially handicapped children—
Education (Elementary)—United States.   I. Title.
LA2317.K64A3 1998
371.1'0092—dc21   97-39214   CIP
ISBN 0-684-81412-9

To Judy
with love

Contents

Chapter 5: Fresh Waters Are Ever Flowing

Introduction:
A Lifetime of Teaching

It is inconceivable how many things children are capable of, if
all the opportunities of instructing them were laid hold of,
with which they themselves supply us.

> —Benjamin Franklin, "Proposals Relating to the
> Education of Youth in Pennsylvania" (1749)

This book is an attempt to share my life as a teacher and reaffirm
the obligation of providing all young people with the richest, most
challenging, and best-crafted education imaginable. The book does
not provide a simple formula for school change, nor does it presume
to address all of the current problems of American education. It
does, however, suggest some specific ways in which education can
work, especially for poor children. It is about education "on the
ground"—about the daily, intimate, and complex interaction between teacher, students, and the content and process of learning. It
is also about what I have come to call the discipline of hope: the
refusal to accept limits on what your students can learn or on what
you, as a teacher, can do to facilitate learning.

Providing hope to young people is the major challenge of teaching. Through engaging the minds and imaginations of children, teachers can help children develop the strength, pride, and sensitivity they
need to engage the world, and not to despair when things seem

stacked against them. Even though hope is not sufficient to provide a good life or even guarantee survival, it is a necessity. However, to teach hope you yourself must be hopeful, must believe that all children have a right to learn and can indeed learn.

When I began teaching in the 1960s I felt that education had an important role to play in solving some of the major social problems in the United States. Many of us believed that the civil rights movement would lead to the elimination of racism, and that the Poor People's Campaign would make a significant contribution to the elimination of poverty. We were wrong about racism and poverty but certainly not about the central role of education in providing hope and opportunity for many people.

Just recently, I have had a number of conversations with old teaching friends, people whose careers are as long as mine and who continue to teach with energy and love for their students. A few of them have expressed a loss of hope, a sense that our society is undoing much of the work they do, that the defunding of public education is symptomatic of the abandonment of the children of the poor. They worry that an effective and creative education is no longer a route to a decent job and life, and they express dismay at the cynicism of many of their students.

They are not wrong. It is not easy to teach at a time when society as a whole does not honor its young and when the young, understanding this, show no respect for the adult world. However, there is no more important time to teach well, and to reach the sources of hope in one's own life in order to project that hope to one's students.

For me, the source of hope lies in teaching itself, hard work requiring ingenuity, patience, and a focus on what is effective with children. At its core, it is not mechanical or technological. I have always thought of myself as a teacher the way other people think of themselves as gardeners, painters, composers, mathematicians, and poets. I am a craftsperson of learning, working to refine what I do with young people to the point where it is both free and structured, spontaneous and disciplined, innovative and classical, fun and very difficult.

I've seen many changes in schooling and society since I became actively engaged in education in 1954 while a student at the Bronx High School of Science; and yet, on reflection, I see that I have also witnessed so many persistent—even intensified—problems and bogus solutions that it's not clear how much we have progressed since that time. The *New York Daily News* published a series of articles on the high schools in New York City in February and March of 1954. They began with these headlines: "Teen-Age Terror Stalks City Streets, Cows Teachers, Trains Kids for Crime" (February 28, 1954); "Fear Balks Exposure of School Terrors" (March 1, 1954); "Dope Pushers Prowl Schools for Teen Prey" (March 5, 1954); and "A Teacher Has to Be Tough or Be Trampled On" (March 3, 1954). The series was described by the author, Jess Stearn, as addressing "the growth and protection of future public enemies in New York City's public schools and the terror which infects teachers, students, and parents alike." It was accompanied by a series of photos: menacing students hanging out in the hall, soliciting sex, holding switchblade knives, smoking, drinking beer during lunch hour. It's interesting that all the students depicted as thugs, gangsters, and other low types were white. Only later did it emerge that these photos were posed, with professional models, and that some of the incidents reported in the series had occurred as many as ten years before (retraction, published March 7, 1954). This didn't stop a public outcry on the need to reform the schools. A public forum was held on the subject, and the series' last article, entitled "How They Could Reform the Schools," was published Sunday, March 7, 1954, along with the retractions.

I was one of the student representatives at the forum. The debates we engaged in and the contradictory recommendations that emerged are still the stuff of educational struggle. One recommendation was "Get rid of 'permissive' discipline in 'progressive' education, where the student does as he pleases—until the teacher can no longer cope with him." Another was "Instill teachers with the need for maintaining a friendly, mutually respectful relationship with pupils—and not let them get the notion that children are a necessary evil."

These contrary views of the relationship between schools and children represent the poles of current debates about schooling. What is different is that we are now at a critical juncture in the history of public education: the very survival of free public education as a right and entitlement is in question. In those days, people were trying to patch up a system that everyone believed could be made to work. Now the belief in democracy is weaker, and to have hope for all children is often put down as naive and romantic.

The conflict between advocates of unquestioned adult authority and harsh discipline, on the one hand, and respect for students and parents (in particular those who are poor and culturally non-European) on the other is at the heart of current debates about school restructuring, testing, curriculum change, and multiculturalism. The 1950s attack on "progressive education" finds its echo in the present standards debate, in which high standards are often mistaken for high test scores. And 1950s conflict between parents and school authorities is reflected in current disagreements about who is accountable for school failure and who should control public education money.

When I began teaching the fifth and sixth grades in Harlem in 1962, I learned that the schools didn't work for my students, most of whom were poor and either African American or Puerto Rican. Most of what I had learned at teachers' college was irrelevant, and I found myself in the position of having to choose between experimenting with teaching or giving up on myself as a teacher and on my students as learners. Since the latter was not an option for me, I decided to explore new ways of teaching that would hook my students into learning. I looked to *them* for clues, listened and read what was available, and every once in a while ventured out into unknown territory myself. The specifics of these explorations, which have continued over the past thirty-five years, make up the substance of this book.

At that time I searched for experimental materials and new ideas and found that most of those available in the schools came from the post-*Sputnik* science and math curriculum projects supported by the Executive Branch of the White House under John F. Kennedy and later Lyndon Johnson. These led to the new math, physics, biology, and social studies curricula that were widely disseminated in the schools during the 1960s. Some of the material was floating around my elementary school. I tried to use it but discovered that, though the material was conceptually interesting, it was developed with no sense of how my children learned or of teachers' everyday lives and the demands made on us in public schools. It was all top-down material, coming mostly from university professors with no public school experience and certainly no experience teaching in poor and culturally diverse communities. I used what I could, but eventually abandoned the material in favor of things I made myself, borrowed from other teachers, or cobbled together from old textbooks and worksheets. I tried the new math, for example, but found that my fifth- and sixth-grade students couldn't make any sense of the abstract concepts they were asked to learn, while they did want to know how to calculate and understand the role of numbers (and especially money) in their lives. I had either to build a curriculum that related to them, or fail them because of someone else's idea of how and what they needed to learn.

What emerged from this experience was a conviction that if school change was to be truly effective it had to begin in classrooms and schools, with caring and creative teachers and administrators who would develop and test the materials out of concern for their students' learning. Useful change would not come from a government grant, a university-based project, or a national or state-mandated program.

Early in my career, I saw that teaching that did not respond to students' needs simply did not work. I also saw that rigid programs that depended upon heavy doses of phonics and rote learning led not merely to many students' failure, but to their confusion and discouragement as well. I began experimenting with more democratic and participatory ways of learning, and especially with imaginative writing. I wasn't the only teacher doing this; during the sixties and seventies many teachers were discovering the power of their students' voices and the importance of beginning with students' interests and experiences in order to prepare the ground for other, more sophisticated learning. Unfortunately, this strategy was often taken to mean simply centering learning on student interests—to me, a condescending way of limiting the scope of learning. This was not at all what we had in mind. Education has to be as demanding as it is giving. There are many things of value in the adult world, and it is our obligation as teachers to balance children's needs and interests with exposure to the social, cultural, and technological achievements that are our gifts to them.

The word "education" is derived from the Latin *educere,* which means "to lead, to draw out, to bring forth" and, by extension, "to rear, nurture, and foster growth." It is in this original sense, of one who draws young people out into encounters with what they do not yet know, while honoring what they do know, that I define myself as a teacher. For me, to be a teacher means to help students move toward a larger and continually expanding encounter with knowledge and experience, while also celebrating what they already know.

Listening to students' voices and responding to their interests meant giving up the authoritarian role of the teacher. I found myself much more at ease in dialogue with my students than in telling them what to do all the time. Through this work, and through the work of many other teachers during the sixties, there came to be a new conversation in education; it was not so much a movement as a different way of talking about children, education, and schools.

In those days, the energy students brought back to us teachers when we simply listened to them and responded to the content of their writing and the sensitivity of their conversation made many of us feel like explorers in new territories of learning. I have since learned that we were reinventing a tradition that reaches back to American progressive-education movements that developed as early as the 1840s.

To call what we were doing anti-authoritarian, though that was how the media characterized it, was too negative and gave no sense that central to our teaching were a positive pedagogy and a faith in our students' ability to learn if only the conditions were right. We believed that an emphasis on the students' own voices would lead to serious imaginative and intellectual work, especially for those students whose voices and communities were marginalized. As African American communities throughout the country voiced their needs and demanded respect for their intelligence, we found, on the more intimate scale of the classroom, our students doing the same thing.

The term we chose to describe this work was "open education." The word "open" stood for both a commitment to dialogue and an understanding that there were many roads to excellence, that no one method or type of education could suit all the diverse and complex communities or children in public schools.

Though there was no national organized open-education movement in the United States in the sixties and seventies, centers for open education sprang up all over the country. And many individual teachers and schools began to explore these practices, which were rooted in ideas of equity and justice emanating from the civil rights movement.

My books *36 Children* and *The Open Classroom* contributed to popularizing these ideas and gave me a wonderful chance, during the seventies, to travel around and meet other educators and community leaders who, in their own ways and in their own communities, were responding to the needs of children rather than forcing the children into rigid and predetermined adult molds. Open education thrived in the ambience and politics of the civil rights movement. The greater sense of free expression and participatory democracy, and especially the faith that everyone could participate in the economic growth of society, fueled a general belief that we needed all of our children and could, through education, bring them into a future in which their success would benefit everybody. In those days, everything I dreamed of for my students was consonant with what many people dreamed of for themselves and their own children. It was easy to imagine oneself as part of a majority of people who cared about each other and the health of the society as a whole. I did not anticipate the retreat from compassion that developed in the 1980s, or the economic stress produced by the global economy.

I have never thought of my ideas or work as anything but what any decent person would do if education was where he or she chose to place energy and love. I came to open education through my work in the classroom, and I find that many of the fundamental ideas developed in the sixties and seventies are still valid.

Open education was discussed, attacked, and advocated with passion; but on the ground, in the classroom, it was never widespread enough to affect U.S. education as a whole. It was under constant pressure, both from conservative educators and politicians and from central school bureaucrats who saw too much openness as a threat to their control of the system.

However, unexpected support for open education came from the federal government. I participated in the Experimental Schools Program of the U.S. Office of Education during the early 1970s and ran one of the schools, in Berkeley, for several years. The idea of the program was to provide federal support for school districts to develop a variety of types of school within the same system. The goal was to find a way for different educational structures to exist side by side, and to open up parental choice in learning within public school systems.

Though most of the experiments supported by the program were eliminated over the years when federal money dried up, in at least one city, Minneapolis, the open schools created under the Experimental Schools Program are still thriving and have lasted long enough to become a permanent feature of the system. I believe much of this success is due to John Davis, who was the superintendent of schools in Minneapolis when the experimental schools were established. He was smart enough to support most of the new open schools from the top while letting power devolve to the school sites and enabling people committed to open education actually have the freedom to do it. He understood the power of teachers taking control of and assuming responsibility for their work.

I am currently working with the same kind of program in the New York City public school system, but now there is wider support for autonomy and diversity within public school systems and, among many parents and community groups, there is greater educational sophistication. The lessons of the sixties and the seventies have not been forgotten and the mistakes, I hope, need not be repeated.

During the sixties I also became involved in developing programs that would support and honor children's imaginative writing. By centering these efforts on the voices of children and the process of imaginative writing, we could provide students with a basis for intellectual and social development rooted in their own experience and culture. As founding director of the Teachers and Writers Collaborative in 1966, I worked with teachers and writers to place creative expression at the center of the curriculum. Now, over thirty years later, Teachers and Writers serves over 10,000 students a year and has published dozens of books on the teaching of writing.

Although the terms of many of these conversations have changed, much of what critics of the public schools were saying in the sixties and seventies is now debated with even more passion. And there are few voices defending the public schools as presently constituted. During my career I have learned to listen carefully to the parents whose children I have served, and to make efforts to understand their values, aspirations, and cultures. This has led me to place diversity, multiculturalism, and cross-cultural communication at the center of my teaching, as well as to understand that no matter how precious my ideas seem to me, I have to measure them against the dreams, needs, and aspirations of the people I serve. This means, for example, that no matter how repugnant I find standardized testing, I must honor my students' need to do well on the tests, and their parents' demand that they be prepared for tests even if the tests are biased. This is mediated education in the real world—that is, trying to change the way education is done without sacrificing the future of one's students in the process. It is very difficult, because it involves negotiating the very fuzzy border between helping children adapt to a dysfunctional system and helping them maintain their integrity and risk being damaged or marginalized for trying to change the system. As a teacher I am always negotiating, moving between possibility and vision.

Listening to my students and to the voices of their cultures and communities has led me to become active in changing the schools through redoing the curriculum. Cultural diversity, the history and voices of women and gay and lesbian people, and the contributions of working people to the making of our country have come to be part of my idea of what democratic education must embrace. I have worked with many other people to make that happen. Even more than open education, the reshaping of curriculum content has succeeded in broadening educational thinking about what children ought to know.

In addition the issue of choice within the public schools—which dates back at least to the sixties, when many parents and teachers decided that they and not some centralized bureaucracy should have control over education on a school and community level—has broadened to include such issues as restructuring school systems themselves, enabling charter schools, and issuing school vouchers; on the far right, the legitimacy of public education as an entitlement is even questioned. What began as an argument for community control of schools in a progressive context has become a major political debate about the future of public education.

Over the years there have been times of despair as well as times of hope. I look back on teaching through times of ghetto riots, of running a high school in Berkeley during the late sixties and early seventies, of being in the classroom during the Vietnam era and the Reagan years of "benign" neglect of the poor and the consequent disintegration of urban communities. I remember the earliest school computers—they had keyboards and no monitors—and have been taught about interactive media by my students, who entered the electronic world quicker than I did. Through all this I've tried to make my teaching both rooted in its time and beyond and bigger than its time. I want to help young people know who and where they are, but I also want them to share what other people know, what work they do, what wonders people have already created in science, culture, and the arts. I want students to explore learning through doing but also through reflection and hard study. I want them to learn hard skills in soft ways. Most of all, I want my students, wherever I teach, to feel part of a compassionate learning community where they are honored as individuals, where they respect each other, and where they respect and love learning itself. In other words, I want it all. I don't get it, of course, and the limits on what can be accomplished in any classroom are the challenge that keeps me teaching knowing that there is always more that can be done.

In this book I've described times in my teaching career when I've learned how to teach better. This book is not a theoretical tract on education, nor is it an autobiography. It is about an ongoing love affair with teaching and about the wonderful growth that can emerge when adults and children come together for the sake of learning.

Chapter 1

SETTING OUT

They sought it with thimbles, they sought it with care;
They pursued it with forks and hope;
They threatened its life with a railway-share;
They charmed it with smiles and soap.

        —Lewis Carroll, "The Hunting of the Snark"

TO NOT KNOW

About ten years ago one of my students left this poem on my desk:

Is a leaf smart?
Does it keep secrets,
   or
Is there a secret
I don't already know?

No
I know every secret
that roams this earth,
   but one,
the secret that breaks my heart.
To not know what I did wrong.

Eva wrote the poem when she was eight, but it might just as easily have been written by an eighteen-year-old. It is not a child's poem so much as a deep sigh that could come from any of us at any age. I think a lot about what she might have meant by "the secret that breaks my heart. / To not know what I did wrong." Those lines express vulnerability and guilt compounded by a profound uncertainty about how the world works. They are sad and, coming from Eva, who projects strength and hope despite having lived through very difficult times, remind me of how susceptible we all are to events, influences, and circumstances we don't understand. However, the lines are also an expression of faith in education, since to give such weight to the phrase "To not know" is also to honor knowledge as a source of liberating strength.

I often wonder whether an unarticulated and sometimes unwarranted faith in the power of knowing isn't one of the central characteristics of childhood—a characteristic that extends into adolescence, and, for some people, into all of life. I think of my aunt Addie who, at eighty-five, lives alone in Co-op City in the Bronx and tells me that she is learning new things in order to keep alive. These days she is struggling with a fading memory, so she memorizes things she never knew before: state capitals, birds, and animals; the names and lengths of the rivers of the world. I asked why she does this and she told me that knowing more is the key to surviving difficult circumstances. Learning is a confirmation of her will and identity, a proof to her that at eighty-five she can still grow.

Addie is one of my most faithful and critical readers, and her comments always bring me back to my own work and struggles. It is harder to teach and nurture hope for young people now than it was thirty-six years ago, when I began teaching in the New York City public elementary schools. This thought occurred to me on a recent trip to New York. I had some time to kill and decided to wander around Grand Central Station as I used to do as a teenager. It was rush hour and the main hall was full of people charging from one destination to another, some making stops at a newsstand, a dry cleaner's, or a fast-food outlet. People studiously avoided looking at each other, clutched their purses and briefcases, and navigated the space with the purposeful intensity of bees heading home with full loads of pollen. I felt deliciously out of place. I found a café, ordered a double espresso, and watched people.

After about fifteen minutes I noticed a peripheral disturbance in the rhythm and movement around me. Five boys, one of whom could not have been more than seven while the others were around nine and ten, wandered through the crowd. They stopped at a newsstand and spoke to a vendor, who handed them something—candy, maybe, or money—and then chased them away. The boys made for the men's room, entered, then emerged in less time than it would have taken to undo their zippers.

The five children were African American or Latino. Three of them bumped into a person and then ran off to meet the other two, who had just emerged from a tourist gift shop. Then the five of them passed by me. Four were talking to each other and the fifth, the youngest, had fallen behind and was slowly following them, getting lost in the crowd. All of a sudden he stopped, put his thumb in his mouth, looked slowly around, and then, as if panic had overcome him, ran straight through the crowd until he joined his friends. They kept moving, ignoring him, and he trailed behind, sucking his thumb.

The image of that child has haunted me for the past months. At that moment I saw those boys, as I've seen all my students over the years, as complex mysteries, people who know only the smallest amount about themselves and what they are capable of, partially formed individuals with semi-defined surfaces and hidden talents, interests, and resources. I know as much about these boys, who haven't the slightest idea of my existence, as I do about most of my students before meeting them on the first day of class. Perhaps I know more.

I can imagine each of them in my class and speculate about how to draw them into a circle of learners so that the energy and intelligence they put into predatory wanderings can be transformed into positive searches that nurture their own learning. Yet how can we entice them into places of learning? I believe that the climate of hope that informed the beginning of my teaching career has dissipated or been replaced by cynicism and rejection, not just in public debate over the schools, but in the hearts and minds of the children.

Teaching begins as an encounter among strangers. This is particularly true for beginning teachers. When I began my first full year of teaching in 1962, the year I wrote about in *36 Children,* I was a stranger to my students and their community and was quite aware of it. I grew up in a working-class Jewish community in the Bronx; attended Harvard and then Teachers College, Columbia, both overwhelmingly white institutions in the late 1950s and early 1960s; and did my student teaching and substitute teaching in schools that had a mixture of white and Puerto Rican students. However, during my first full year of teaching at P.S. 103, all thirty-six of my students were African American or Caribbean. The community was African American, bustling with all the complex and, to me, unfamiliar institutions of African American life. I remember a bounty of churches and mosques, some in storefronts or basements, others in imposing stone edifices. There were offices of antipoverty and community-based organizations, including the Harlem Tenants Committee, which during the 1964 New York World's Fair in Flushing Meadows, Queens, ran its own "World's Worst Fair" calling attention to the terrible living conditions in Harlem. There were beauty parlors and barbershops, bars, candy stores, small restaurants, coffee shops, a diner, and an occasional family-run supermarket or bodega. The community was poor but cohesive, and many of the families had lived there for several generations.

P.S. 103, however, was a monument to the nineteenth-century commitment to public education that had barely survived into the mid–twentieth century. My mother had attended the school sometime between 1915 and 1925, when the community was Jewish and Italian. By the time I got to teach there, the imposing five-story brick building was in a state of terminal disarray. The high ceilings of my classroom, which was on the top floor, were falling down in several places. The room had little alcoves where bay windows looked out over the brownstones below. In two places you could see through the walls to the external structure of the building. The tongue-and-groove wooden floors looked as if they hadn't been cleaned in a half century, and the desks—thirty-five of them for my thirty-six children —had once been bolted to the floor. Half of them had come unscrewed and slid easily across the room, leaving track marks in the floor. Pushed into the corner was an old grand piano with a fifth of its keys gone. It was soiled with plaster that had come down from the ceiling, and piled with old and torn textbooks, wall charts, and the tattered remains of what must once have been beautiful cloth maps that could be hung at the blackboard. Half of the blackboard was usable. From my perspective as a twenty-five-year-old first-year teacher, this classroom was very exciting. It may not have been much, but it was mine.

As it turned out, the piano, the alcoves by the bay windows, and the unbolted desks were blessings. They helped me overcome my biggest problems: getting to know the children and getting them to trust me. They provided me with some of the first experiences that led me to a critical understanding: that what often seem like obstacles to learning and potential distractions from it are in fact the keys to making connections with students.

Take the piano, for instance. At first, instead of thinking of all the wonderful music we could make in the classroom, I thought of how to keep it locked away from the children, or how to use it as a reward for other, more "serious" learning, such as reading and math. I worried about students sneaking over to it and making noise to distract me and the rest of the class. I worried about control, about my planned curriculum, about what other teachers and my principal would think if they heard kids playing around with the piano during reading time.

However, during the first few weeks of school my students put me to the test with the piano. It was irresistible to two children in particular: Larry and Ellen. *Everything* seemed irresistible to Larry, except for sitting in his desk and working. During the course of a morning he and his unbolted desk would migrate from one side of the room to the other and often make a stop next to the piano, where he'd sneak a tune.

As for Ellen, the other children wanted her to sing for them; they begged me to let them come in the classroom at lunchtime and listen to music and sing and dance. They had heard her in church and at parties and said she was fabulous.

I was not prepared for Larry's tunefulness, Ellen's singing, or the articulate way in which my students asked me to do reasonable things that nevertheless would offend the administration and were not part of the sixth-grade curriculum. I was tested by my students before I had enough craft or experience to make informed decisions. Instead I acted on intuition and curiosity and asked Larry to play and sing a tune for the class, and helped the students plan a time for Ellen to sing and for them all to listen to music in the classroom. (I wasn't allowed to let the children into the classroom during lunch and was too new at the schooling game to know how to get around the rules.)

The piano became a center of learning and a social center for the children rather than a dumping ground for old textbooks. Over the first few months the same thing happened with the alcoves. They became private areas for reading, for small-group work, or just for gossip. As the school year developed we became like an extended family for whom formal learning, informal learning, and just hanging out and sharing time and conversation filled the day. It was not chaotic, yet each step we took toward being relaxed with each other was shaky and clumsy, like a baby learning to walk.

I had to learn how to deal with cursing and fighting in a way that would not lead to permanent warfare between me and some of the children. My intention was to find a way to keep everyone involved in our class as a community; I knew that neither punishment nor admonishment worked, and that sending students to the principal or depriving them of privileges didn't solve problems but rather created pockets of organized resistance to learning. I didn't know then what *would* work, so I fell back on a combination of my belief in democratic processes and in the curative power of writing.

In November of that first year there were rumblings among groups of students. The conflicts threatened to blow up. I didn't know who belonged to what clique, or anything else about the history of the conflict among the children. It seems, according to student writing I've saved, that on November 14 there was an incident serious enough for me to call a trial in the class. I had been reading about experiments in democratic schooling, such as those described by Homer Lane in *The Children's Commonwealth,* and I decided there was nothing to lose and perhaps a lot to gain by instituting a trial. I had no idea who had done what to whom, and amid the screaming and threats of fights I wouldn't find out. Besides, even if I did find out, doing so wouldn't get to the larger problem of finding ways to adjudicate disputes without disrupting learning or excluding children.

There was one thing, however, that I had already begun to understand as a teacher: moments of tension and conflict can be turned into occasions for learning if managed sensitively. I realized that having a trial was an opportunity to teach the complexities and virtues of a jury system. If the goal became to teach about our system of justice in the context of resolving a problem, rather than to find guilt and institute punishment, the negativity in the class might be turned into greater understanding of civil and community life, both in the classroom and in the children's futures.

I spent time explaining the jury trial system, including such notions as reasonable doubt, jury polling, testimony, proof, and evidence. I also had the contending students choose attorneys and prepare cases, had the whole class select a jury, and even appointed a court reporter. Then, after three or four days of preparation that took up about three-quarters of an hour a day, we had a trial. By this time the conflict seemed to have died down and there was no longer a threat of all-out warfare among the students.

Here are some of the students' comments on the trial:

Rachael
Wed. Afternoon at 1:30 my class had a trial. My teacher Mr. Kohl, was the judge. Some children were selected to be the jury. The two defendants were Belinda C. and Joyce. Belinda's lawyer was Sam, and Joyce's lawyer was Ruth.

It started when someone said Ellen, and Theresa had notty hair. There were witnesses for Joyce and Belinda. Joyce won the case.

I think the whole case was ridiculous. But I also think the jury made a good decision.

Connie   *November 15 1962*

COURT'S DISCUSSION
Yesterday we had a court discussion as you all know it of course was between Belinda and Joyce and you wanted to know my opinion well you think Belinda was wrong not everybody but almost the whole class except for a few others I think she was wrong because I how Joyce is you might not Think so but I almost know her as much as she knows herself (and you know much she knows herself) and she's a very nice girl I think she is (except for a few other people on her side which is one or two) but Belinda is very rude and kinda complicated child and she's always starting something or in something that she don't know the first thing about and always starting fights or something I'm not trying to say that she's not better than anybody else but she's kinda you know coo coo and doesn't know what she's talking about half of the time. And if Joyce talks about somebody (but

she really doesn't) it in a nice way of saying they're nice or pretty or you know! But Belinda every time I look over there she's running her trap (and so and so and so and this and that and bla bla bla she's always talking about somebody. maybe I'll stop looking over there and think of her as a nice person.

Belinda

I think the trial was not fair because the jury was prejudiced because all of them said I was guilty and I wasn't guilty. Many of them said I was right until I accused them of being prejudiced. And they know I was right that is why they took that vote.

Ruth

I think the Trail was very fair. I made up a story about two woman one woman's name was Clara and the other's name was Phillis. One day Clara was putting her garbage in Phillis' yard. Now Phillis saw her but said it was nothing. Clara kep doing it and the more Phillis kept it in her the more Clara put in. Phillis began to turn *pale* and then. Everyone was looking at her and wondering what was wrong. She wouldn't say a word of it not even to her husband. She got so sick of it 'til she had to take the case to court. The jury listened and said the case was dismissed. Phillis won, and Clara had to pay $200.00 fine because of littering. I think the guilty person should be made to pay five cents fine.

I wasn't on Brenda Thacker's side or Belinda's. How my name was in it was beyond me. P.S. Mr. Kohl, if you were there what would you have done?

Sandra

I think that wasn't a fair trail. You was on Joyce's side. The whole class seems like they dosen't like Belinda but I do I don't care if you don't like me and Belinda or Janette but I do you talk nice to the other kids but don't nice to us if we say something you jump down our thouts. Mr. Kohl I know you believe Joyce and all her friends so you don't have to hide it because me and Belinda Now and I still say that wasn't a fair trial the kids don't like Belinda that why they charge us guilty.

Fred

I think the most important thing of our trial was when the dession was made. and when we dug down deep and got the facts which Samuel and Joyce dug down and got.

The most troubling aspect of the trial was Sandra's comments. Was I playing favorites? Was there some deep division in the class that I was insensitive to and that affected the comfort with which some students learned? How complicit was I with the tensions within the group? Frankly, I had no way to answer these questions, and I was very sensitive to wanting all of the students to like me. I now know that desire for approval is characteristic of many caring young teachers. It can be helpful in giving students who have a history of rejection in school a feeling of being welcome and important, but it can also make the teacher vulnerable to manipulation by youngsters who will try to charm him or her into letting them not learn.

In those days I didn't explicitly understand the nature of the personal bonds that have to be created in order for serious learning to take place, but I was determined to become an effective teacher and brought everything I knew and cared about to bear upon teaching that class. In 1962, for me, that meant creating a resolutely Eurocentric curriculum. I wanted my students to like me; I wanted us to trust each other; and I wanted the classroom to be a nonviolent place, but that wasn't enough. Imaginative engagement with ideas, and the development of literacy in both reading and math were and continue to be at the center of my work with young people. No amount of good feeling is adequate without that pedagogical dimension, without students actually knowing more and being able to do more at the end of a school year than they could at the beginning.

Before coming to P.S. 103 in September 1962, I had spent six months—January to June—teaching fifth grade at P.S. 145 on the Upper West Side of Manhattan. During that time I became convinced that text-based and workbook-based learning would simply not do for much more than memorization of disconnected information. Such rote learning didn't work with many of my students, anyway. I had to find out how to spark excitement in the classroom, and at 103 I found two ways, one based in the children's own experience and the other based in Greek and Mesopotamian mythology.

I discovered the power of rooting learning in what students know outside of school, of tying what I teach to what they understand of their own lives and experience. Early in the school year one of the students—Rachael, I think—came up to my desk before class and told me she couldn't do any homework the previous night because there was a fight outside and she was scared. Another child corroborated her story and said the cops tried to break up the fight but beat up the wrong people. A third student, Fred, told me his cousin was hurt in the fight and had to sit for hours bleeding in the emergency room of the hospital.

A few days later Fred and Larry handed me this paper:

> Last night on 117th St. Liebowitz collected the rent. They told him not to come himself but he came for many years. The junkies got him last night. He wouldn't give them the money so they shot him and took it. They was cops and people runny all over the roofs and streets.
>
> There were people from the news and an ambulance took Liebowitz.

After reading this, I decided to share it with the class, who affirmed that everything was true. In fact, the reality was even worse: 117th Street between Madison and Fifth Avenues, the worst block in the neighborhood, was known as "junkie's paradise," and several of my students lived in the midst of this twenty-four-hour chaos and violence. As we discussed what it was like to live on 117th I found myself becoming silent and respectful. The children's stories didn't seem like horror stories so much as sad tales of resignation or heroic narratives of survival. Even though I grew up in a working-class neighborhood in the Bronx I did not know what it was like to live so close to the edge. I realized how free I had been as a child from the burden of constant wariness and worries about imminent death.

As an assignment I asked the children to write about their block. Over thirty papers were turned in, the most ever for a homework assignment. Perhaps this was because I had asked them to write about something they knew and wanted to talk about. Phyllis began her paper: "My block is the most terrible block I've seen." Nancy wrote "My block is the worse block you ever saw people getting killed or stabbed, men and women in building's taking dope."

Not all the papers were completely negative. Frances wrote: "From Madison Avenue to about the middle of the block the houses are kept clean. The back yards are kept swept and the stoops are clean. I like my building and block." Other students also indicated that they lived on islands of stability and decency in the midst of a violent and depressed neighborhood. What struck me was how life had forced adult awareness and sensitivity upon the children. They were not protected from death; they saw or lived poverty. Rats and garbage were themes in their experience, accompanying all their attempts to create more harmonious lives. One student invited me to come and see the reality for myself; another described how she stayed holed up in her apartment.

My follow-up to the children's responses was to ask them to write about what they would do if they could change their block. I wanted to tap into their dreams as well as their immediate reality. Phyllis's response was full of the rage all the children felt about what they were forced to live with:

> If I could change my block I would stand on Madison Avenue and throw nothing but Teargas in it. I would have all of the people I liked to get out of the block and then I would become very tall and have big hands and with my big hands I would take all of the narcotic people and pick them up with my hands and throw them in the Oceans and Rivers too. I would let the people I like move into the projects so they could tell their friends they live in a decent block. If I could do this you would never see 117st again.

The students' responses to these two assignments entirely changed my plans for that school year. Originally I had intended to take a fresh approach to the material in the standard curriculum. We would study the frontier, the industrial revolution in the United States, and world geography in hands-on ways. My impulse was not so much to reject the curriculum as to transform it from a mechanical and rigid sequence into an interesting series of projects based on inquiry and experience. I wanted to motivate my students to learn what the system wanted them to, only in a more creative way. I did not intend to raise issues such as poverty, racism, sexism, and pervasive violence. I wanted to be a creative teacher, and it was the students' responses that moved me to understand that I couldn't be one without also being militant and passionate in defense of their right to a decent childhood and to the hope of a welcoming place for them in the adult world.

My class was 6-1. That meant that of the seven sixth-grade classes in the school they were academically the top. Yet many of the students acted as if learning were their enemy. They ran around the classroom with abandon, interrupted class discussions, and in general tried to make my life miserable. I noticed that although most of them could read on a fourth- or fifth-grade level, and some—like Rachael, Fred, and Larry—could read just about anything you put before them, none of them wrote well. There were also a few students who could barely read at all. Except for Rachael, the children had formal mathematical skills way behind what the system expected of sixth-graders.

My pride and my expectations for my students pressured me to find a way to have the class acquire skills and exceed the expected grade levels. Never in my whole teaching career has it occurred to me that there are limits to what any student can do. The limitations I perceive are to do with how ingenious or sensitive I can be in devising the right situation or discovering the right materials to reach into my students. I am hopelessly optimistic when it comes to believing in people's capacity to grow and learn. Such optimism has occasionally led conservative educators to accuse me of romanticism, but I readily accept any accusations of being positive and hopeful in the service of my students.

That first year of teaching, I was torn between being creative within the system, and following my instincts and the children's responses to what I presented to them. There were no guidelines or formulas to follow, but the students' voices spoke to me so strongly that the authority of my supervisors, the instructions in teachers' manuals, and the practices of my colleagues weren't collectively strong enough to keep me from listening to those voices, learning from them, and then teaching to my conscience. Besides, the school around me was a shambles. Students roamed the halls; many of the teachers screamed themselves hoarse every day or simply gave up teaching and presented the children with coloring books and crayons to keep them seated and silent. Racism was rampant, though not explicitly articulated except in the teachers' lunchroom, which, after a few encounters with bitter and defeated colleagues, I avoided. Sticking within the system didn't have much to recommend itself to a young teacher.

It was also easier for me, in 1962, to break with the system than it might be for beginning teachers these days. It was the heyday of the civil rights movement in the South, and many of us new teachers considered ourselves part of the northern branch of the movement. We worked in communities that were as segregated, impoverished, and victimized as any in the South. P.S. 103 had over a thousand students, only one of whom was white. Once he graduated, the school never had another white student. It was torn down a few years later and replaced by a new building renamed P.S. 79. So far as I know P.S. 79 has never had a (non-Latino) white student.

The words of the students obsessed me. What was my responsibility when they hurt so much? I couldn't change their block but could I give *them* power to change it in the future, or the skills to leave and to succeed in the larger city? *Should* they leave? What would happen to the children left behind? How could I change the whole school, when I didn't even know what to do in my own classroom?

At times I felt these questions were interfering with my teaching. How could I focus on spelling tests, on introducing new concepts in mathematics—on the industrial revolution—when bigger moral issues were untouched? I tried to talk to my colleagues about my dilemma, but it was impossible. None of them wanted to talk about teaching or children with a first-year teacher. Some of them warned me not to raise questions that might upset people. As it was, I had been involuntarily transferred to the school and didn't have tenure. I decided it was best to shut up, at least until I could get union protection.

By Halloween, I knew I had to do something for my children. In many ways, that Halloween was the most important day of my life. The school day itself was uneventful, except that the students were more restless than usual. There was an air of anticipation. I sensed an unusual glee in the kids that morning. People were waiting for the night—for the celebrations, the costumes, the tricks even more than for the treats. My students told me that they ran around with socks full of chalk and marked up everyone in sight. Anthony and John told me about going up to the rooftops and throwing water and "stuff" down at people partying in the streets.

I had my own fantasies of Halloween in Harlem, a white man's fantasies mixing fear and admiration. I wanted to stay in the community and be part of the celebration, and indeed I was invited to a few parties by my students' parents. But apprehension about being stranded in Harlem at night got the best of me, so I retreated to my apartment farther down Madison Avenue, where I felt safer.

Back on Nineteenth Street, I spent the evening reading papers and trying to figure out a response to "My Block." At about ten I got restless and went out for a few beers. On the way down from my apartment—a fifth-floor walkup—I noticed that someone had moved into the vacant apartment on the first floor. The new tenant was at the door saying good-bye to friends. I got a glimpse of her face, decided I wanted to know her, and vowed to knock on her door and trick or treat if her light was still on when I got back from the bar.

It was, and I did.

Teaching tales poured out that night, and stories of her return to New York after a year of traveling in Europe. Perhaps it was that passion and my obsession with the children that moved her. To this day, thirty-some years and three grown children of our own later, I don't know what originally attracted her to me. However, my thirty-six children very quickly became hers as well. I read my students' papers to Judy and began to formulate a strategy to respond to what the children were teaching me.

There are many ways to respond to the truths children can tell in school if trust develops in the classroom. One might be to shape the curriculum around neighborhood studies, collect local oral histories, and become involved in community-based organizations. Another might be to examine and celebrate the children's cultural heritage. A third would be to directly confront racism, explicitly teach civil rights, and figure out a way to engage in particular struggles over equity and justice.

I tried a bit of each of those methods, but without confidence or direction. Finally I turned to a fourth, inspired by the second of my exercises, "What I Would Do If I Could Change My Block." My idea was to rethink, with my students, the creation of society and the potential for people to live in groups governed by compassion and mutual aid. I would begin with Egypt and Mesopotamia (I didn't know anything about ancient Chinese civilization), and then focus on Greece. I was intrigued by the idea of a pantheistic universe in which many gods with differing powers fought, made love, and created trouble for people and for themselves. I guessed that a world in which ideas such as revenge, justice, respect, deceit, honor, pride, and dignity were played out in mythical adventures would appeal to my students, whose lives were laden with moral dilemmas and social problems. Moreover, Egypt, Mesopotamia, and, more fully, Greece, which I knew more about and had visited, might give us intellectual distance from the children's immediate problems and allow them to think and speak and write about issues without being overwhelmed by them and giving up.

There was another, crucial bonus for centering the curriculum on Greece. I had noticed that, though the great majority of my students had mastered basic phonic skills, they had major difficulties comprehending material that was supposed to be on their grade level. Vocabulary was the main problem. The children could speak and think on mature and complex levels, but they did not have a mastery of the standard language of ideas and emotions. When they encountered such language in a text they panicked, and the other reading skills they had developed were of no use to them. Guessing could take them just so far; then they were lost. I reasoned that, given the Greek roots of much English intellectual language, I could build vocabulary through an encounter with word-origin stories and indirectly increase my students' reading power.

My vocabulary lessons worked. I remember explaining to the class that the word "sarcasm" meant "flesh cutting," and referred to the Greek Dionysiac ritual of stripping the flesh from a living person. For a week, everything negative was described as "sarcastic," and we had some wonderful discussions in class about how bad a comment had to be to qualify as sarcasm rather than mild joking or simple ridicule. I followed up that lesson by introducing words such as "skepticism" and "irony," and then "hyperbole" and "metaphor."

One of my great pleasures that year was to watch the children's faces light up with recognition as they came upon a word from the vocabulary list in their reading. They expressed the joy that comes from being able to use something you have learned, and I felt like a gardener who has prepared his soil well.

Vocabulary, however, was just a small part of the program. I wanted the children to imagine different, better worlds, to think about their city and their block as temporary, as made by people who could also remake them. I created a curriculum to tease their imaginations into hope for themselves and for the communities in which they would later live. I wanted to connect, through a study of the early history of humanity, to the current civil rights movement. My curriculum was about the making of culture, and for me the civil rights movement was about the remaking of culture. In both cases everyone's effort was required to make the world better; I wanted my students to feel that their voices counted and that their intelligence and ingenuity were important.

I began my teaching career fully committed to both a Eurocentric curriculum and civil rights. I did not see them as contradictory. On the contrary, they enriched each other through the study of society-making. My use of Greek mythology and culture was neither didactic nor normative. We did not memorize facts about the Greeks, or drill and practice the names of Greek gods and goddesses. Nor did I waste time praising Greece as superior to other cultures. To me it was one among many I could have chosen as a starting point, but it was one that I knew well and that excited me.

I did not teach Greece in order to produce experts on Greek culture. My goal was to draw my students into the creation of new myths and the development of their own social visions. I encouraged them to rewrite old tales and change them. The goal was to have them draw upon their own experience and, through the structures of Greek mythology, classical fables, and other traditional genres, develop larger conceptions of the world.

Writing was a vehicle for exploring thoughts and feelings. It was a starting point, a way of setting things down so we could talk about them, dramatize them, and discuss how the world was and how we might make it different. The sheer volume of my students' writing, combined with the variety and complexity of thought it contained, elicited some unanticipated depth of response that required a major shift of my early lesson plans. The students at first responded out of their own experience when they talked about their block. When they wrote of reconstructing their environment, hope was drawn into the mix. Now, through mythology, fables, poetry, autobiography, adventure, science fiction, and mysteries, their imaginations became inflamed and a hunger to write seized them.

I, too, had developed writing fever and began work on a book of my own. In the classroom I let writing time grow and grow, until there were days with no math or social studies or science. The students wrote about everything. Then we spoke about their work, in terms not of grammar and pronunciation but of substance and content. In February, before we moved into a new school building, the children wrote about their dreams for the new school; then we talked about what a good school might be like.

New School February 4, 1963

Delores
The changes I expect to be by going to the new school; Is that our room will look like something + have a new set of rules. The third change I expect to have is to change from a cold lunch of beans. Then quit the writing on the walls + keep us sanitary and clean! Enough is enough + I'm just fed up with not only beans with some teachers that are employed; Like Mr. Charles in room 401 + the teacher in 414.

Gregory
I expect many changes in the school but not much in me. I think the yard would not be so crowded. There will need more monitors in the yard, an office. Some kids will learn more some will learn less.

Theresa
First thing I am going to thank God that they're getting out of 103. I expect we won't have no beans and glue soup. I expect that we won't be on the top floor. I expect that we'll go home earlier and go to lunch earlier and when it is cold out side they will let us come in on line. And some other children will get a chance to be monitors. I expect we'll have movies in the classroom I expect new desk and chairs to write and sit on. I expect no writing on walls and I hope to graduate.

Belinda.
I hope that in the knew school we will have a better program. One of the changes I would like is that we would have more activities. Many of the small children would have a separate play yard. It would be nice if we could have cake sales, parties where the children join in so we can feel we helped the school. I hope down in the lunch room we have a change of things. Like a new group of lunch ladies who don't steal the lunch. I don't think we should use spoons so much I think we should have knife and fork. I think we should have different kind of dessert

Connie
I expect P.S. 103 to fall and if it doesn't it has to be a miracle because people's great grandmothers were going to this school and I expect the new school to be like Cooper a little bit and in every way the food has to be nothing like 103. I don't expect to see children outside or inside of the school or street fighting all the time. I don't expect to see drawing all over the school or writing all over the walls and the most thing I don't expect to see which is disgrace, mess in the toilets that isn't flushed.

Regina
In the new school I expect the children to learn how to read and learn how to do arithmetic and learn how to spell more words. I expect the children not to tear down the whole building and not write on the walls, and not to throw paper, candy papers thumb tacks and I expect me to study more harder so that I can pass all the final examinations and try to graduate so that I can go to junior high school and I expect for to learn more arithmetic so that when I get in the seventh grade I might know some of the arithmetic. I expect to get more then we usually get like franks, rice, cornbread, chicken, greens, mash potatoes, sweet potatoes instead of beans.

Nancy
I expect that we won't have to walk up all these flights anymore. I expect to get into a new school and graduate I expect that we will get a better lunch. I expect that we will have new and better equipment. I expect that we will have new chairs and tables to sit on. I expect to have a new gymnasium. I expect to have a new auditorium. I expect to get hot lunches. I expect to be

served on plates instead of tin trays and plastic bowls and saucers. I expect to have napkins instead of paper towels.

I hadn't paid much attention to the lunchroom before reading the children's papers, but I decided to spend time there the next week. The children were right. Their soup was ladled out of what looked like large garbage cans. Each child was given a bowl and a soup spoon and had to line up for a bowl of gruel. It was absolutely Dickensian. The kitchen workers were angry and demoralized; the children rushed to finish, and if they took too long their spoons and bowls were seized from them. And the "lunchroom" itself was just benches in a dismal room with a few stoves. It was exactly how children were fed in the 1920s, according to my mother. Forty years later what should have been a decent and nourishing place for children to eat and socialize remained a minimalist soup kitchen. I resolved to take on the issue of food and children someday, and did get around to it ten years later. In those days I had to deal with the children's anger and hunger as part of all the other challenges behind my classroom doors.

Another example of the children's writing shows the passion and intelligence they brought to bear on troubling events during the civil rights movement. In May 1963, during the Southern Christian Leadership Conference's "Children's Crusade" in Birmingham, elementary and high school students in that city demonstrated against segregation. Police Commissioner Eugene "Bull" Connor retaliated with police dogs, fire hoses, and mass arrests. My students wrote about those events and tried to make sense out of them.

Rachael
I think that all the Negroes and all the whites are very brave to go down south and parade. I know that it is easy to fight but hard not to fight. Some people say that people will never get freedom but I know they will.

Phyllis
BIRMINGHAM ALA.
I think that the white people in Birmingham are not treating the colored right because every time a colored person goes

somewhere a white person says something bad about him. The white people always turn everyone else against the colored. The white people think they are so good but the colored are just as good. The whites are jealous of us because they think we will get a better education and they don't want us to get ahead of them if the Negroes get their freedom. They would treat the white better than they are being treated now.

Every man is created equal.

Deidre

I think that the white and the colored peoples should always be friendly with each other. And that they should not be slaves for the big shots. They should have their freedom like other people do now I don't know what the white and colored people have against each other. But I know that it is horrible it will be a miracle if the white and colored people come together to work and play like human beings and not like animals.

THE END

Rachael

I think that the whites should be friendly with the colored should be friends because after all colored came over from Africa to let the cotton and crops grow while the whites don't even know what's going on. It was also a colored man taught the people how to preserved plants and vegetables I think its just a horrible that they are like this.

Elsa

I think that it makes sense. The only way that anybody can win this fight is by using their brains and not their hands. The way they are going (the Negro) the whites will give in, because its a constant strain on people. Every body should join the freedom rides.

Allan

I think that the Negro in Alabama are right to be non-violent. Because if they fight back they couldn't get what they want. And I think that its a pity that people have to go out and parade for what they want. After the Bill of Rights and The Declaration of Independence was signed. I hope that the Negroes in Ala. And that the word segregastion disappears off the face of the earth.

John

INTEGRATION

I think the world should be completely integrated so that no matter what race color or creed you can go to any store and be waited on any restaurant and be served and go to any school and learn. Just as much as anyone else without being picked on or ridiculed.

Why! Because all men are created equal and because if everyone were all alike this world would be a great bore looking at yourself all the time and living just the same and hurting the same thing as everyone else

My students and I felt equally powerless to act in the South, and we knew that there were serious racial problems in the North. Writing and talking explicitly about segregation, nonviolence, and the need to act against racism was a way of engaging in the struggle within the classroom. My students had no problem writing their own versions of Greek myths one day and turning their attention to the civil rights movement the next day. Their energy, which in September had often expressed itself in random acts of disruption, was now focused on trying to understand the world.

Time was a major problem: When to write? How was I to fit in math and science, social studies and the industrial revolution? How could I, at least minimally, comply with my supervisor's demands and the curriculum guidelines of the system so I wouldn't get thrown out of the school? How to get other teachers, the assistant principal, and the principal as excited about the children's work as I was, and to get them to understand how brilliant the students were?

I carried around a portfolio of my students' writing and read it to anyone who was willing to listen or whom I could corner and force to listen. I must have read their papers to dozens of people—at parties, in restaurants, at dinners with friends. My principal wasn't interested.

A few of the other young teachers listened, but for the most part they didn't see anything important in the children's writing. They didn't, as I did and still do, see this writing as one key to help the children open up to learning and become strong enough in themselves to dare to oppose all the forces that conspire to force them to accept less than a full place in the society and the economy.

Nor did my colleagues comprehend how the content of children's writing suggested a complete revision of standard educational ideas about who the children were, what they knew, how they thought and could think, and how much they could learn if we only knew how to tap into their brilliance. The ideas the children wrote about, the feelings they expressed, and the dreams and schemes they spun out shaped my thinking about teaching and learning in ways that have permanently affected my life and work. The children developed the courage to show me and each other who they were and what their dreams were. These expressions of trust and hope became the driving force behind my commitment to children, whatever the systems, tests, and experts say about their performance or potential. The authentic voices of children are a challenge to the pious pronouncements of experts and politicians who believe that children can be reduced to test scores and manipulated to meet the needs of an economy that does not honor the value of their lives.

This selection is from the beginning of Arnold's fictionalized autobiography. I must have read it to dozens of people:

The Story of My Life: Foreword

This story is about a boy named Maurice and his life as it is and how it will be. Maurice is in the six grade now but this story will tell about his past, present, and future. It will tell you how he lived and how he liked it or disliked it. It will tell you how important he was and happy or sad he was in this world it will tell you all his thoughts. It may be pleasant and it may be horrible in place but what ever it is it will be good and exciting but! there will be horrible parts. This story will be made simple and easy but in places hard to understand. This is a nonfiction book.

WHERE I WAS BORN
In all stories they beat around the bush before they tell you the story well I am not this story takes place in the Metropolitan Hospital.

When I was born I couldn't see at first. but like all families my father was waiting outside after a hour or so I could see shadows. The hospital was very large and their were millions of beds and plenty of people. And their were people in chairs rolling around, people in beds, and people walking around with trays with food or medicine on it. Their was people rolling people in bed and there were people bleeding crying yelling or praying. I was put at a window with other babies so my father could see me their was a big glass and lots of people around me so I could see a lot of black shapes. And since I was a baby I tried to go through the glass but I didn't succeed. All the people kept looking I got scared and cried soon the nurse came and took all the babies back.

The details and images in the writing amazed me: the baby's seeing shadows within an hour or so of being born and attempting to reach through the glass, as well as the sense of the chaos of the hospital. Arnold's ability to project himself into the baby's mind and to conjure up an emergency-room scene that must have been familiar to him from some more recent experience made the grammatical and spelling errors seem insignificant compared to the more important matter of recreating a world. This provided me with a dual challenge: how to nurture the students' writing while providing them with the skills necessary to do it well and correctly. I knew how easy it was to close down children's creative efforts through excessive correcting and criticizing, but I also believed it was important for them to know and be able to use the rules of standard English. It was, and still is, my conviction that student writers can break any grammatical or linguistic rule or convention they care to if they do it consciously. Many contemporary novelists, poets, and even journalists do it all the time. Knowing the rules of grammar, spelling, and syntax provides the license to break them while staying in control of your writing.

As my first full year of teaching class 6-1 at P.S. 103 progressed, I decided to respond primarily to the content of students' work and teach skills only when it seemed necessary. I wanted to keep the writing flowing and see how far it could take us. After reading Arnold's autobiography, the "My Block" assignments, and the fables and other writings I abandoned any sense of being able to predict or know the limits of what my students might do. As a first-year teacher I was overwhelmed by my students' imagination:

Barbara
Once upon a time there was a pig and a cat. The cat kept saying you old dirty pig who want to eat you. And the pig replied when

I die I'll be made use of, but when you die you'll just rot. The cat always thought he was better than the pig. When the pig died he was used as food for the people to eat. When the cat died he was buried in old dirt.

Moral: Live dirty die clean.

John

Once a boy was standing on a huge metal flattening machine. The flattener was coming down slowly. Now this boy was a boy who loved insects and bugs. The boy could have stopped the machine from coming down but there were two ladie bugs on the button and in order to push the button he would kill the two ladie bugs. The flattener was about a half inch over his head now he made a decision he would have to kill the ladie bugs he quickly pressed the button. The machine stopped he was saved and the ladie bugs were dead

Moral: smash or be smashed.

Barbara

Once upon a time a girl was walking up the street with her little brother. Her little brother loved to suck a pacifier all of the time. One day he met a little girl that loved to suck her finger. The little boy asked her how does you finger taste? The little girl said it tastes delicious. The girl asked how did the pacifier taste and the boy said delicious. They traded and the boy liked the thumb the best and the girl liked the pacifier best.

Moral: Enjoy them all.

Nick

Once upon a time there was two men who were always fighting so one day a wise man came along and said fighting will never get you anywhere they didn't pay him no attention and they got in quarrels over and over again. So one day they went to church and the preacher said you should not fight and they got mad and knock the preacher out

Can't find no ending.

These fables didn't emerge from the students' imaginations spontaneously. I read the class Aesop and James Thurber's *Fables for Our Time.* We invented variations on morals from dozens of traditional fables. Together we transformed "A stitch in time saves nine" into the following:

A stitch in time saves none.
A stitch in time is fine if you don't have to go to work.
A stitch in time saves glue.
A hit on time saves nine. (A ball game.)
A snitch in time gets everyone in trouble.

The students' work came from the internalization of the reading and class conversations. I had no specific expectations when I asked them to write their own fables; I assured them that anything goes. What was unusual about the writing was the frankness and humor with which the children expressed bitterness, cynicism, and a very hard sense of life. They weren't writing for me; they were writing the truths they lived. I realized that the freedom to speak out in this way was essential to any good education I could provide them.

Phillip's "A Barbarian Becomes a Greek Warrior" and other writings like it convinced me that the Greek and Latin vocabulary and the time I took to tell stories were not incidental diversions but central strategies for eliciting learning and developing the students' comfortable use of their imaginations. Phillip's novella began:

One day, in Ancient Germany, a boy was growing up. His name was Pathos. He was named after this Latin word because he had sensitive feelings.

For most of the year I was unsure of myself. There was no road map to where the students and I were going. However, there was no question but that I would respond to the students' work with whatever ingenuity and resources I could summon. I chose not to follow the standard curriculum and the school system's demands since it was clear to me that these would lead to failure. Still, I didn't feel on solid educational ground. I was telling stories, spending mornings discussing events in the neighborhood, reading from Robert Graves's *The Greek Myths,* and whenever possible bringing in articles from the *New York Times* about the civil rights movement. Once I tried to lip-synch *Rigoletto,* an opera I knew and loved, with the class; students acted out the murderous events at the end of the opera. Another time I suggested the students build a large (five feet square and five feet high) model of a Sumerian ziggurat; we ended up with a messy mound that resembled a beginning archaeological excavation more than a functioning city complex.

According to the curriculum experts I had read while taking classes to qualify for a teaching credential, sixth-graders had outgrown storytelling. They didn't need to make large-scale art projects. Discussing "my neighborhood" was part of the kindergarten curriculum, irrelevant for twelve-year-olds.

There still is a feeling among educators that storytelling and open-ended conversation have no place in a "serious" curriculum. For me, however, the idea that one should stuff as much "substantial learning" as possible into the limited time children spend in the classroom involves a grave educational miscalculation. When I began teaching I knew that intuitively, and now I feel secure in my conviction that education has to be shaped so that the timbre of students' voices can emerge. This is essential if substantial learning is to develop. The teacher's voice must emerge as well, and students must have the opportunity to engage in dialogue with their teachers. Students and teachers have to learn to speak to each other across culture, class, age, gender, and all the other divides that inhibit the development of intelligence and sensitivity.

Every new class presents that same challenge: how to create a situation in which teachers and students can speak with each other comfortably in their own voices and turn their attention to an open examination of content. My goal, as a teacher, is to allow all of us in the class to explore complex issues in ways that minimize ego involvement and social posturing. That means providing students the safety they need to develop intellectual relationships with each other and with the subject matter, relationships not mediated by worry over grades, laden with self-doubt, or burdened with the wounds of previous schooling. This implies creating a climate where the common focus is on what is learned, not on how one has performed. The objective is to have students come away from class with a sense that they have journeyed into some unknown territory and come home the stronger for it.

It's very difficult for a teacher, in the context of evaluation-obsessed and product-oriented schools and universities, to teach well if teaching well includes creating intimate, personal, and thorough engagement with content. The screens created by grading systems, grade-point averages, career paths, and other forms of sorting and ranking people distort learning. This is as true in kindergarten, the middle grades, and high school as it is in college. If a teacher considers her or his work centered on the quality of learning, then other, structural aspects of the social organization of schooling have to be reconsidered. You cannot be indifferent to the infrastructure of learning as you plan your teaching. *Everything*—from the size, shape, and decor of the classroom to the time of day and the number of hours a week the class meets—affects how learning happens. Add to these the system of evaluation and the other learning obligations of the students, and you get a sense of how dependent learning is upon context and situation and how much craft is called upon if a teacher is to do an excellent job.

LISTENING AND LEARNING

To teach well you have to be able to listen carefully and learn from your students. You also have to come to know the community in which you work and be sensitive to the issues that people take seriously. That certainly wasn't true for me when I began teaching the sixth grade at P.S. 103 in Harlem in 1962. As a first-year teacher I spent a lot of time learning how to listen to my students and trying to understand their needs and lives. I learned, for example, that almost all the students in my class lived in extended families and that considerable authority lay with their grandmothers, who were major allies in helping me educate their grandchildren. I also learned about social and cultural differences within the class. Some of the children's families had lived in New York for generations; other children, born in the South, had been part of a recent migration north. A few were from the West Indies and one was from Panama. Family friendships and networks of support existed, but I had to discover them. Doing this meant spending time at the children's homes.

Larry was the first student to invite me to dinner. After that Ann and Ruth conveyed invitations from their parents. I readily accepted. When Judy and I started dating we were both invited to dinners and family gatherings.

I will never forget that first dinner at Larry's three-and-a-half-room apartment on the fourth floor of a walk-up on 116th Street. I was an honored guest; an elaborate table was set for me in the middle of the living room, which doubled as a bedroom for the two youngest of Larry's five sisters. Larry's mother, Mary, his grandmother, and several neighbors had made a fancy meal for me. There was fresh cornbread and a spread of potato salad, fried chicken, vegetables, cooked greens, chicken, ribs, and sausages, all garnished with an amazing hot sauce. The centerpiece of the table, which was set for ten, was a bottle of Manischewitz wine, purchased out of respect for my Jewishness. Though I detested that particular wine, I drank the glass Mary offered.

In our conversation it emerged that no teacher had ever come to dinner before and that everyone in the building wanted to know what I looked like. The gap between the children and the people who taught them astonished me. With the exception of one of the other sixth-grade teachers, who had grown up in the neighborhood, none of P.S. 103's teachers or administrators spent any time in homes in the community.

Before we sat down to dinner the phone rang—or at least, that was what I thought I'd heard. The sound was muffled and it was hard to tell where it was coming from. Mary and I were talking about Larry and I was praising his creativity while avoiding the issue of his wild flights across the classroom, knocking things off people's desks in an effort to amuse everyone and disrupt whatever else was going on in the classroom.

Alison, the oldest, asked Mary what to do and then went to the kitchen and pulled a telephone out of the bread box. Larry explained: "They don't let us have a phone."

It seems that the welfare system had decided that for someone on AFDC, telephones were out of the question—even if, like Mary, you had seven children in school. Answering the phone with a guest like me in the house was a dangerous thing. This was a revelation. What were simple events for me, like answering the telephone, had been turned into furtive activities for many of the children's families. The episode provided insight into the kinds of pressures the children lived with every day and made me understand why getting emergency phone numbers for the children was so charged with secrecy. The numbers couldn't appear on school records, which might be checked by the welfare department.

Dinner was wonderful. All the children had a spark, a brilliance and wildness, that a good teacher has to love. They are the kind of children who challenge you in class, sometimes by annoying you but mostly because their minds are racing with ideas and they want to talk, to know, to touch things, to play, and to learn. They don't have patience for the formal rituals of learning, but want to jump into the process itself without any preliminaries or ceremonies.

Dinner conversation started with school, then turned to Larry's father, who had died a few years earlier, and to hopes for the children. At first I felt very uneasy. It was a cold evening, so the burners on the stove were lit to warm the apartment, since there was no working central heating in the building. Every corner of the small apartment was crammed with clothes and toys and books. Eight people were stuffed into the three and a half rooms and, except in the living room where everything had been cleared for me, there was no space to move or breathe. The whole apartment had been rearranged for my visit.

I was twenty-five and being treated as if I were an expert, a professional who knew how to educate their children, a person of importance. This was hardly true. I was a novice, an apprentice, and as much of a learner as the children were. The awkward part of the evening came from the disparity between what the family thought of me and what I wanted to be as a teacher and the actual struggles I was having in the classroom.

The conversation turned from school to the civil rights movement in the South, and then to neighborhood gossip. During that evening and many others like it, with other students' families, I learned about the vibrant, complex, and often difficult lives of people in the neighborhood. And I came to honor and to care about them—to care not just about my students but about their sisters and brothers and parents as well. I developed friendships that lasted beyond the time I spent teaching at P.S. 103, and my involvement in the community led me into political and social struggles in East Harlem over the next seven or eight years.

Judy and I stayed in touch with the family for about ten years, from 1962 when Larry was in 6-1 until about 1972. Larry came to live with Judy and me in Berkeley, California, in 1968 and 1969. He worked at Other Ways, a high school I ran there, and for a while wrote poetry. In 1968 he joined a group of our students who transformed their own poetry into songs using rhythm backgrounds provided by other students on congas. The group traveled to teachers' conferences throughout the country, performing and talking about changing schools. I believe they were among the forerunners of current rap artists.

Judy and I also stayed close to the family until we moved to California. In 1967, when I ran a storefront learning center in East Harlem and became the founding director of the Teachers and Writers Collaborative, they were moved by the welfare department to Brooklyn. The house they were assigned to was bigger than their apartment, but the neighborhood was much more dangerous and the children's lives became more difficult. Three of the children died young.

The loss of gifted people, the loss of students to violence and poverty, is often felt by teachers as a personal loss. We must know and care enough about our students to grieve for them as well as take part in their joys. It is this personal bond that harnesses the energy to teach creatively despite the often negative momentum of the system in which we teach. The bond between teacher and student is a special kind of intimacy, based on personal commitment of energy and affection to the lives of others. It is easy to understand this kind of reaching beyond oneself in the case of one's own family or lover but the situation is more complex with one's students. It is almost as if the family life cycle is repeated each year, with the birth of a new relationship, the development of mutual bonds and common activity, growth, and finally separation. That is the emotional structure of the life of most teachers (though there are schools that function more like communities and in which teachers and students spend a longer time with each other).

There is a special quality in the parting of teachers and students who care about each other. For the teacher, it has to do with the pleasures of witnessing growth and knowing that one's work has some lasting value. Knowing and caring about your students is not merely an academic matter but is essential to shaping learning for them and a challenge to take them into your life and fight for their survival and growth as if they were your own children. This is not all pleasure; the more intensely you care for your students, the more you grieve for them when they are brutalized by a violent world and the more enraged you become when an unfair distribution of the chances for a decent life contributes to the destruction of one of your students.

I am astonished that teachers are not more militant, considering the number of young people lost on the streets these days. I believe that one key to making sustained changes is finding teachers who care about their students and are willing to become personally involved with their lives. The craft of teaching can develop; the love it requires cannot be legislated or trained.

At one time or another I spoke to almost all of my students' parents and had dinner with or visited about half of them. I got to see lives in disarray and lives held together by faith and ingenuity. Ann's home was a haven, a calm, beautifully cared for place with an atmosphere of love and welcome. So were most of the places I was fortunate enough to be invited into. My picture of the neighborhood, of the children and their families, was complex, though what framed the whole was the problem of being Black in the United States. Not one person I met had escaped the wounds of racism or had not, in some admirable way, resisted the dehumanization perpetuated by white society. All this was new to me, and very troubling. To my mind, the education I was trying to provide was color-blind, and yet the world obviously wasn't.

It took at least half of that school year, 1962–63, for me to feel confident as a teacher. The constant outpouring of intelligence, sensitivity, and creativity in my students' work, from their "My Block" essays to the fables and stories they wrote, kept challenging me to push things further and further. Some children embarked on long forms of writing; the class produced novels and plays, volumes of short stories, and memoirs. They explored genres from science fiction to romance. I couldn't bring enough books to class to keep up with the children's insatiable desire to read.

In March Judy and I were married at the Bronx County Courthouse. Both of us were so caught up in the lives of the children that it seemed natural to take only half a day off to get married. The children and their parents threw a wonderful surprise party for me the next day when I came in.

That year ended in a peculiar way. P.S. 103 was moving two blocks up Madison Avenue and changing its number to P.S. 103/79. The principal decided that the sixth grade had to move right away so that in June the new school could have its first graduating class. The first and second grades were moving too. But since the building wasn't completed, the third and fourth grades had to be left behind until the next school year. By that time I knew many children in every grade, and I listened carefully to the bitter complaints of those left behind. The divided school was like a family moving from a slum tenement to a suburban home and leaving the middle children behind. I suggested that instead of rushing to have a new graduating class for P.S. 103/79 we have a last graduating class for P.S. 103, and I volunteered to stay with my class in the old building. It would be a way to express appreciation for the sacrifice of the older children and wish the younger ones well.

The principal turned me down. I tried to fight the decision but there was no mechanism for talking to parents or staff or making the issue public, so we moved. From March to April a number of the left-behind children spent hours at night and on weekends breaking windows and vandalizing the new building, which soon looked no better than the one it replaced.

I spoke with my class about the dilemma of the students left at the old school and they decided it was our responsibility to do something about it. We began visiting P.S. 103 and inviting some of the third- and fourth-graders over to visit us. The children's concern for each other should have been reflected in the administration's attitudes, but it wasn't. At that time Judy was a substitute teacher in one of those fourth grades; I visited with her and her students a few times. The demoralization of both students and staff at the old building was agonizing to witness. I never imagined, when I dreamed of becoming a teacher, that I would have to witness such disorganization, lack of learning, and feelings of abandonment and neglect in a school. I was full of admiration and sorrow for all the children and teachers who forced themselves to come into that half-empty, filthy building, which was in such a state of disarray that the custodians had abandoned the empty classrooms to the rats and the roaches. It was amazing that the school administrators could turn the move into a new building into an experience of humiliation and rejection, while seeming completely untroubled.

My class's efforts to visit the left-behind children and bring them over to the new school for visits were discouraged. With all the other pressure I felt as a first-year teacher, I gave up trying.

However, that experience made me sensitive to the children who are abandoned when an experiment takes place or a special program comes into a school or a school district. I always ask myself, "Are there leftover children?" and, "How can anything that is good for some group of children be made available to everybody?" And now I am willing to fight for the abandoned and left-behind children even if it means risking my job.

Listening and learning as a teacher has many consequences. It makes you conscious of the environment you work in—aware not merely of whom and where you are teaching but of the social structure imposed upon your work. In many ways it is dangerous for teachers to listen too carefully or learn too much, because doing so often leads to opposing conditions under which no sensible person could teach and no healthy child could learn. I discovered how teachers, for the sake of mere survival, have learned not to listen and not to learn things that would force them into action. Those of us who did listen and learn became involved in school reform movements that continue to the present.

My involvement in school reform has always arisen directly from my work with children and my relationships with people in the communities I served. It has not arisen from books or theories, although I read a lot and honor the task of creating theory as a way of understanding and communicating the ideas that emerge from practice. As a consequence, most of the attempts at school reform I have been involved with are either community-based or grow out of direct work with children. I've never been in the business of school reform—and it *is* a business, more so in the 1990s than ever before. People have systems to sell, and yet I've never encountered a system that meets the needs of all children or that measures its success on the basis of how every child does. Just about every attempt at school reform seems to try to fit the child to the system rather than help teachers, students, and communities build education that works for them. I believe that is why testing is so prevalent. Educational experts don't trust children, communities, and teachers enough to let them judge the effectiveness of education. School bureaucrats are afraid of children's voices, community control of schools, and critical scrutiny of their work so, for the sake of survival, they use tests, no matter how biased, to evaluate the results of specific efforts and remove the evaluation process from the people most directly affected by programs. "Objective" testing is often a ruse to protect people who do not have a moral commitment to see education work for all children.

The end of my first full teaching year was marked by a sixth-grade graduation both grand and pathetic: grand in that everyone, from the children and their parents to the entire staff and administration, was dressed up as if for a college commencement ceremony; sad in that the staff knew from experience that this was the only graduation ceremony most of the students would ever participate in.

I was assigned to guard the main doors to the school during the ceremony. The principal was worried that a number of teenagers or nonparents from the community might crash the event. I thought they should be invited, be allowed to show pride in the young graduates, but they were seen as the enemy even though most of them were products of the school and had passed as much as seven years of their lives there.

The principal's fears were realized. Two teenagers came to the door and tried to enter. I said that all of the tickets to the ceremonies were taken and they had to stay outside. One of them got very angry; I could see that he was getting ready for a confrontation that I wasn't prepared for. I couldn't understand why I was arguing with him or preventing him from walking into the ceremony, and I felt like a fool enforcing a rule that made no sense to me. In addition, I was scared. If I feel morally right I'm usually able to face down my fear, but not for something as trivial, wrong, and bureaucratic as guarding the school against the community. I backed down and told the young man that I'd escort him and his friend in and find them seats. He told me to fuck off and left muttering something I decided not to hear.

After the ceremony the staff had a party and celebrated the end of a hard year. After a few drinks, conversation turned to how terrible and stupid the students were and how silly the parents looked in fancy clothes. The chatter depressed me; I felt alienated from the group, as did several other teachers who cared about the children and had worked very hard all year. Those teachers and I, along with Judy and several other spouses and friends, went out later for a few drinks. We determined that the next year things would be different and better for the students. Then we told teaching tales, those funny, self-deprecating stories that teachers tell each other by way of recognition that they love their work.

My class for the next year was 6-7, the bottom rung of the sixth grade. It was smaller, with twenty-seven students, but presumably much more difficult to handle. Students were put in the class for one of the following reasons: they had failed in or been thrown out of other classes in the fifth grade; they were identified as having learning problems; they were Spanish-speaking and couldn't manage the English-only curriculum; they were older than other sixth-graders, having either started school late or been left back somewhere in their school career; or they had some history of violence and were in school on a form of probation. Most of them could barely read—though several could read well and had the reputation of being too smart for their own good.

On the whole, the class was a wonderful teaching challenge and, with a half-year of substitute teaching and a full year of teaching behind me I was excited about beginning again in the fall of 1963 with greater experience and more resources. I felt free to experiment more broadly with curriculum and space and time in my classroom. And new educational ideas were stirring within me, provoked by my students' writing; my growing knowledge of the community and greater understanding of how children thought; the events of the civil rights movement and the hopes created by the early days of the Kennedy administration; and my discovery of Sylvia Ashton-Warner's book *Teacher,* which had just been published in the United States, and Homer Lane's *The Children's Commonwealth,* which had recently been reprinted. I believe these were the first books about education that influenced my teaching.

Ashton-Warner's book helped me early on in my struggle to figure out the best way to enrich my students' learning. Perhaps this was because the book was a story of specific children as well as an account of how one might reach other children by learning about central concepts and themes in their lives. I think what appealed to me mostly was Ashton-Warner's respect for the four- and five-year-old children she taught, her uncanny ability to listen to them, and her faith that the list of key words they chose to learn would help her learn about the substance and content of their imaginations.

A child's "key vocabulary" consists of the words that tap into her or his inmost experience. These are words that children ask to learn when given the choice. Children connect reading with experience, and although there are some words most children request, no two lists are alike. If a child learns a word a day, after three months she or he has a new vocabulary of at least forty words and the teacher has a tentative portrait of the children's world, fears, and dreams.

The power and importance Ashton-Warner ascribed to children's own organic language and the books they created influenced me to push writing and speaking in my own classroom. *Teacher* confirmed what I was discovering through reading my students' work and helped me trust my own teaching instincts. These words of hers have stayed with me over the years, a reminder of the power of imaginative expression to transform children's worlds and provide a hedge against the overwhelming violence they too often encounter:

> I see the mind of a five-year-old as a volcano with two vents: destructiveness and creativeness. And I see that to the extent that we widen the creative channel, we atrophy the destructive one. And it seems to me that since these words of the key vocabulary are no less than the captions of the dynamic life itself, they course out through the creative channel, making their contributions to the drying up of the destructive vent. From all of which I am constrained to it as creative reading and to count it among the arts.
>
> First words must mean something to a child.
>
> First words must have intense meaning for a child. They must be part of his being.
>
> How much hangs on this love of reading, the instinctive inclination to hold a book! *Instinctive!* That's what it must be. The reaching out for a book needs to become an organic action, which can happen at this yet formative age. Pleasant words won't do. Respectable words won't do. They must be words organically tied up, organically born from the dynamic life itself. They must be words that are already part of the child's being.

The power of her children's writing didn't surprise me, as I had already discovered, through the work of the children in 6-1, the amazing range, variety, and complexity of young people's imaginative work. The specifics of Ashton-Warner's techniques weren't of interest to me at that time, though I've found successful ways to adapt them for older learners since. What she planted in my mind was the power of listening to your students, reading their work carefully, and learning what was important to them and to their community. I believe that her faith in five-year-olds could easily be extended to twelve-year-olds, and over my teaching life I have come to believe that it is never too late to learn and love learning, nor is it ever too late to rechannel the energy coming out of the vents of destructiveness and open up the creative vents.

In another, equally important way Homer Lane, too, influenced me and confirmed the path I had set out on as a teacher. In his book *Talks to Parents and Teachers* (first published in 1928) Lane describes his work with young British delinquents at the Little Commonwealth, where he developed a student-governed democratic learning environment. The trial I had students conduct in my 6-1 class was influenced by this early experiment with student democracy. Homer Lane actually ran a whole living and learning community for young people on the basis of one person, one vote, himself included. Though this doesn't work well in a classroom with young children, Lane's experiment was a challenge, especially when it came to issues of discipline and the development of mutual respect and responsibility in a school or classroom setting.

These remarks by Lane stayed with me as I reflected upon the basis of my teaching after a few years in the classroom:

> Even confirmed anti-social tendencies in children may be re-leased by educational methods. The energy occupied in destructive activities is always capable of being turned into social service. Harsh repressive methods will not do this, although the energy may sometimes by long confinement in a reformatory be subdued by fear. The problem of correction is, however, not one of destroying the energy of mind which is so much needed by society, but of transforming it from vicious behavior into social service.

Lane gives dozens of examples of this transformation of defiant and often self-destructive behavior into participation in students' democracy. Though none of my students had been in prison and only a few had had problems with the law, they had been confined to bad schools, trapped in poor communities, and thoroughly accustomed to functioning in a chaotic and undisciplined way in school. I had to take this energy, work with it, and make an educational environment that my students felt compelled to defend and protect.

Lane kept my courage up—as, later on, did other writers, such as Fritz Redl, August Eichorn, and A. S. Makarenko, all of whom discovered ways of turning defiant behavior into democratic self-governance among children who had lost hope. Moving children from a school life in which they feel unwelcome and are angry and resistant to learning, into one that allows them to let their guard down and dare to be intelligent and compassionate is very difficult. Beyond patience, it requires a great love for your students and an inner strength that I wasn't sure I had. Reading about other people who had gone through similar—though often much more difficult—situations and succeeded with their students provided me with more strength than I ever got from books on teaching techniques, curriculum methods, or educational philosophy. I've always felt comfortable with the management of curriculum. The management of love in the classroom is much more difficult. However, as Lane said, also in *Talks to Parents and Teachers*:

> When authority, in [the poet] Shelley's sense of power, is recognized for what it is the only revolution that is of any vital importance will begin to take place, and it will take place in the hearts of men. This will affect not only the attitude of parents and teachers to children, but also the attitude of men and women towards each other and to themselves. Then it will be seen that love (the creative impulse) is a deeper and stronger instinct in human nature than fear, upon which the fabric of our society is at present constructed, and that love is indeed, as Shelley declared it, synonymous with life.

HOW MANY CHILDREN?

For those people unfamiliar with the New York City schools or the way teaching careers develop within that system, I should mention that "P.S." stands for "Public School"; the numbers that designate elementary schools run from 1 up into the 200s. Each borough's schools are numbered, starting from 1, for a total of more than 600 elementary schools within the system. In my New York City elementary school career, which was confined to Manhattan, I did six weeks of student teaching in the fall of 1961 at P.S. 41, which is on East Twenty-second Street; got my first teaching job, at P.S. 145 on Amsterdam Avenue and 105th Street, in January 1962, the middle of the school year; and was involuntarily transferred to P.S. 103 on Madison Avenue and 118th Street for the fall of 1962. P.S. 103's number was changed to P.S. 103/79, for reasons no one seemed to know, in the spring of 1963, when the old building was replaced by a new one two blocks away. Three schools and four numbers in less than two academic years.

During the first years of my teaching career I began to know my students and their communities better and to see the effects of my work. As the thirty-six children I taught in class 6-1 at P.S. 103 grew older, I was confronted with major reasons for shifting my thinking about learning and culture. During the summer of 1963 and the next school year, there were major events in the lives of a number of these students and in the society. Just two weeks after the school year ended in June, I got a call from a welfare worker who had befriended one of the children in 6-1. She told me that he and his brothers and sisters had been removed from their home and were in a temporary shelter on Fifth Avenue and 105th Street. It was a case of child neglect.

I immediately went up to the shelter and, after spending a few hours going office to office, managed to convince someone to let me talk to the child. I was led into a large open hall. There must have been over a hundred children in the room, which was filled with sleeping mats, blankets, suitcases, clothes, and a random assortment of other possessions that the children had been allowed to take with them. It was a summer roundup, it seemed, of children the welfare department deemed neglected. I was told that this happened every summer when school was out. Many children were found wandering the streets unsupervised; they were accompanied home by social workers and probation officers. If the home was chaotic and the parents in disarray, the welfare department had a right to remove the children.

I asked where the children would be sent, but no one seemed to know. They might go back home, they might be put in foster care, or even, someone told me, sent to juvenile hall—a youth prison—until someone in the family claimed them or some placement was found for them. Some of the luckier ones might find themselves going home to new neighborhoods and apartments if the welfare department decided to provide better living facilities for the family. There was no clear authority and no clear criteria for action.

I called Judy and we started phoning around, trying to find decent placements for the children. We visited their mother, who did indeed need some care herself. Finally we found decent placements for all the children.

Several other children from 6-1 had problems during the summer, as did some former students of mine from P.S. 145 and from my student-teaching days at P.S. 41.

Through 1963 I had kept in touch with students from all three classes I'd worked with. But my mind was on my new class and the challenges it presented. So early on in my teaching career, after only two years of full-time involvement in the schools, I faced dilemmas that caring teachers everywhere experience: how far into your personal life and career do your love and responsibility for former students extend? What is the nature of the affection between teacher and student, and how long can it continue? And how big can your family get? How many children can you have and nurture over a lifetime?

These questions go to the heart of the relationship between teacher and student. For me, there are some central obligations of teaching that go beyond concern for the mastery of content, beyond the academic support of students. These obligations have to do with the personal quality of life in the classroom and involve giving yourself as fully as possible to every student, playing no favorites, and being as supportive and ingenious as you can in the quest to bring out what is strong and special about each youngster. This is not easy, since there are some students who just about drive you crazy and other students who make it clear that they don't like you and want nothing from you but to be left alone. Equally, there are times when you develop a deep emotional bond with students that tempts you to treat them in special ways. These bonds may arise from personal identification with a child or from ways they support and validate your work. It's easy to begin to care for someone who acknowledges your help or whose work indicates enormous growth that you know you contributed to. And then there are some children whom you simply find beautiful or brilliant or inspired. Teaching is an emotional matter as well as a moral and academic one; being with children day after day over a school year means that the emotional tone of your presence affects the nature and quality of what is achieved in the classroom.

I remember this being made explicit years later when I was teaching a combined kindergarten and first-grade class in Berkeley in 1972. My oldest child, Tonia, was six at the time; she could have been in my class but I was afraid of the pressure being there might put on her, so I had her placed in a class next door to mine. In retrospect, that was a dumb decision. I had underestimated the pressure of *not* being in my class, of wondering every day what I was doing with other parents' children. After a few weeks Tonia made it clear that she wanted to be with me. We got her transferred into the class and I told her this was fine, only she couldn't call me Daddy in the classroom.

Once she slipped and then apologized for calling me Daddy. One of the girls objected and said that my daughter should be able to call me Daddy anytime she wanted to, only I shouldn't favor her. That was perfectly reasonable, and I agreed. However, a boy named David added a twist: he started calling me Uncle Herb (all the children called me Herb), and it stuck. I was "Daddy" to Tonia and "Uncle" to everybody else. David made it possible for all of us to be related without having to violate the special relation between father and child. Everyone in the class knew that I was their teacher, not their father, but they also wanted to be related to me in a familial way. They were explicit about the need for an intimacy which, though personal, wasn't parental.

It's important to reflect upon the nature of the emotional bonds between teachers and parents, as well. These bonds have changed for me over my teaching career. When I was younger, and especially before I met Judy and became a parent myself, much of my social life revolved around the parents of my students. This first happened when I was a student teacher in a sixth-grade class at P.S. 41 in the fall of 1961. My supervising teacher assigned me a small group of students for individual tutoring. One of the children was African American; one was Chinese and had recently arrived in the United

States; two were Puerto Rican. They were the only students of color in the class of thirty children, but not the only ones with reading problems, so it was noticeable to everyone in the class that at least one criterion for being in my group had to do with ethnicity.

I still remember all of them. James Chou was a good mathematician; he knew how to read and write Chinese and had mastered about a thousand characters (I still have samples of his calligraphy), but couldn't speak much English or read or write it. Betty Johnson was a delightful storyteller and could read and write with some effort; she was a fair student. Her problem was that she was a few years older than the other fifth-graders and her social life was more sophisticated and complex than theirs. Also, she was poor and the rest of the children (except for those in my group) were middle-class and white. Betty was socially and culturally isolated in the class, and my supervising teacher saw to it that that isolation was completed by academic isolation. Betty was sent out of the class whenever possible and passed most of her time, when she wasn't in my group, doing errands for the principal.

Robert Levin, who was half Jewish and half Puerto Rican, was, at thirteen, the oldest student in the school and the one who seemed to produce the most fear in the teachers. His name was mentioned in tones usually reserved for people like Dillinger and the James Gang, though no one ever told me anything he did wrong. I saw him with quite different eyes. He was an artist, quiet and very observant. His father had been a sign maker in Puerto Rico, and Robert knew woodworking and a bit of drafting. I got to know him pretty well because I had set up a complicated art-related project for a sample lesson I had to plan and teach by myself. Robert volunteered to do the artwork, so I delivered the art material to his apartment one weekend. I got to meet his mother and chat with both of them in that informal environment.

Robert was indeed much more mature than the other students at the school, yet he had a history of failure since arriving from the island. At first, the problem was just that he didn't have the language. Then it was that he was bigger than most of the other students. Then it was that he was Puerto Rican in a white middle-class public school where most of the children lived in the middle-class and upper-middle-class housing developments of Peter Cooper Village and Stuyvesant Town. Robert's final problem was that he was a Puerto Rican with a Jewish Puerto Rican father who was cultured and a member of the Puerto Rican Socialist Party. Robert did not tolerate even casual racism and often got into trouble for confronting white students whose offhand comments reflected the racism of their parents.

During my second weekend of visiting Robert and his mother and finishing up my project, I ran into another student, Alma Rodriguez, on the street. Alma was with two of her sisters: Graciella, who was in fourth grade, and Emilia, who was about fourteen and was in junior high school. They pushed Alma up to me and forced her to make introductions. Alma was the shyest student I had encountered until then. She would not look directly at me, although once in a while I caught her looking my way in the classroom. Her sisters were not shy at all; Emilia invited me to meet their parents, Gloria and Julio, who told me that afternoon that they had heard all about me from Alma. Evidently my group was a great success, though I wasn't sure why. I had James teach everyone Chinese characters; Betty told stories while the others collectively transcribed or illustrated them; and Robert illustrated some simple bilingual stories that Alma wrote. I improvised these learning situations, knowing from my own growing up that learning new things emerged from doing, in new ways or contexts, what you already knew and loved. There was no theory behind it. I just watched the students and tried to build new lessons on the basis of how they responded to my experiments.

I felt at home in the Rodriguezes' railroad flat. There were always lots of people around. A pet turtle would emerge unexpectedly from under a chair or the couch. An uncle or neighbor would wander in. Julio and his friends played music and sang on the weekends, and Gloria was always busy cooking, sewing, or chatting with friends. Sometimes we would move outside to the stoop and play dominoes or cards and listen to music. I felt like a member of the family and also became a learner as my students and their families became my teachers.

I grew even closer to the family when Gloria, who worked at a doll factory in Brooklyn, threw out her back and was hospitalized in traction. She had never eaten the "American" food the hospital served, and the children and Julio were told that it was against the law to bring her Puerto Rican food. For days she refused to eat anything and got very sick. Consequently I volunteered to sneak her good Puerto Rican food under the pretext of making parent-teacher visits. I made up a bogus project with an academic-sounding name and wrote out a description of it on borrowed Columbia Teachers College stationery. The hospital staff let me come and go as I pleased, with Gloria's food in my ample briefcase. Fortunately a number of the nurses were Puerto Rican and felt I was performing a medically appropriate procedure, so we were never turned in.

After Gloria came home I was never allowed to leave her apartment without taking some food home with me. This was wonderful and familiar: the same thing happened (with Italian food) every time I visited my aunt Addie Gallardo and her husband, Rocco, in the Bronx. I knew food was an important personal and family matter and felt honored to be included in the circle of both Addie and Gloria's caring.

After my student teaching ended and I got my first job, at P.S. 145 on the Upper West Side of Manhattan, I still visited the Rodriguezes on weekends. I got to know other members of the family and was invited to weddings and larger family and social gatherings. In the family I became El Maestro, "The Teacher," a title that thrilled me then (and still does), though in those days I did not feel I had earned it. A few times, before I met Judy, I was fixed up with older cousins; I went out with them, though nothing ever developed.

Throughout the time I knew her, Alma remained shy. I became more friendly with Emilia. When I ran a summer project at Teachers College during the summer of 1962, she was my teaching assistant. I stayed in touch with her and the family while I was teaching at P.S. 103, and I introduced Judy to the family when we began going out. I still have pictures of Julio playing his guitar and singing at our wedding reception.

During my first two years of teaching, other families and other communities, too, became part of my life. In March 1962, while I was teaching at P.S. 145, my students Jaime and Consuela invited me home to meet their parents. Jaime and Consuela lived across the hall from each other, and most of the people in their building and the one next door were relatives.

I didn't spend much time visiting their parents during the school year but was in the community every weekday that summer. A few days after the school year ended, the police picked up a number of my students and their older brothers. I was told that this was part of an annual summer roundup: as soon as school was out the police would pick up young men they identified as potential troublemakers, citing them for minor violations such as loitering or creating a public nuisance. The exact charges didn't make much difference, as there was no intent of bringing anything to court. The arrests were usually made on Friday night; the kids were kept in jail over the weekend and then released. It was a warning that the police wouldn't tolerate anything during the long summer.

Worried for my students, I responded by developing a summer program for some of them and their relatives. I ended up with students who ranged in age from five to fourteen and were all cousins of either Consuela or Jaime, both of whom were also part of the program. Actually my project wasn't really a program but an improvised learning community, in which I had the kids take responsibility for each other. For the sake of Teachers College, whose facilities we used, I dubbed the program an each-one-teach-one summer community education experiment. Each child in the program was both a learner and a teacher. Children read with each other and told stories. If one child knew how to read on one level that student taught someone else who wasn't quite there yet. The group was convival enough that a junior high student felt no humiliation about being taught phonics by an eight-year-old.

At the end of the school day I often had dinner with Jaime's family. They ate early, because Jaime senior worked the night shift and had breakfast when everybody else had dinner.

Jaime Cortes was a very bitter man and it took a while for him to trust me. But he was delighted that I was willing to help his son and nieces and nephews, and I realized that the family meals were initially a way of paying me back for that work. Friendship came later.

What happened with the Rodriguezes and the Corteses has, over the years, continued to happen with the parents of many of my students. They feel that public school teachers do not go out of their way for poor children or children who have a hard time adjusting to the social and cultural system of the schools. Therefore, when a teacher does recognize their children as having worth and intelligence they feel grateful and go out of their way to return the gift with whatever they can afford.

Jaime and Maria Cortes fed me well and I learned to appreciate the nuances of Puerto Rican cooking. The family came from the south of the island and many of the men had been fishermen at home. The fish and pastelles they prepared and the large family meals reminded me of my grandmother's meals in the Bronx, especially the ones she prepared when there was a strike and people came in exhausted and hungry from the picket lines. Eating was celebration and nourishment came from the company of others as much as from the food.

Jaime senior loved to tell stories, and my presence at dinner gave him the chance to pull out all the old tales that the family was tired of hearing. He told me about growing up on the island; I especially loved the stories of how people encountered the spirits of their ancestors when they were out fishing, and of miraculous rescues at sea. I also heard many healing stories and first encountered the medical powers of *curanderos* and *curanderas* through those conversations.

I loved to share stories about my grandparents and the Yiddish world I grew up in, as well as stories of the foibles of the children of the rich and famous that I'd picked up at Harvard. I believe that after a few weeks I shared as much about my life as the Corteses did of theirs.

After a while our conversation turned to racial, cultural, and political issues. Jaime had served in the U.S. Army during World War II. He told me about the racism he faced during basic training in the South, and of the fights between whites and Puerto Ricans throughout the war. Just when the animosity began to wane and some camaraderie to develop, the firing war ended; he returned to the States, only to face the race war once again. Jaime believed that after the war racism was more intense than before. Many soldiers who came home from Europe and Asia felt that by risking their lives for the country they had become full citizens. They mistakenly assumed that the victory in the war would also have been a victory for democracy at home. Instead they found attempts to "return to normal."

Returning to normal meant, for the white soldiers, getting back to business as usual and taking advantage of the new economic opportunities of the postwar period. For African Americans and Puerto Ricans, a return to normal could only mean a return to segregation, poverty, and resistance.

For his part, Jaime had no intention of returning to normal. He felt he had earned his freedom and often got in trouble for going where he wasn't wanted, speaking out too boldly, and making demands that, as he told me, people constantly said were "ahead of the times." He was attracted by Puerto Rican nationalism and had friends who were members of the Puerto Rican Socialist Party. However, he wasn't entirely persuaded that Puerto Rico would be best served by independence from the United States. The question of what it meant to be both a Puerto Rican and an American haunted him. He knew the history of his nation and hoped his children would learn about Puerto Rican culture and history and be proud of who they were. He pressed me—what was I doing to help children feel strong in their own culture? I had to admit that I hadn't thought about that being part of my work.

My conversations with Jaime opened up a whole series of educational questions that had never been touched on at Teachers College or in staff meetings at P.S. 145. In addition to reaffirming what I learned growing up with my grandparents, who couldn't read or write English—which was never to mistake intelligence for schooling —Jaime set me to thinking consciously about the social and cultural dimensions of my work. He was an intellectual, and he pushed me intellectually. He wanted to know how I analyzed the curriculum and how it affected Puerto Rican students. He wanted to know what I thought about the New York City public schools' English-only policy and affirmed that it could only damage Puerto Rican students. I revealed to him all my frustrations about the school, and he wanted to know how far I was willing to challenge the system. This was hard for me to know: I wasn't a good teacher yet and felt overwhelmed by the everyday classroom demands on me. Besides, my job at P.S. 145 was the only work I had ever done that I could unambiguously say I loved. I didn't want to jeopardize it lightly or quickly.

Our conversations and growing friendship and my sense of being part of the community around P.S. 145, as well as my thoughts about incorporating bilingualism and Puerto Rican culture into the classroom, were abruptly terminated toward the end of August 1962. I received a letter from the New York City Board of Education informing me that I had been involuntarily transferred out of 145 and assigned to a new school, P.S. 103 in Harlem.

I had already known who would be in my new class at 145. Now all my plans for them became irrelevant. I would teach sixth grade, not fifth, and it was unlikely that I would have any Puerto Rican students in my class (indeed, there were none).

Several teachers at 145 had told me, late in the school year, that they knew I would be transferred. The principal didn't like my socializing with the students or getting too close to the parents, though I suppose the same thing would have been fine had I done it on Long Island, where the principal lived and sent his children to school. I was picked out as a potential troublemaker and was dealt with in the usual way. It was okay for poor children of color to fail; teachers who stirred things up had to be sent to Harlem, where worse schools than his would chew them up.

I believe that in many ways the principal was right. I do speak out and sometimes stir things up. Getting rid of me by sending me to P.S. 103 as punishment was like throwing Brer Rabbit into the briar patch. But I didn't feel that way the summer before school began. I felt abandoned and rejected. I had lost not just a teaching position but a community I was beginning to love. I tried to hold on to the connections and enter a new community as well, but the combination was impossible to sustain.

In September 1962, at the beginning of my year at 103, I had to face the question of what exactly was my connection as a teacher to the community I served, and to all the children I would come to love over a lifetime of teaching. I threw myself into teaching and, as I mentioned before, became involved with the families of my students. But there had to be a breaking point; there simply wasn't enough time to spend with all the people whom I enjoyed being with and who seemed to enjoy my company. For me, at twenty-five, it was very flattering and moving to be so connected with my work and with people whose children I served. However, my social life in the community had to be tempered by my obligations and commitments as a teacher. I worked with new children each year and had to give each class the same love and energy. Nostalgia for former students and classes was not fair to my present students, nor did it interest me. I found my commitment to teaching was primary. I could not keep a social life going that inhibited my teaching. So, slowly, I came to remove myself from the community of 145, though for as long as we remained in New York City Judy and I kept up a relationship with the Corteses and the Rodriguezes. (In fact, when I was working at Teachers College, Columbia, from 1965 to 1967, a cousin of Jaime's and her fiancé were my research assistants.)

I have thought about my relationships with students and their parents a lot these days. Sexual relationships between students and teachers are in the news, as are questions of the sexual exploitation of children. I'm appalled by some of the cases that have been exposed, but I worry a great deal when suspicion of the potential for abuse is extended to any personal closeness between teachers, students and parents. This suspicion has sanitized the student-teacher relationship, which, if anything, needs to be *more* personal than it has traditionally been. It's ironic that at a time when teachers are being urged to care more for their students and create higher achievement scores they are also being warned to stay away from close contact with students and keep their relations formal and safe.

I find it essential to know each of my students in an individual, personal way, and feel that my ability to teach them is enriched by knowing their families as well. I need to speak with students informally, chat with them when no other people are around, provide special tutoring services on occasion, introduce them to people outside of school who can help develop their talents or show them what it means to be a successful adult. Yet in the past few years I have felt uneasy about doing some of this. Along with the erosion of trust in the public schools there is a general distrust of teachers, which I sometimes feel in communities where my family and history with teaching are unknown.

Still, the personal is at the heart of my work with children, and I have found that efforts to get to know people in the community are essential to being a teacher. I believe we need to demonstrate our concern for the children not merely through test results but through involvement in their lives and care for the well-being of their families. We have to be, at the very least, honorary members of the communities we serve as teachers. A teacher has to be more than a technician or a visiting stranger who is in the community for work and for nothing else. Many of the problems of public education would be solved if teachers were more visible presences in the communities their students live in, with personal commitments to those communities. This is not always possible, especially when schools serve a multiplicity of communities; but even so, teachers can know parents, can make an effort to be present when there is trouble or when important events happen in the community. Teaching for me has never been an 8:40-to-3:30 job; if a teacher is to be effective, I don't believe it can be. We need not more child time in the classroom, but more teacher time in the community.

I don't like ending relationships, so I have kept in touch with students from almost every class I've taught over thirty years. August seems to be the month when former students contact me. During August 1996, as I'm writing this, I've heard from about twenty of my former students. Two students from Carleton College visited on their way back from a Chicano students' conference. A former elementary school student called to say she was getting married, and another called to say one of the other students had died. A number of teachers who were graduate students of mine called for advice about doctoral programs and to keep me posted on their own students and the foibles of their school districts. Two called to ask if I knew of any interesting teaching jobs. Three former college students called to talk about their dream of creating their own school, and two former high school students called to ask for help shaping their college schedules for next year. I also got one call from someone who got the job of their dreams and wanted to share that with me. It is a delight, though too often tinged with pain, to be able to touch all these lives; it is an affirmation that the energy that goes into teaching comes back throughout life.

By my third year of teaching, after working at P.S. 145 and teaching 6-1 at P.S. 103/79, I had begun to understand how to maintain relationships with former students and their families that did not interfere with the energy and attention a new group of children demanded. So long as my focus was on the present class, former students and their parents understood, better than I originally did, that there was a clear and unambiguous line between being a teacher and being a parent or a friend. I was expected to move on to other children while maintaining casual friendships with those who'd come before. It wasn't as hard as I had anticipated, once I realized that there was a rhythm to my life as a teacher that meant getting close to young people for a fixed period and then, while caring about them and continuing to be interested in their lives, withdrawing and refocusing my attention on the next educational challenge.

My concerns with children have always been pedagogical and not psychological. I have never seen myself as a healer or a counselor, though at times healing and counseling become part of the job. I am concerned with learning, with acquiring skills and understanding, and with eliciting all the creativity and intelligence possible from my students. I become very close to them—but within the framework of their learning and their growth. It is important to make this distinction, because many young people who enter teaching do so to heal hurting children or to overcome social and political oppression. I believe in those things, but what characterizes good teaching above all is concern for the process and content of learning. If I taught in a perfect and untroubled society, I would still be challenged by helping children learn. As it is I teach with what exists and try to make things better. But it is learning and growth that are at the center of my thought and work.

The first time I was consciously aware of this teaching cycle as an integral part of my own life was in September of 1963, when I taught 6-7, the year after the class I wrote about in *36 Children.* In many ways that year was pedagogically more interesting than the earlier ones; I was beginning to understand how learning could be structured for the children and how schools might work. That year also brought my teaching solidly out of Greece and into twentieth-century America.

On September 15, 1963, four African American children were killed when the Sixteenth Street Baptist Church in Birmingham, Alabama, was bombed by white racists. The need to shape learning on the basis of the complex interaction of academic content and current social reality was forced on me that year, as I voyaged with my students through school boycotts, freedom schools, protest demonstrations, and the assassination of a president.

Chapter 2

TEACHING WELL IN A TROUBLED SYSTEM

But it's beautiful to love the world
with eyes
that have not yet
been born.

—Otto René Castillo, "Before the Scales, Tomorrow"

EXCESSIVE SOCIALIZING

When I was a student teacher, my supervising teacher remarked that
I had developed a bad habit: saying hello to any and all of the
children at the school when I passed them in the halls, in the lunchroom, in the schoolyard, and even, when school was not in session,
on the street. I paid no attention to her and eventually got a bad
evaluation for excessive fraternizing with students. These greetings
were not planned or calculated as part of some educational formula;
it was just such a delight to be among children that greetings and
casual conversation came naturally. The informal community of the
children was and is wonderful to behold.

Despite that evaluation and a similar one during my first year of
teaching, enjoying informal and joking relationships with children,

whether they were in my class or not, has always stood me in good stead as an educator. By the time I graduated from 6-1 to 6-7, the bottom class of the sixth grade, which included the students nobody else wanted, many of those in the class were already casual friends. I had given a few a hand with their homework, had helped one of them when he was in trouble with the police, and had an extraordinary series of conversations with one future student, Manuel, whom I met one day after school. He was sitting on the steps, half asleep, and I asked him if something was wrong.

Manuel was a well-dressed—almost formally dressed—boy whom all the other students treated with fear and respect. He had strange eyes that seemed to see beyond and through and within everyone he looked at. Feeling the same strangeness in him that the other children described to me, I mentioned it to some of my colleagues. Some had noticed it, but no one paid much attention to him. He was quiet, a straight-B student with good English whose parents had come from Cuba and owned a corner grocery in the neighborhood. He was the kind of child who slips through school unremarked if you do not choose to look at him closely. If you do, however, it's unlikely you'll ever forget the encounter.

In response to my questions that day, he told me he had been up all night and had received several visitors, who exhausted him: his dead grandmother, an old man who had recently died in Cuba, and an ancient ancestor whom he had never heard of had all spoken through him. If not for his eyes, I would have thought he was putting me on. I offered to buy him a soda and walk him home. On the way we talked about school, homework, everyday things. He didn't want to talk about the séance and it made no sense to intrude upon his privacy.

I know other teachers might have gone to the school counselor or thought there was something psychologically wrong with Manuel. However, through my relationship with the Rodriguez family, I knew that in parts of the Puerto Rican and Cuban communities there were traditional forms of communicating with the spirit world. In my own life, I had encountered the ecstasy of Hasidic Jews and seen dervishes in North Africa. I knew older people who swore they communicated with the dead. I didn't presume to have any definitive knowledge of what went on in such circumstances. Though I was skeptical of such claims, I knew that the people who made them lived perfectly normal and complex lives; I felt that their spirituality was not a matter for me to judge.

I got to know Manuel's younger brother and cousin, who confirmed for me the special role he played within their family and community as a medium for spirits. Manuel himself told me that he never knew who would speak through him and that many of the voices that came out were so strange that they frightened him. Yet he reassured me that no one forced him to do anything, and that often he felt exhilarated and happy after a session.

Nothing he did in the spirit world affected his school performance, which was excellent in my class and, as far as I have been able to discover, throughout his subsequent years in junior and senior high school. Our friendship stood me in good stead with the many students who admired him or knew his special gifts and were awed and perhaps frightened by them.

When I mentioned this episode to some other teachers a few years later, they questioned my judgment; they would have referred him for psychological counseling. I askd whether they would do the same thing for a Pentecostal Christian who had talked in tongues and whose family were believers. Their silence made me feel that they might have, if they could get away with it—but they understood that Christianity is mainstream and Santería isn't, so behavior that they would let pass in a Christian context might not pass if the context was less familiar.

For me the issue was one of respect for Manuel, his family, and their culture, as well as a deep suspicion of all stigma systems. In those days students were stigmatized by notes on their cumulative record cards indicating they had been referred for counseling, had been suspended or expelled at one time, received AFDC, or were considered discipline problems. Children who did not learn in the ways the school tried to teach them were treated differently by teachers and so, in addition to the problems that had caused their trouble in the first place, they had to deal with the consequences of being singled out for special treatment. I felt an obligation to protect Manuel from that stigma system.

Stigmatization was not as institutionalized then as it is now. Dyslexia, educational handicaps, and the attention deficit disorder syndrome were not part of the armory of weapons educators used to protect themselves against their failure to educate the resistant student. Those sham categories of stigma, created to blame students for unimaginative education or adult impatience, were not yet sanctioned; and Ritalin was still considered a dangerous amphetamine, used only for weight loss. I find the proliferation of learning-handicapped programs a distressing development. We have designated more and more youngsters academically deficient and are on the way to creating a permanent educational underclass. Instead of examining our own work, our own lack of creativity, and changing the organization of learning in the classroom, we have put the blame on children.

This trend is likely to grow as the movement for "high standards" kicks into gear and more and more students either resist the pressure of unreasonably intensified demands or crack under it. I believe educators have to take a serious look not merely at what they want students to achieve but at how they expect them to get to those goals. The whole stigma system, ranging from enforced drug use (Ritalin) to separating students in special-education classes to creating specialties and master's degrees based on categories of student resistance to rigid and contentless learning should be abandoned. Instead of creating more degrees in special education we should be spending more time developing creative teachers and complex learning environments.

There was no "educationally handicapped" apparatus in 1963, but those little notes on students' cumulative record cards were a covert way for teachers to warn each other about who was a troublemaker and ought to be treated as such. In June, the day after graduation at P.S. 103, when the classes for next year were assigned, a few colleagues suggested that I take a look at the record folders of some students who were to be in my class the next fall. That way, one of them said, I could arm myself and be prepared for trouble. If I could get on top of potential troublemakers during the first week of school, the students would quickly learn how tough and smart I was and trouble would be minimized during the rest of the year.

I knew some of the teachers used that tactic, picking on the toughest students in their class in order to intimidate the others. However, I refused to anticipate trouble. I intended to give all my students a chance to learn, whatever their prior educational histories. This was considered naive by most of my colleagues, who responded that young teachers always begin as romantics and get toughened up

after they learn how hopeless it was to educate most of the children
—that is, if they survived and went on teaching.

Instead of forewarning myself about next year's students, I spent
time during the summer of 1963 reflecting on what I had learned so
far as a teacher. I planned my next year using that knowledge. I had
to find a way to acquire the kind of knowledge about my students
that was not to be found in test scores or cumulative record folders.
To know that a student is in sixth grade and reads on a 4.7 grade
level is not very useful. All it tells you is that on a standard test the
student is somewhat behind. It does not reveal what she or he *can*
read, or whether she or he likes to read or hates reading altogether.
It does not tell you whether the student is fluent in Spanish but not
in English, or whether the student reads well one day and is hesitant
and discouraged the next. It does not give any specific sense of which
skills have already been mastered and which ones cause trouble. It
provides no indication of how well a student understands a text and
can talk and write about it. Yet all this information has to be part of
the everyday working knowledge of a skillful teacher. You have to
internalize (and continue to update) the specifics of your students'
current skills and be able, for each child, to tell whether she or he
can read a certain book or understand a science manual, read an
article in a newspaper or comprehend a word problem in math.

Having this knowledge is not merely a matter of enabling you to
teach skills better. It helps you avoid humiliating children by asking
them to do things they just do not yet have the skills to do, or by
pitching a creative curriculum at the wrong level for your students'
current state of knowledge. It also makes it possible to slip skills
teaching into every area of the curriculum and to use time efficiently
by pulling aside individual students and feeding them skills that will
allow them to grow as learners.

I learned this painfully in 6-1. Once I decided to do a series of
scene readings from current American drama. I described all of the
scenes to the class, then did what I thought was a creative job of
casting so that the balance of personalities would create just the right
tension to bring out each scene's humor or pathos. What I had
forgotten, to my disappointment and a few students' agony, was that
the casting required a few of the students to read, out loud, material
that they simply could not get through unassisted. On a first reading
of one such scene I had to think on my feet and become a bit of a

clown, reading all of the parts in different voices on the pretext that the scene's complexity required a first reading. This was in order to prevent one of the students, who couldn't read his part, from being humiliated.

Had I internalized all of the students' reading skills I would have handled the situation more effectively. I would have cast the students in the same roles, but would have introduced the text either by giving it a reading myself or by telling the cast that the reading might be difficult for some of them but that they could pull it off if they all worked on it together. Also, I could have rehearsed all the actors in each scene after school myself, prompting the students who had reading problems. In other words I could have solved the educational problem gracefully if I had been accustomed to using qualitative information about how well each of my students read.

I knew this information would be particularly important for class 6-7, which, in our homogeneously grouped school, would contain the worst readers in the grade as well as some students who could read but who were a bother to other teachers. This meant, for reading, figuring out a way at the beginning of the school year to sit down with each student individually and have him or her read to me. This can be very difficult for a teacher who has not figured out how to create a learning community where children do not have to be controlled and monitored all the time. In the case of writing it meant having a sample of their daily writing as early as possible; for math, I needed a take on how well they could do a simple math worksheet. These three items, which would provide pedagogical information I needed to teach that particular group of students well, determined, to a large degree, how I organized the first two weeks of school. To that gathering of information, I added the consideration of some topic that I believed would provoke the students into interesting conversation and further reading and research.

The first task for the summer was to gather a wide range of books so that I could sit and read with my new students. Given that I had no class library—at best, I had a miscellany of books most of which were in bad shape and had been rescued from P.S. 103 during the move—I had to buy the books myself. There was no time to mourn the inadequacy of the school's supplies, and I certainly had no intention of depriving myself of the tools of teaching, or my students of resources for learning. Judy and I scoured used-book stores for children's books and picture books that would interest my new class. Fortunately, from the time I was in junior high school I had haunted the used-book stores on Fourth Avenue and had made a number of bookseller friends, so we could get a lot of good books for very little money.

To teach writing, I decided to modify Sylvia Ashton-Warner's ideas about key words. I would provide each student with a writing notebook the first day of school. Every student would begin the day by writing in the book. I would make a number of suggestions for topics, and also leave open the option of writing whatever they chose if my ideas didn't interest them. That way even students who could hardly write at all could put something in their books and be part of the process. In the event, I was glad I'd chosen to allow that: one of the students, Jerome, could not write at all. He copied out of storybooks, which was fine with me. It improved his handwriting, gave him some familiarity with books, and, as he began to read better during the course of the year, reinforced the skills he was developing.

I had no creative ideas for math at that time, so I made a series of math worksheets that started out very simply with single-figure addition and subtraction and moved through to sixth-grade math. Some of the examples came from worksheets left by a previous teacher, which served me fine as a starting point.

Coming up with themes for study was more difficult, though I felt confident that my previous students' responses to Greek mythology and planning their own dream cities provided a good basis upon which to build. I also planned to spend more time giving the class an idea of what kinds of things people did to make a living in New York City. Once I mentioned that a friend of mine was a pharmacist and another an editor. The kids looked puzzled and asked me where they worked. When I told them, they wanted to know how these people got to do such things. In other conversations I began to realize that my students didn't know much about the kinds of work people did, so I took it upon myself to let them in on the nature of interesting work.

I began gathering information and resources to share with the class. Instead of telling students that there were a few ideal professions to be aimed at—say, law and medicine—I wanted to introduce them to public service work and to work in the arts and crafts, in science, and in small business. I wanted to expose them to dozens of jobs, each of which employed a modest number of skilled people. My idea was to spark in each student, one by one if necessary, some inner desire for satisfying work, and through that desire and the connection to ways to realize it, help them see a way out of the poverty they lived in.

Recently I was reminded of how little has changed for poor children and how limited are the opportunities presented to them. I was doing a demonstration lesson in a junior high school and one of the students asked me if I knew how to fight. I answered that when I was younger I knew how to protect myself but that as I got older I discovered different and more powerful weapons than knives and fists. In fact, I told the class, I would take out my weapons now and share them. Then I reached into my pocket and it was as if the dead had awakened. Even the most bored student looked up with anticipation as I slowly took a fancy pen and leather-covered notebook out of my jacket pocket. They are beautiful objects. We talked a bit about writing as a weapon and about the power of words and ideas. They understood what I was talking about. One of the students said it was a bit like the Bible, whose words can change your life.

Then one of the young men in the front row, the one who had asked me if I could fight, asked, "Where could I get one of those?" At any stationery store, I said. The kid looked blank so I asked, "Who knows what a stationery store is?" No one raised a hand. From conversations with the students after class I realized that *none* of them had ever been in a stationery store or knew where you could buy pens, paper, notebooks, binders, and so on. I found out where the nearest store was and drew a map for the kids.

A few weeks later the teacher called to say that a number of the students had actually bought pens and notebooks and begun to focus on reading and writing in a way that she hadn't seen before.

Back in 1963, I wanted not only to introduce my students at P.S. 103/79 to the complexities of work, but also to spend more time on projects that integrated the arts with other subject areas, to perform experimental science, and maybe even to begin one of my favorite hobbies, model building. One of my goals was to create what resembled a workshop as much as a classroom and where it would be normal for many different activities to go on simultaneously. The year before, I wound up with that by following the students' lead and my instincts as a teacher. Now I wanted to formalize it, to create a learning environment in which most of our time was spent in individual and small-group projects. I didn't abandon full class discussions, class meetings, lectures, or any other means of bringing the children together in learning, as did some of my peers in other schools who were experimenting with classroom organization. I saw, and still see, value in integrating many different ways of approaching learning. Lectures have their place, as do group projects, individual learning, and simple messing about and experimenting.

As I prepared for the school year, other things were also on my mind: the social problems some of the students from 6-1 faced during the summer; the increasingly violent struggles of the civil rights movement in the South; the threat of a school boycott in New York City; and the philosophy book I was contracted to finish by the end of the summer.

My notes for the book had sat untouched on my desk since 1960. It wasn't until 1962, when I was teaching 6-1, that I was inspired by my students' writings to begin it. I largely finished the book over the summer of 1963 and honored my students' influence on it by dedicating it to them.

Several things strike me on rereading *The Age of Complexity* now, over thirty years after it was published in 1965. First, I find that I stand now where I stood then, with a wider view of personhood and a clearer sense of how moral values underlie everything one does, but with the same acceptance of responsibility for creating a decent world and the same understanding that, despite our longing and desire for theological solutions to human problems, we must accept complexity and finitude as the basis of our existence:

> Throughout this book I've attempted to illustrate how many apparently divergent and incompatible philosophies are actually concerned with the same problems. The starting point of modern philosophy is ordinary life. Through a close scrutiny of the daily, ordinary lives even the most extraordinary of human beings must lead, a sense of the complexity facing man emerges. There is no single explanation of all phenomena, no single characterization of language, and most of all, no one point of view from which man "must" be considered. . . . Modern philosophy is not the philosophy of despair, decadence, and anguish it is so often depicted as. It recognizes these aspects of our life, but only in order to overcome them and to resolve our daily confu-

sion. Much of modern philosophy comes to grips with the central problem each of us must face these days—What must men, and more particularly, we as individuals, do in order to create some order out of our chaos, and to produce something constructive in the midst of all our destructiveness? Modern philosophy is a philosophy of difficulty. It asserts once and for all that there is no cheap hope for man. We must work hard or we will not survive in this complex world. But we can survive and possibly thrive through soul-searching reflection, action, and feeling. We must choose what Albert Camus called "the only original rule of life today: to learn to live and to die, and in order to be a man, to refuse to be a god."

The notion of complexity has been central to my thinking about education as well as about life. There is no one road to democracy, no single method for teaching reading, no pat solution to a discipline problem or a question of motivation or hope. There is no single, simple canon that represents the best of human effort, no absolutely clear list of things every child must learn to be a successful human being. I believe that children, guided and informed by self-respect, respect for others, confidence, and compassion, can find many roads to decent and rewarding adulthood, few of which we can reliably predict. In my teaching I'm as concerned with the values children take with them into the future as with the specific things they learn.

I have never felt that science and technology will open the door to the solution of human problems without political and social struggle based on moral principles. I am a cynic when it comes to believing in some abstract notion of "progress," and the Yiddish sensibility I learned from my grandparents and my father has made me too wary of simple answers to complex problems to have any confidence that ideas alone, no matter how progressive, will make life better. We have a lot to learn from other people's dreams, struggles, and history. Voices of the past, speaking in poetry, drama, and literature, have always been a central part of my work. I identify with past struggles for equity and justice and with stories about simple personal struggles to achieve and sustain love. My educational philosophy has always drawn inspiration from past understandings and insights as well as from contemporary ideas.

I have often argued with progressive educators, friends, and colleagues over issues of curriculum content and the role of the past in the development of educational programs. Their strong reaction against teaching the values of the past comes from taking conservative tradition to represent all tradition; consequently they focus on the present and the future to the exclusion of their own progressive past. This has sometimes led to an uncritical acceptance of children's work and a neglect of history and literature. I've been guilty of some of that over the years myself. It is easy to become carried away with the wonder of young people's creations, especially if you witness their flowering in your class after years of being bored and resistant learners.

My concern for what could be called the justice face of tradition, for historical struggles for equity and democracy, and for the incorporation of culture and literature into the content of learning has continued to grow over the years in ways that have further separated my ideas from those of many progressive educators. This separation has widened most recently over issues of multiculturalism. I have increasingly included in my teaching the way different groups of people experience and record the same historical events and worked to learn about my students' cultures. This is no small project, as my students come from over a dozen cultures, half of which I am just beginning to know about.

Ironically, many progressive educators, though acknowledging the need to respect diversity, resist incorporating different cultural modes of learning and understandings of history into their work. For example, issues of adult authority and the role of passing on traditional wisdom often divide progressives from other, equally caring, educators of color. There is as much resistance to Afrocentric education among progressive educators as there is among conservatives.

I first began to think about Afrocentric education and the cultural implications hidden within the standard curriculum while I was planning for 6-7 during the summer of 1963. At the time, the debate over integration of the New York City public school system was in the news. A group of African American organizations, including the NAACP and, locally, the Harlem Parents Committee, was calling for Schools Chancellor Calvin Gross to come up with a satisfactory integration plan and threatening to boycott the public schools and set up their own Freedom Schools in storefronts and apartments. I sympathized with the community groups, yet I was skeptical about the possibility of integrating the New York schools. I even discussed the issue of the desirability of integration with a number of African American friends and colleagues from other schools. Some of them thought that busing African American children would not benefit them educationally; they believed that improvement of the schools would more likely come from increasing the number of Black teachers and teaching Black history and culture. At the time I resisted that idea: I thought it would be wonderful if African American children could learn both Black history and culture and "regular" history and culture. I still saw Eurocentric history and culture as "regular" and Black culture and history as somehow supplemental and inessential. It would take me the entire next year, with the help of several new friends and colleagues at P.S. 103/79, to fight and think my way through the role of culture in learning.

However, I decided to include in my teaching some Black history and, since a number of my new students were Puerto Rican, some Puerto Rican history and culture as well. I also decided to concentrate more on the whole question of civil rights and on segregation in the North, including northern schools. The students would be affected by these issues and in particular by the boycott organizing, which was going on during the summer and would continue into the fall term. It seemed clear to me that there was no will on the part of the white community for the desegregation of the New York City schools. Consequently, whatever plan Gross developed was bound to be some unacceptable evasion. African American community leaders knew this, so it seemed quite likely that the school boycott they threatened to hold during the school year would take place. I felt it imperative to help my students understand what was happening and articulate reasoned personal positions on it.

My position on the boycott was ambivalent. I did not want to think about leaving my class unsupervised in an understaffed school. In addition, to have integration as one's whole goal seemed to be to neglect the glaring need to improve education for my students and the other children in the community here and now, within their young lifetimes. At that stage in my life I did not know and trust activists in the community except for the parents of my students, so I undervalued their knowledge of the kinds of struggles that had to be organized to help children. My life was within the classroom, no matter how much I tried to reach out to parents. It was more than a full-time job learning how to teach well, and until I could do that I didn't feel comfortable getting involved with anything else.

Though I understood the importance of the struggles for desegregation in the South and was committed to the civil rights movement, here on 119th Street and Madison Avenue, where I was surrounded by 400,000 African American and 250,000 Puerto Rican people, the whole battle over integration seemed insincere. Calvin Gross knew that the most he could achieve was token mixing at the boundaries, and his proposals reflected that. The Harlem Parents Committee and the NAACP must have realized it. In June, at the end of the school year, I discovered that some powerful members of both groups despaired of ever seeing any integration plan implemented in the New York City public schools.

My uneasiness with the idea of a boycott was also based on another, more visceral, response I had to how the integration battle was framed in New York. I resented the notion that my students could not learn unless they were in schools that also had white children. As a teacher and an advocate of my students' intelligence and creativity, I refused to accept the idea that even if the educational context was right and the teaching good, they still needed the presence of white students in order to learn. My inclination, that summer of 1963, was to refuse to become part of the boycott for these reasons, and to articulate them in writing for my colleagues and the community if we came to having to decide what to do if a boycott occurred.

The NAACP and the Harlem Parents Committee, being patient and reasonable as they were throughout this struggle, agreed in August 1963 to wait until December for an integration plan before deciding whether to go ahead with the boycott. I knew that the issue of the boycott would be alive in the community during all of the fall semester, so I decided that at the very minimum these words and their histories had to be part of my curriculum: "boycott," "protest," "negotiate," "proposal," "settlement," "agreement," "integration," "segregation," "opportunity," "achievement."

I researched the origins of these words and selected examples of protests, strikes, and boycotts, and of conflicts that had been resolved through negotiation. I decided to explain to the children how their own achievement was measured, what their test scores meant, and how the tests were created. Since a struggle was taking place over their education I felt obliged to let them in on it and, if they chose, become partisans. I felt that the worst that could happen was that some students would become angry enough to become literate about their own lives and thus would acquire the academic skills that such literacy implied. Among other things, my plan was a way of helping the children help me teach them.

The civil rights movement was shocked that June by the murder of Medgar Evers; Judy and I were tempted to join the struggles in the South. Instead, we kept in touch with my students, both from 6-1 and from P.S. 145 and P.S. 41. There was so much to do to help the children get through the summer that our contribution to the struggle in the South was marginal: it consisted entirely of babysitting a whole group of preschoolers while their mothers and fathers took buses to attend the August 28 March on Washington.

When the 1963 school year began I was eager to teach again. The summer was too long for me—and, it seemed, for several of my new pupils. When I got to school on the teachers' prep day before the year began I found Rosy, Richie, and Roger waiting for me outside the building. They had learned which room we would be in and walked me there.

I believe that Rosy and Richie had decided to adopt and protect me for the year and had brought Roger with them as enforcer. They had decided, from observing me during the previous year, that they could learn many things in my class if I didn't become discouraged and abandon the school. They showed, as many children have done since, how much they wanted a good teacher, how badly they wanted to learn, and how much they feared that yet another adult would abandon them.

(I learned later in the year, from one of Richie's older cousins, that protecting good teachers was a common idea floating around the community. In a school where the annual staff turnover was about 40 percent and disrespect for the children and their parents was the norm, the few caring, decent teachers were treated as community treasures. I didn't know this then or have any insight into the sophisticated analysis of the schools that was current in local churches and community organizations.)

That day before school began, Rosy chatted all the way up to the classroom and then proceeded to give me recommendations on how to decorate it. Her suggestions were, for the most part, brilliant: she was giving me a guide to decorating the walls in ways the kids might enjoy, urging me to make our place of learning beautiful and comfortable and begin laying the groundwork for a convivial community of learning.

I told Rosy to look around the room, gave her the keys to the desk and the closets, and suggested she make an inventory of what we had available to make the room ready for the class. I also told her that she could make plans for only one corner of the room, reminding her that the idea that the class should be like a home implied that other students had to have the same power she did to build the environment. She knew exactly what I was talking about and reluctantly accepted my conditions, at least for the moment. It was clear that if left unchecked Rosy would move into any power vacuum in the class. She was also smart enough to comprehend that I understood her desire to control things and would not allow her to become a negative force in the group.

Rosy turned out to be more complex, wiser, and more compassionate than I anticipated. The writing she did in her notebook the first few weeks of school made that clear. Here are some of the revealing pieces she wrote during the first three weeks of September 1963:

Church

A church is the best place were you can go Saturday. A church is a place were you can study and don't be disturbed. A church is everything. I love to go to church on Saturday.

Poems

New moon, true moon, true and bright
   if I have a true love, let me dream of him tonight.
New moon, true moon, true and trusty,
   tell me who my true love must be.
Gypsy, gypsy please tell me.
What my husbands name will be.
Who's table shall I spread?
For whom make the bed? Who's name shall I carry?
And whom shall I marry.

Poems

A mole on the arm.
Will do you no harm
a mole on the lip,
your little to flip.
A mole on the neck,
money by the peck.
A mole on the back.
money by the sack,
a mole on the ear,
money by the year.
If you got a mole above your chin.
You'll never be beholden to any of your kin.

Having a Wife

I say a wife is good to have. When you are tired you don't have to make her breakfast for your wife, she would know about cooking herself. I want a wife because I don't want any children.

Travel

I have never traveled the only place that I have Been was in Brooklyn. I am glad I have been in Brooklyn, in Brooklyn some things are different. Manhattan is a very nice place. Some children wish they live in Manhattan that are in far away places. I would like to go to California because my father was born there.

My Story

Do you know when Abraham Lincoln signed The Emancipation Proclamation that all the Negroes was to be free. Now in Washington they was marching for freedom and they had supposed to have freedom already.

Study

I love to study. Many people like to study but some people don't. When you study you can learn more by studying. Study

and you don't have to ask you teacher how to spell a word. And
when you study you can find yourself around the world. I study
lots of time I hope you do to.

Educationally

I would like to be an educationally person. And educationally
person can get a good job and get more money. I would like
that I want to go and finish school I want to graduate from
college and really get a good education.

During the first few weeks of school I read all of my students'
work several times. Doing so gave me insight into their reading and
writing skills and helped me figure out where to pitch my teaching
and how to shape the curriculum. It also provided tentative insights
into the children's experiences, dreams, aspirations, and worries.
Rosy's writing was particularly revealing. I asked her about the first
piece and suggested she meant Sunday, not Saturday. She said no, the
church was loud and busy on Sunday, but on Saturday she was the
only one there. Her poems were more puzzling. I couldn't tell
whether they were her spontaneous creations, memorized poems, or
simply copies from a book. Each of these options provided teaching
possibilities. Here was a student who seemed to enjoy playing with
language; there were a thousand ways to use that basic pleasure to
develop sophisticated learning.

The first poem probably was copied or memorized. The second
poem was more like a jump-rope rhyme or playground song with
remembered verse and a few variations of her own. Both of these are
the beginning material for the development of poetic sensibility and
the grounds upon which to build a love of literature. Many other
teachers would not be so generous; and instead, they would take
Rosy's writing as an attempt to put something over on them. But
because I set up the writing notebook so that students could choose
the nature and shape of the entries, I had precluded the whole cate-
gory of cheating on the assignment. I wanted my students to develop
some intimacy and fluency with writing and with these notebooks I
hoped to create a free space for written explorations. There were
other assignments demanding more formalized writing and revision.

I wanted the opportunities for formal and informal writing to be as diverse in the classroom as they had been for me several years before in Paris, where I wandered around preparing myself to be a writer. I took notes in an informal writer's notebook, wrote sketches while sipping espresso in cafés, tried (mostly unsuccessfully) to write formally for several hours a day, and took notes on what I read. All these ways of experimenting with written forms were part of the larger task of learning how to write, which now, over thirty years later, still engages and enchants me. For 6-7, I hoped to help my students experience a language environment that did not merely teach the formal skills of writing school papers but also brought them closer to themselves through explorations of their own written voices.

After reading the first entries in Rosy's notebook I thought she might like to be a poet or writer. Why not? Several of her entries said that she aspired to go to college, that she loved to study. I took the line "when you study you can find yourself around the world" to mean that reading and learning, teasing the imagination and discovering things beyond what one learned at home or on the block was liberating for her. Hers was a beautiful way of describing a love of books and learning. My interpretation was not far off. Rosy could read everything I had in class—and in a few weeks, she did. She was always a few steps ahead of the rest of the children, and I had fun keeping up with her. Books were a feast and she loved a well-laid table.

She was the next to youngest of five children. Her three older brothers must have been as brilliant as she, to judge by the way she spoke of them. Two of them were lost to the streets—one had made it to college. Her mother, a strong, wonderful woman, was an informal doctor and adviser who helped people in the neighborhood. When I asked Rosy about her statement about wanting a wife she said that was exactly what she meant. When she grew up she wanted to find a wonderful woman to marry and raise a family with. Men were too much trouble, and raising a family alone was too difficult.

During that year I learned from listening to Rosy and following up on suggestions she made or insights she expressed in casual conversations we had during lunchtime or after school, while she helped me clean up the classroom and prepare for the next day. She took me on walking tours of the neighborhood and pointed out the cops who took bribes, the dealers, and the junkies. She showed me the storefront churches and gave me a running commentary on where helpful and kind ministering took place and where there was trouble. She warned me about what white people shouldn't do in her neighborhood; she was the first student I had who spoke explicitly, openly, and sensitively about race. She talked about the problems she had with some light-skinned children and about how she learned to think about race because she was dark.

Before my first trip to her apartment she warned me that she lived in what the kids called junkies' paradise and told me to stay close to her as we walked up the five flights. She reassured me that there was nothing to worry about from junkies so long as they had their fix, and that the only junkies we'd see in the stairwells were nodding. As we went upstairs she greeted everyone, the junkies included, and confided that these were all people she loved. It hurt her to be where she was, but her pain was bigger than that. She told me again and again—and her actions confirmed it—that she wasn't scared for herself, but for the whole neighborhood, for the block, for what people had to live with.

What Rosy gave me on that and subsequent trips through the community has stayed with me, both nurturing and troubling me. As we toured the neighborhood, it became clear that she saw all the pain people suffered from poverty, racism, neglect, and an excess of worry. She kept her eyes open to it—and yet she saw all the joy, too. Her thoughts and ideas were tempered by a clear and painful vision of the present. This didn't prevent her from dreaming, from imagining a better world, or from being very playful, a bit of a trickster, in fact. But it did prevent her from fooling herself into believing that her fate wasn't tied up with the fate of everyone she cared about. This made her one of the most unselfish people I have ever encountered, and at the same time one of the toughest. She would not let herself be bullied, yet she had no resentment toward those who tried to get at her.

Rosy taught me to keep my eyes open to what is horrible without being overwhelmed by it; to keep hope and a sense of humor alive while being fully aware of the desperate nature of the struggle for decency. I learned by watching her and responded by feeding her insatiable desire for literature and learning.

Richie and Roger, who were brothers, were my other guides to the neighborhood. I never got to know Roger as a student, but by the end of that first morning before school started, we did arrange for him to spend time cooling out in the back of my classroom instead of getting into trouble wandering the halls. Roger was very big and broad. He had a clubfoot and seemed to hop along, dragging it behind him. He also had the largest hands I'd ever seen on a youngster. Other students made fun of him and often challenged him to chase them. The few he caught were messed up pretty bad, which gave him a reputation for having a violent and uncontrollable temper and made some of the teachers fear him. He was always kept under some kind of surveillance, as I had noted the previous year. Yet I never saw him attack anyone or initiate any aggression. My impression was that he was peaceful and troubled, that he was saddened by his disability. I felt he needed to keep his mind busy in a productive way, so one day the year before, when I was on yard duty I showed him how to make a lanyard key chain. After that I kept feeding him some of the small craft projects I provided for students who wanted extra things to do and we agreed to continue the relationship into the new school year. I offered him free passage into my classroom as long as he wouldn't disrupt things, and he accepted. The principal and other teachers agreed; it was better for them to know where Roger was than to have him wandering around the halls, which often happened since his teacher threw him out of the classroom on a regular basis.

Roger's brother, Richie, was wild. He and Rosy hung out together and loved to argue. Where Rosy was thoughtful and clever, Richie was impulsive and extravagant, sometimes even bizarre. He preached when he spoke; even his writing had a biblical quality. He tried to describe and explain everything and his words tumbled over each other. The morning when he and his friends "adopted" me, he tried to tell me a dozen things simultaneously; I needed Rosy's translations to make sense of what he was saying. The few pieces of writing that survive from his notebook illustrate his rhetorical flourishes and his attempt to grasp the complex flow of events and actions:

Richie Jones
(fire)
One day I was in school ad the teachers name Mr. Moldow and
a friend name Bobby, Alex and me were playing basketball and
a friend named Alfred ran in the gym and said it was a fire in
my building and Bobby and me run out the gym and we did not

stop until we got there and Alfred's mother was crying. She said that Jimmy sent a diamond ring from the boat. Jimmy was in the Navy. Jimmy just send the diamond ring the same day too. The diamond ring was under the bed and she told me Bobby and Alfred her son to go over the roof and we did and one of the fireman were putting the diamond ring into his pocket and Alfred said "no you don't" and the fireman gave it to him and told him to go down stairs and we here Bobby crying and I open the door and took a baby out and the soon I was getting to go out the fire separate and went on my face and body and I almost dropped the baby and then I gave it to Alfred and then Alfred run downstairs and Bobby helped me and we went downstairs and Alfred told my mother that I was brave and she told him to go help me. It was burn me and they put me in cold water. The fire was almost over.

Best Wish Stories:

(I think . . .)

I am the greatest writer. I think I remember more then I think. I think I like to writer story. I think I could be the greatest writer in the world. But I think I want to be lawyer but I have to go to school four years. I hate to go to school. Maybe when I get big I might get use to going to school. I hope Mr. Kohl will be my teacher. But when I get mad you better move because I am going to murder you.

Best wish to all teachers.

(color)

Color doesn't make any difference—suppose I am white and you are color and I told you to get out of my store, don't you feel mad and you are very to fight wouldn't you. So I will be mad to. Anyway we have the same blood in us. Why are we fight about you about you are the same, as me but you are fighting. So let go home so color and white can be friendly now until a color man drink want to fight. So color and white start to fight again.

Best wish to color and white.

(my jaw hurts . . .)

I don't like to think because my jaw hurts and when it hurts I don't like to think. and when I think about people I hurt more, and when I think about old people. They more and more, and when I think about sentences they hurt more, more and more and more, and when they hurt, I don't like to think. And when I think about arithmetic they hurt more, more, more and more, they hurt so bad they feel like they are going to fall off.

 Best wish to all jaws that hurt.

(a good thing I did die)
A good thing you can run fast because I will die. And when I die my father will cry and my mother will cry. I don't want my father to cry—a good thing I didn't die. A good thing I didn't die because my mother will fall and went she fall she will fall on no good—I didn't die. No good thing I didn't die because my father will fly and when he fly he glide—a good I thing I did die.

 Best wish to all who glide and who will. die

Some of Richie's flights can be attributed to trying to fill up a page or two a day in the notebook. However, his writing manifests a delight in the flow of narrative and an intense engagement with everything that is happening. Richie was everywhere at once, full of anxiety and insight, always moving, trying to get a sense of a complex whole that was too large for him to grasp. His view of the world was active and fluid; he fell right in with the drama we did later in the year. He could improvise a plot based on almost any idea and could carry on an endless monologue. When shaped, his work was both funny and moving.

 His writing scared me because it dealt with death, violence, disruption, and confusion. Formally it seemed wild and uncontrolled, but it was realistic. The more I understood life in the neighborhood, the more I came to appreciate that the most insidious effects of racism and poverty had to do not with incidents of violence or instances of prejudice, but with a more total sense of threat and marginalization. This, when it did not sink people into hopelessness, was redeemed through the church or through street loyalties. Richie, the eyes and ears of the class, knew too much to be calm; all the other students respected and feared him, because whenever something was happening Richie was there. It seemed ironic that with his eyes so open Richie was close to being functionally blind; he could not even make out shapes without his very thick glasses.

All together there were twenty-seven children in 6-7, and every one was as unusual and interesting as Rosy and Richie. Ronnie James, the tallest and heaviest student in the school, was a born orator who led the passionate debates and discussions that emerged during this very political year. Paul, Allan, and Harold, who along with Ronnie and Richie made up the starting five of our class basketball team, were older than the other students, tougher, and more resigned to being school failures. They were just waiting to be pushed on to junior high and it took a lot of work to convince them to try academics after having failed all the way through school. Intelligence had nothing to do with it, nor did the ability to concentrate and do schoolwork. They were just a defeated trio who were able to maintain status and respect at the school through athletics and fighting ability. I had to win them to learning through content, had to convince them that their understanding of the world and their ability to succeed in it depended on academic skills as well as physical force. I had some success, although to the end of the year Harold and Paul kept defying me. Every little bit of work they did was accompanied by complaint or disruption. By April this became a game, but one that, for reasons of self-respect, they never gave up. They had to show the rest of the class and the other students in the school that I had not conquered their independent spirit. I acknowledged that show of strength and fought meaningless little battles with them over unimportant assignments in exchange for their full participation in most of our activities and their help in developing a spirited, congenial learning environment.

I never reached Allan.

At the center of busy activity in the class from the very first day of school was a group of Puerto Rican girls, Roberta, Maria, Luisa, and Rosa, and their friend Ciro. Ciro was younger than the other students and academically just about as advanced as Rosy. The only reason I could ever come up with for his being in our class was his Puerto Rican accent, which some teacher must have mistaken for a learning problem. He had no learning problems, and in fact was the biggest and most delightful gossip as well as the hardest worker in the class. Everyone seemed to confide in him, and with the protection of Roberta, Maria, et al. as well as of Harold and Eugenio, who was the leader of the Puerto Rican boys in the class, Ciro gossiped from student to student and group to group in ways that informed me of where centers of influence and power lay in the class and the school.

With the exception of Ciro, who talked to everyone, there was a major separation in the class between the fifteen African American students and the twelve Puerto Ricans. Students resented doing group projects across this ethnic divide; until I began an after-school basketball team and league I could only rarely create personal and learning bonds that either used ethnicity positively or overrode it.

Solving the problems of educating all my students, of providing respect and pride across the three ethnicities in our small community (mine being the third), and of engaging in exciting learning was a welcome challenge, into which I threw myself during just about all my waking hours. That year I was on top of things in the classroom and taught with an ease, confidence, and joy I hadn't known before. My plans for the first week went very well. I gave the students their writing notebooks and had my vocabulary lessons all well planned. The presence of dozens of books in the room excited the children; the many small arts-and-crafts projects I seeded throughout the room, as well as the chess and checkers sets I brought to class, got an enthusiastic response. The children knew me from the previous year, and I got the feeling that these so-called problem children understood that this might be a good year for all of us.

BUSINESS AS USUAL

On Sunday, September 15, 1963, during the first weekend of the school year, Denise McNair, eleven, Carole Robertson, fourteen, Addie Mae Collins, fourteen, and Cynthia Wesley, also fourteen, were killed by a bomb planted by white racists in a church in Birmingham, Alabama. That was a very difficult day, spent grieving for those poor children and worrying about what to do the next week, about how to memorialize the girls' lives within our classroom.

When I got to school on Monday I expected all the administrators, teachers, and students to be agitated, wanting to talk and to protest what was happening in Birmingham. I was wrong. The white teachers were clearly tense but refused to discuss the issue. Several told me that we had to get on with our work and not upset the children anymore. The principal agreed that we should teach as usual; when I protested that our obligation to our students and to the ideas of democracy and equality required us to take a stand and show the children our outrage, he commented that I was naive and inexperienced and shouldn't get so excited. The African American teachers, grim-faced, stayed away from the white teachers. The usual casual greetings still passed, but I distinctly remember feeling overt hostility coming from both sides of that unspoken divide that day.

As is my wont, I opened my mouth when other people kept quiet. While walking up the stairs to my classroom, I ran into two of the African American teachers, Joshua Robbins and Joseph Rogers. Joseph was a veteran teacher and a professional classical musician who played in chamber groups and in the American Symphony Orchestra. He taught fourth grade. I'd never had a chance to get to know him the previous year, though I did notice at faculty meetings that everyone in the school treated him with respect. Joshua Robbins was new to the school and maybe thirty-five years old. He kept to himself, much the way I did. He was teaching third or fourth grade and until that day I had never spoken to him, either. When I saw them I blurted out my outrage and my frustration at how the principal and other teachers wanted to ignore the whole event. Joshua gave me a cynical look and Joseph said, "Business as usual." Their rage was tempered by resignation to the culture of the school, in which race was an official nonissue. Neither African American nor Puerto Rican cultural studies was taught; the only person at the school whom I had heard advocating it was Joshua Robbins. He was put down as a hothead who would either be tamed or not last until tenure.

My students didn't seem particularly agitated. I wondered whether they had heard the news. When everyone had arrived and settled down, I told them to put their books and writing notebooks away. It was time for a class discussion of the bombing. My face must have looked particularly troubled: I recall Ciro or Roberta asking me what they had done wrong, assuming that such a negative response had to be their fault. I told them what I had heard on the news, spoke about how awful the murders were, and wrote the word "racism" on the board. Before I could ask the students what it meant and launch some ideas for how we could study racism over the next few weeks,

Paul, who up until that point had never raised his hand in class, muttered, "That ain't nothing new."

I asked him what he meant and he said he and his family had come north to New York from South Carolina because of the racism. The church bombing didn't stand out to him as particularly horrible; it was one of a continuing series of violent actions Negroes suffered at the hands of whites. I was naive, he said, in thinking this was anything unusual.

Ronnie agreed and became angry, even menacing. He turned on several of the Puerto Rican students and talked about getting even with whites. Eugenio objected that he wasn't a white person and that Puerto Ricans had it just as bad as Negroes. I began to be afraid that things would get out of hand and became acutely aware that I was the only white person in the room. I still had the chalk in my hand, though, so I decided to do something to shape the conversation and focus the anger on some issues we could all talk about. As a teacher one learns to react quickly and intuitively in situations like this and turn what could become discipline problems into learning opportunities. This, one of the craft aspects of teaching, develops when teaching rather than controlling becomes second nature.

I drew a very large rectangle on the chalkboard and added two large circles and one small circle inside it. Then I suggested that the rectangle was the class; one large circle was the group of African American students, the other was the Puerto Rican students, and the third was me. Then I asked if someone else could draw another diagram that showed a different way to divide the class. Rosy caught on right away. She jumped up and drew a rectangle with two circles, one containing males and the other females. That way, she said, I was included in one of the circles. She provided me with a second word for study (the first being "racism"): "inclusion." From that word came a series of others I decided later in the day to use for the regular spelling list of ten words for the week: exclusion, integration, segregation, violence, civil rights (this counted as two words), demonstration, and protest.

I didn't worry about the difficulty or grade level of the words; I knew that once their meanings were elucidated none of the students would forget them. The passion and rage I sensed submerged in the classroom and implicit in the exchange between Ronnie and Eugenio were enough to motivate learning if I could provide ideas, content, and shape to our consideration of the causes and consequences of the bombing.

After writing "inclusion" on the board, I asked for more ideas about how to divide the class. Richie cynically suggested we do it into rich people and not-rich people; he drew one big circle, and then an "X" for me. Although I protested, there was no way I could convince the class that teachers weren't rich—we were, from the perspective of the residents of the neighborhood.

I brought the conversation back to Birmingham and we talked for a while about how horrible it would be to die young and how terrible the victims' families and friends must feel. Maria suggested we write them letters, though I can't remember now whether we did. What stumped us was understanding what kind of people would perform such an act and why racism would be such an all-consuming, ugly force in their lives.

I spoke to Joshua Robbins later in that day and told him about our class conversation. He told me my approach was completely wrong, that I had a white perspective on things and should be teaching cultural pride and Black history instead of trying to deal in a sympathetic and understanding way with racism. I wasn't sure what he was getting at, but I did persuade him to meet me after school that Friday for a cup of coffee so we could talk about his objections to my work.

That Tuesday the following article, which I shared with the class during reading time on Wednesday, appeared in the *New York Times:*

WHITE BIRMINGHAM 4TH GRADE CLASS
BACKS NEGROES IN CLASS THEMES
by John Herbers

(Special to the New York Times)

Birmingham, Ala., Sept. 17
    "It [The bombings] would stop if the people would quit waving Confederate flags and other things like that."
    "I think the Negroes have a right to fite back."
    "If the I was a Nigro I would threw rock and thing fuilish."
    These are some of the opinions of white 9-year-old school children in Birmingham, as expressed in essays on Sunday's church

bombing that killed four children and set off racial clashes in the city that resulted in the deaths of two others.

The papers were written by students in a fourth-grade class of a public school situated in a lower-middle-class section of Birmingham. The woman teacher, who asked not to be identified, said she had asked for the children's opinions without attempting to influence their thinking.

ALL VOICE SYMPATHY

All 25 students in the class expressed sympathy for the Negroes. A number connected the bombing with anti-integration demonstrations in Birmingham during the last two weeks.

The poor spelling was explained by the fact that the class is made up of students who were not the most advanced. Those with higher I.Q.'s are in a separate class, so they may advance at a faster rate.

"I think the person that bombed the church should get a trial and sinunst for life," one boy wrote. "And I think the Negroes have a right to fight back. and I think if the people wood stop waving the Confederate flags [the bombers] wouldn't do all this."

"I think [the Negroes] should be free like the white people," another boy wrote. "If I was a Negro I would threw rock and thing foolish. They should have a right to go to our school. They have to live just like us. They are like us but they have a different skin. We are white and they are black. There is know different in color."

A girl wrote:

"There was a car honking there horn. There were Confederate flags all over the car. They were yelling 2, 4, 6, 8 we don't want to integrate."

"SORRY FOR CHILDREN"

"I think the people who bombed the church ought to be put in jail for life. And I feel sorry for those 6 children who got killed."

A boy said bombing the church was "foolish ... that man, well what they call a man, was mean. He must be put in jell."

"I don't believe the children had nothing to do with it," a girl wrote. "The one who did that should be asham doing that in church, because that is Gods house.... God loves all his children."

"Who started all this?" a boy asked. "who ever bommed the church is a killer. I think he ought to be in the electric chair."

A girl wrote:

"There is a colored man and woman that works for my grand

mother. They help her in the garden ever summer. My grandmother gives them vegetables out of the garden for helping her. They are very nice."

We discussed the article. Ronnie, in the lead once again, challenged the *Times* for only asking the opinions of white kids. Another student wondered why people were always talking about how dumb some kids were. She wondered whether the article implied that only white kids who weren't smart liked Negroes. As the students continued to critique the article I realized how much I had to learn about issues of racism and how important it was for me to try to think my way into my students' perceptions of the world.

The most frightening immediate consequence of making this effort was the realization that the students had no reason to trust me as a person and every reason to think of me as white above and beyond thinking of me as Mr. Kohl, the nice teacher. If they offered me their uncritical trust, as I had hoped would happen, they would be acting contrary to their experience and their parents', and exposing themselves to potential harm. To win their trust was a complex, long-term, and sensitive matter. I chose to win it—not through psychology, but through reading, writing, science, and math. I could provoke and shape the kind of discussions and projects that led to trust while at the same time helping the students develop their intellectual skills and learn to read and write with greater ease and sophistication.

This was a critical time in my growth as a teacher, a time when I began to articulate what it meant to be an activist teacher. I began to see that the key to my role and effectiveness was the ability to develop the skills and hone the intelligence my students needed to both maximize their chances of personal success and sustain a commitment to the nurturance of their community. In other words, I saw myself primarily as a teacher trying to live out in the classroom the values I held as a person.

After the bombing in Birmingham and the subsequent demonstrations, the hosing of children on the streets of that city, the arrest of Martin Luther King, Jr., and other leaders, and the escalation of violence in the South, talk of Freedom Schools and boycotts increased. Many teachers at 103/79 felt a need to express solidarity with the civil rights movement and believed that a temporary school boycott and Freedom Schools would make it clear that there was also a struggle for civil rights in the North.

My summer resistance to the boycott was strengthened by the way in which people talked about Freedom Schools. Many of the people talking boycott were terrible teachers whose classrooms were chaotic or sterile. Much of the pro-boycott lunchroom talk implied that integration would solve the children's learning problems by giving them proximity to well-behaved, motivated white students. I agreed that there was a deep problem with the school but couldn't see how the proposed action would affect that one bit. When the principal implied that he would, at least covertly, support the boycott and the Freedom Schools, I became even more skeptical. In my view, if he wanted to change things and challenge racism in the school, he could simply take some chances and do it.

During that fall semester I started thinking beyond my classroom. Before then, most of my thoughts had been about how to make education work for my children. As soon as I began to understand how to do that, I had energy left for thinking about other children and the more general organization of education.

My conversations with Joshua Robbins the week of the bombing and throughout that school year were very troubling. Joshua informed me that he thought my curriculum, with its emphasis on Greek and Latin word origins and Western European culture, was not good for the children. He didn't deny that much of my work was effective, but insisted that without Black history, study of the African origins of Western culture, and an African-centered view of the world, the children would be damaged no matter how well I taught them to read, write, calculate, or speak. Useful education was a matter of inculcating in the students the pride that would enable them to resist the racism they would inevitably face in the white world. Such an education would also let them see the strengths within their community and culture, strengths much less visible than the terrible consequences of racism and poverty.

Nowadays this sounds like an old and common argument; it has transformed many people's perception of how education should be done. In 1963 it sounded strange and not fully credible. Joshua knew and honored Western culture, to an extent; he was a percussionist and performed Renaissance and medieval music. However, mastering part of the culture of Europe, he explained, also gave him insight into the way in which racism and exploitation were integral parts of the thinking that also led to the great achievements of Western culture. For him, without a heavy and continual emphasis on Black culture—without what is now called Afrocentric education—Black students would be damaged by what they learned. Students had to see themselves in what they studied, or they would always be struggling for full dignity and an appropriately affirmative vision of their place in society.

Joshua's words disturbed me but fit with what I saw happening among a number of my former students from 6-1. Phillip told me he was tired of white superheroes; he began a comic called "Combinative Man, the First Black Superhero." Larry began to write poems referring to Black pride and culture. Many of the ideas of the Student Nonviolent Coordinating Committee and the beginnings of the Black Power movement were absorbed by the kids on the streets. And the results were impressive: students who couldn't read became interested in reading about themselves and their people; small reading groups of adolescents formed to deal with provocative texts; despair was refocused on the militant texts that were everywhere in the community. There was a sense on the streets that literacy was for the people even if schools weren't. Malcolm X, preaching on the streets a few blocks from 103/79, had the kids talking and thinking. It was clear that I had to learn what was coming from within the community rather than just bring what I knew to it.

I integrated a study of the events in the South into my program and began, very slowly, to change my curriculum. If Joshua was right, there remained the problem that I didn't know enough African American or African history to teach it well and had no resources available to begin to do a credible job. Furthermore, almost half my students were Puerto Rican; their culture and history had to be honored as well, if Joshua's underlying argument about the relationship between the curriculum and the student was correct. Not least, there was the problem of how a white man could teach these subjects in ways that did not seem arrogant or condescending.

I began by introducing great people and events from Puerto Rican and African American history. I knew this wasn't what Joshua had in mind, as he wanted African American history at the center of the curriculum, but in taking a step toward his ideas, I had to watch my students' responses, had to get an intuitive feeling that this was a sensible way to shape the curriculum, before I plunged in. I wanted to keep what was working and use Rosy and Roberta, Eugenio and Ronnie, and the other children as my guides through what seemed a perilous and very bold experiment both with culture in the classroom and with my cultural attitudes and biases.

Meanwhile, two events finally convinced me, much to my subsequent regret, not to become involved with the boycott or the Freedom Schools. One was a nightmarish effort at school reform that came from within P.S. 103/79; the other was the demise of my experimental basketball league for the fifth and sixth grades.

The basketball league had begun when I started staying after school for an hour or two in order to meet privately with current students and be available to help some of my former students with their junior high school homework. Harold, Paul, and Ronnie asked me if I would spend one or two afternoons a week with them in the gym so they could play basketball. I agreed, and since the custodian stayed at the school until five we could use the gym without having to get permission to keep the building open.

The first day about ten of my students showed up. I set some very clear rules. First, no one could leave the gym during the time we were there. Second, we all had to leave the school together. And third, when we left the gym it had to look as if we'd never been there. The custodian was doing me a favor by letting us use the gym and I wanted to be sure he didn't get into trouble because of it.

My students' first time out on the court was a combination of shocking and hilarious. I divided the ten students into two teams based on my intuition about how well they could play, and set up a scrimmage. After the jump ball, Harold ran down the court, tried some fancy moves, and missed a simple layup. Paul, who was the opposing center, grabbed the rebound and looked around. Eugenio, his teammate, was unguarded under the basket at the other end of the court. Paul saw him, muttered something, and refused to pass to him, instead throwing the ball to Ronnie, who was triple-teamed and immediately lost the ball. After a wild scramble, Philip, the smallest boy in the class and one of the most agile, came up with the ball and ran to the nearest basket and shot. He missed and Allan punched him. As a fight ensued, Harold picked up the ball, dribbled untouched to his basket, and made an easy shot.

I grabbed the ball and called an extended time-out. It was time to talk about basketball as a game. I told the kids I wasn't sure whether to shout at them or laugh at how silly they all looked. Then I got everyone to line up and do layup drills. I put on my best coaching demeanor and explained how important teamwork and cooperation were. I used the word "team" so many times that some of the boys must have dreamed it that night.

After shooting and passing drills, things settled down. I think the group was developing a feeling of possibility, a sense that this was something they could do well. Everyone was in good physical shape, and as I structured the drills each player could feel himself improving. The fourth time Eugenio dribbled at full speed up and down the court I could sense him relaxing and see grace emerge. Paul, the tallest player, began to dance around the keyhole and get a feel for what it meant to play center. And Harold, who never smiled, who was feared by all the other children at school, who could not read or do math unless I sat with him one on one and provided constant encouragement—Harold, who intrigued me and made no move to express any feeling toward me whatever—clearly had the potential to be a fine player in all facets of the game. He was the only one who had what could be called basketball knowledge. Whenever he had the ball during scrimmage he looked around to see where everyone else on the court was. When he didn't have the ball he was always moving around, setting up things on offense, going after the ball on defense. He never stopped moving or thinking, had a fine eye, passed accurately, and shot well. The only thing he lacked was spirit. He played with a combination of grim determination and mechanical efficiency. The spirit of the team had to come from elsewhere—perhaps from Ronnie, once he learned not to beat up teammates who missed their shots.

After a few weeks the ten students had grown to fifteen or eighteen per session. Some of the girls showed up and became a self-organized cheerleading squad. I believe these one or two afternoons a week contributed more to school spirit than anything I could have done in the classroom itself. And the results did spill over. In the classroom, the African American and Puerto Rican students mixed reluctantly, and only when I forced the issue. But on the basketball court and in the cheerleading squad, the more the students enjoyed the game the more they seemed to forget ethnicity. After a few instances when students used "nigger" and "spic" to express their feelings about missed shots or dropped passes I made it a condition of my participation that such expressions were prohibited. When someone used a racial slur after that, I ended the session and told everyone that if it happened again the whole basketball venture would be closed down. That was a gamble on my part; I don't know how I would have responded had the insults and slurs continued. Though things might've been muttered under people's breath, I didn't hear any racial slurs again.

Word got around in school that we were playing basketball. Other students wanted in, too, and my students, tired of scrimmaging with each other, agreed that it would be great to have a league. I tried to get another teacher to volunteer an afternoon or two but didn't succeed. So I came up with a plan: I would work as a coach for a day with any other sixth-grade class if they could form themselves into a team of five or more. Then later that same week I would referee a game between that team and my class's team. This gave us more games than any other class, and some students complained, but I saw no other way out. Besides, my method saved me from the complaints of my own students, who I was sure would feel abandoned if I stopped our twice-a-week practice.

The league progressed through the fall and winter and, astonishingly, we had no fights. (Minor skirmishes on the court were part of the game.) Everyone came and went together and there were no complaints from the community or other teachers or the administration—or so I thought. One day before the Christmas break I got a note from the school's union delegate. He instructed me to stop the basketball league immediately: I was running an unpaid, illegal after-school center.

I talked to the delegate and protested that what I was doing helped the kids, was on my own time, and was costing the school nothing. I had even provided the basketballs so as not to be accused of using the school's equipment. My arguments were useless. I was accused of being young and naive; of getting too close to the students; and of creating a program without going through proper channels. When I offered to go through those channels I was told that there weren't any, since no after-school basketball program had been funded. When I begged the delegate, who was backed up by the principal, who did not want to confront the union, he just laughed and told me that the program was over.

This delegate was one of the school liberals. He supported the boycott, made it clear that he would volunteer at a Freedom School for a day or two, and believed that integration was the solution to the school's problems. And he did, indeed, close the basketball program down. I told the students that the season was over and shared my powerlessness with them. They understood defeat and shrugged it off as another example of "business as usual," of the way they expected to be treated by white folks. Harold even reassured me that we were still a good class and could do other things together.*

I felt that if people like our delegate were supporting the boycott there was something deeply wrong with it; even if it had the support of community organizations, it was coming from people who cared more about the system than the children. I wouldn't have felt this if I'd been more closely related to leaders in the community.

The other event that caused me to resist the boycott also got me to look more closely at the pathologies built into the organization of public education. Our school became a MESS school—a mess, indeed. MESS, as I remember it, stood for More Effective Special School. A MESS school was one participating in a program designed by the New York City schools chancellor and the teachers' union, the United Federation of Teachers, to improve the quality of education in the schools with the lowest reading and math scores. The idea was to provide after-school tutorial programs so that students who needed help could work with their teachers in small groups or one on one. (The program resembled somewhat President Clinton's current proposals for reading volunteers in the schools.) The program included funds to pay teachers for their time so the work wouldn't have to be done by volunteers. In fact, it was a very attractive way for teachers to supplement their income.

As far as I could tell, very little thought went into planning the program. The basic idea was that if the same teachers, using the same books with the same educational ideas and holding the same attitudes toward the children, could only work with small groups or individuals academic skills would flourish. This was the same thinking that

---

* One small result of this short-lived program was that Harold became a disciplined, highly skilled basketball player who was recruited out of junior high to a high school in the Bronx and made all-city for several years. Paul, Allan, and Eugenio also played varsity high school basketball.

looks toward small class size and small schools as the solution to educational problems. In my experience, these may be necessary conditions but they certainly aren't sufficient. Bad teaching can take place in schools of any size, with any number of students. One has to look to educational changes for the solution to educational problems, to how teaching happens and not just to numbers.

There was a general call for staff to participate in the program. About twenty teachers volunteered, though there was funding for only ten or eleven, plus a supervisor. One of the assistant principals became the supervisor. I volunteered since I stayed after school every day anyway, but was turned down because of my of lack of seniority. Assigning places by seniority was a formula for disaster. With a few exceptions, the teachers who had been at the school the longest were the most cynical about the children and the community. They had low expectations for their students and made no effort to develop or discover curricula that worked. They were also the biggest gossips; they said things about students that decent people just don't say of anyone. They turned out to be the majority of the MESS teachers, and I witnessed the tragicomedy they put on after school for a few months before the whole experiment collapsed.

The program's first problem was getting students to stay after school with teachers they didn't like. An effort was made to identify qualified students and make their parents responsible for getting them to stay after school. Though the program was supposed to be voluntary for the students, covert coercion was necessary: teachers wouldn't be paid unless they could fill the classes. But students simply didn't want more time with these people doing the same things they had failed to do during the school day.

When the parent-pressure route failed students were given incentives: books to take home, candy, and other tokens for attendance and performance. There were no clear lines of adult responsibility, and thanks to this disorganization half the students wandered freely through the halls during the hour of the program. I saw all this because I kept up my old habit of staying after school with some of my present and former students.

To an outsider the program must surely have seemed like a crazed parody of education. Teachers who screamed at their classes during the school day screamed at groups of four and five children after school. Soon all the parental pressure and token rewards in the world couldn't keep most of the children in the program. In addition, the idea of unsupervised halls delighted many junior high kids, who came over from James Fenimore Cooper Junior High School, which was across the street, to check out what was going on.

Perhaps some parts of the program were effective, though I didn't see any. Eventually I was asked to substitute-teach, as many of the teachers stopped showing up. MESS was not pleasant for them, either, since many of the children, sensing that things were out of control, refused to cooperate with the teachers in any way. It was a game for the kids—an unfortunate game, in that they were the victims, often sinking deeper and deeper into a dysfunctional rejection of reading and writing that could only disempower them. I quit as a substitute, unwilling to be complicit with manufactured failure that masqueraded as reform.

I had many arguments with the assistant principal who ran the program. A decent person, she had supported some of the first- and second-grade teachers who were trying to be creative. She was also a great boycott and Freedom School advocate and a committed integrationist. Yet she defended the program and, in particular, the idea that reduced class size was the key to school reform. Before she became an administrator she had been a union activist and supported, as a springboard for educational change, the reduction of student-teacher ratios. I kept asking her what the failure of MESS meant in terms of reducing class size. Certainly, it makes sense to have a reasonable number of students, and classes comprising more than twenty-five students are challenging to teach, but, I wondered, what reason was there to think that teachers who had failed with thirty students would be any better with twenty-five—or ten, for that matter. MESS proved to me that there were other important considerations to face having to do with the quality of teaching and learning, even if they led to getting rid of some teachers or confronting them for being terrible with the children. I told my colleague that some teachers at our school were unsuited for the job, period. That comment ended our conversations, and did little to encourage my interest in the impending school boycott.

To feel so critical of the school I taught in was troubling. I wanted to be part of the staff, to have my work understood and even praised. There was so much I didn't know about teaching or understand about learning that I felt a need for mentors and friends. I worried about appearing arrogant and snobbish. But my eyes were open and the school, as an institution of learning, was dysfunctional. Most of the teachers had given up on the children and learning was not taking place.

Fortunately, I was not alone in my perceptions. Judy substitute-taught that year and perceived the same disarray and disillusion I felt every day. I had also made a few teaching friends at 145 and 103 and we used to get together and tell teaching tales.

Rob Williams, a teaching friend from my semester at P.S. 145, had taught a sixth-grade class a few doors away from mine. He could hear our afternoons of music and watch the comings and goings of my students. I noticed him observing me on the playground with my class, or after school when I sat and talked with High Lee and Jaime, or provided extra reading for Haydee or Vincent. After a while we started meeting for a beer after school or spending evenings at Count Basie's or Small's in Harlem talking about school and life. Rob loved the kids and knew all their tricks. As an African American male who had attended the New York City public schools, he had some perspective on the multiple routes to failure faced by most of our students, and though he kept quiet at faculty meetings he had a thoroughgoing disgust with the way the school was run and the children were treated.

Rob's feelings came out during our late-night conversations. It wasn't just the schools he attacked, but my work and relationships with the children as well. According to Rob, I was just another white do-gooder, a temporary charity worker in the lives of the children. I denied it but didn't have a life's work with which to prove myself. Rob's attitude toward me changed when I was involuntarily trans-ferred to 103. Many of my former students became his pupils and he grudgingly admitted that they had learned something through the chaos he perceived my work to be. In fact, not only did they read and write, but they asked questions to learn and not just to provoke; they were mischievous and slightly wicked but nevertheless had the makings of scholars and engaged and knowledgeable citizens.

It struck me that we had become friends over my students' per-formance, and not over my philosophy or pedagogical stance. Rob saw the children—*his* children just as they had become *my* children —become stronger, more knowledgeable, with greater hope and promise. That was what counted; he couldn't have cared less whether

I used magical incantations or the latest research and technology. The reason, one that I concur with, is that it is in the personal, intimate, everyday working out of teaching and learning that effective education takes place. Pedagogy and theory must emerge from success on the ground rather than being imposed upon children for intellectual or political reasons.

There were other teachers, more experienced and patient than I, who had become my friends. The problem we all faced was how to thrive surrounded by people who resented good practice and were supported by institutional indifference to the children's personal lives and learning. The problem of teaching well in a bad school raised questions and provoked our fantasies. Could we all get assigned to the same school? Could a few of us eventually become administrators and create good schools with teachers of our choice? Might we one day get a foundation or government grant to run an experimental school within the public school system? The question that never was raised within our small community of educators was whether the children could learn. We all believed that every child could learn and that it was our job to make that happen.

Interestingly enough, many of our fantasies have become realities within public school systems now, over thirty years later, and many of the people who longed for the power to make education work when they were teachers are now doing it as school directors, administrators, and educational policymakers. If you hang in there long enough, you have a fair chance of gaining the power to do good things for children.

TEACHING STEADY
AND GETTING ANGRY

One of the biggest challenges for me with 6-7 was keeping up a steady rhythm of learning through the traumas of that school year. The events in Alabama shaped my social studies curriculum and informed my students' writing and thinking. But there are other, less dramatic things that have to be done in an elementary school classroom, such as math and science. And there were also some long-range challenges that I found worrying. They had to do with the future of my students, with their lives after our time together. Teachers like

Rob had been around long enough to experience the pain of seeing promising young people get lost on the streets, die too young, or live lives of quiet despair, marginal and poor. Of course, there were occasional successes, all the more important because they made a life of teaching seem useful and rewarding. But those of us who are "lifers" in education get less pleasure than one may imagine from the successes; it takes quite a bit of will and unknown reservoirs of love not to be brought down by all the children who get lost and damaged.

These were new worries for me, ones that had not been part of my childhood dreams of being a teacher. After almost two years of teaching, however, it was clear that I had connected with something very deep in myself and that those early dreams had represented something necessary for me. I didn't have to put away my toys anymore; I didn't have to stop learning; and I could use what I knew in the service of others. I believe it was during my year with 6-7 that I realized I was a "lifer" and that my childhood dream would be my adult reality.

It's very difficult to be equally excellent across the curriculum as a beginning elementary school teacher. This is particularly true when you are not provided books or other resources and are left to your own devices to cover all of the subjects in the curriculum, as I was. For my first few years of teaching, math was a matter of my staying a few worksheets ahead of my students. The only interesting things I did were to teach my students how to teach each other and to invent elaborate stories or situations that involved simple math word problems. For example, I might create a small grocery business and have the students calculate a day's profit or loss using the prices actually charged in a local store as well as the usual wholesale margins; or I would have the children price a trip to Puerto Rico and have them figure out how to save that amount of money based on an actual salary one of their parents might be earning. I found that these practical situations interested the students and made it easier for them to grasp mathematical ideas.

The main theme of the class that fall was the work people do. During my year with 6-1—and even more so during the first few weeks with 6-7—it had become clear to me that the students had a great deal of anxiety over their futures. They would be leaving elementary school in June. Without major changes in their learning opportunities many of them would not graduate from high school, and only a few would go on to college. Naturally, they were concerned with work and worried about being caught on the streets, or trying to make it in the underground economy, or being trapped in low-paying, demeaning jobs. At the time high-status work for people in the neighborhood was a job in the post office or in some city department, or a post as a minister, secretary, taxicab driver, nurse, beautician, or barber. A few ran small businesses out of their homes. Some people sold cosmetics; others provided child care, gave financial advice, or practiced informal traditional medicine. Many of the children's parents did backbreaking labor at small factories for minimum wage or took care of other people's children or cleaned houses downtown, in white Manhattan. All the local shops were owned by people from outside the community, and as far as I knew nobody who worked at the bank, which was about six blocks from the school, lived in the neighborhood of 103/79.

And then there were people who worked in the underground economy—people who ran numbers, made bootleg whiskey, fenced stolen goods, and sold drugs. The kids knew about all of this work and had to place themselves somewhere in the spectrum of these activities unless provided with other options. Many of the parents had high expectations and dreams for their children. I learned this from Ann's and Larry's mothers, and from Roger and Ruth's mother and father; I assumed it, anyway, knowing that my own parents and neighbors had hopes for us as children that went beyond what people on our block currently did.

My role as a teacher was to validate these larger dreams, widen the fields of possibility, spark the children's imaginations and help them on their way to fuller lives. I devoted two of the four classroom walls to an evolving floor-to-ceiling chart of what people did to make a living and build a life in New York City. I also imposed upon as many of my friends as were willing to come to class and talk to the children about their work. We had visits from journalists, doctors, artists, musicians, writers, accountants, scientists, contractors, and perhaps several dozen others. I added their information to the chart and tried to arrange for interested students to visit my friends' places of work. Many of the children had never been downtown into the white world and I made sure that they were well treated and welcomed.

After I had been building this map of vocations for several months, a number of parents and teacher aides asked if they could attend these career talks. By the end of the school year the class was crowded every time we had a visitor to talk about work. In fact, Richie's mother asked me if I would be willing to give an evening class at her apartment—not on vocations, but on how to pass civil service exams. Judy and I bought civil service exam books and for several months, along with several friends of ours, met once a week with some community members and had a small volunteer tutorial program.

Just as I was figuring out how to integrate our study of the origins of English and of Greek mythology with the civil rights movement, Black and Puerto Rican culture, basic skills, and the theme of work, President John F. Kennedy was assassinated.

What do you tell children when the president is assassinated? What do you say about stability, about legality, about hope? Like most people who lived through that time I remember where I was on November 22, 1963, when I learned about the event. Judy and I were home; we noticed teams of armed policemen moving slowly across the roofs of buildings across the street on First Avenue and St. Mark's Place. We heard helicopters overhead. This clearly wasn't an ordinary police chase, so we turned on the TV and got the horrible news. My thoughts turned first to my children. I remembered how, as a child, I was bewildered and frightened by my parents' and grandparents' response to the death of Franklin Delano Roosevelt. His last days were tied up with the last days of World War II and the Holocaust, and my grandparents responded to the radio announcement of his death with cries and screams. My parents were more restrained but equally upset. As a child I got the feeling that the world had been shaken, that even the tenuous and unhappy stability of wartime was undermined.

Later that November evening the magnitude of the event sank in. I had not been a Kennedy aficionado; I felt his response to the civil rights movement was much too slow and his support of the counterrevolutionaries in Cuba misguided. Nevertheless, it was difficult not to feel part of the larger spirit of his presidency, which promised that the most intractable social and economic problems were indeed solvable. And to see life stolen from someone so young was horrible in itself—horrible on the streets and in my students' neighborhood, and horrible at the top.

I didn't sleep much that night. Nothing came to me to tell my students and I went to school the next morning feeling blank, wondering how they would be that morning, and how we would get through the day.

I was met by two surprises. First, many of the children were not particularly upset. They looked upon Kennedy as another white man who had made promises he didn't keep and who had to be pushed to help Blacks and Puerto Ricans. Malcolm X's comment on the assassination, "The chickens coming home to roost," was greeted with considerable sympathy in the community and by many of the older children. The fact that Kennedy died young, which had affected me so much, was nothing unique. As they saw it, he had simply shared the fate of many people they knew who had gone before their time. The second surprise was that his being president was not necessarily a matter of honor. Given segregation and the everyday reality of racism and poverty in their lives, reverence for those in power was less than universal.

However, some children and other members of the community were deeply grieved. One moving sign of that was the name given to a baby born late the morning after the assassination: President Kennedy Gonzalez. At first the name seemed awkward to me, but the honor of it—the conscious attempt on the part of the baby's mother and father to memorialize the person and to give him new life in their own child—was wonderful.

In class we talked about President Kennedy and President Kennedy Gonzalez, and I raised the sensitive issue of indifference or even scorn toward Kennedy. This opened up one of the most difficult and emotional conversations of my teaching career. Ronnie was the most adamant in feeling that Kennedy got his due. He said that Kennedy should have gone to Birmingham after the church bombing; because he didn't go, he got what he deserved. Several of the other boys agreed.

Rosy was angry at them and, for the first time in the class, almost out of control. A number of other girls, too, were clearly grieving; several were crying. Most of the children, though, were silent; I read everything from sorrow to rage to confusion on their faces. There was no unified sense of mourning, no feeling of bringing a grieving community of children together and helping them recover hope. For some of the children there was little hope in the first place. For others, the monster of racism stood between them and grief for the dead president, who was looked upon as a stranger and potential enemy, a leader of a foreign country. Only a few of the students—Rosy, Roberta, Maria, John, and Eugenio among them—had shared in a sense of "Camelot" and had heard that this was supposed to be a president who cared for them and would improve their lives.

I held the discussion under tight rein, not letting the children yell at each other or turn away from a direct response to the death. No one was forced to speak, but all I could think to do was talk this through together, feeling that we could be bound together, despite our differences, through open conversation and continuing dialogue. I did not and do not believe that it is useful to compel anyone to play-act grief—to simulate the emotions expected of them or to sit in compulsory silence when they are in complete opposition to what is being said or done. The only authentic response for the class was to participate in the complex process of seeking wholeness and understanding through their own pained and aggrieved consciousness.

During the discussion I occasionally raised a question, and one of these led us off in an unexpected direction: What happened in our country when we lost a president? Only half a dozen children knew there was a vice president. Some thought there would be a new election; others were sure there would be riots in the streets and chaos. One child asked what happened to the laws and the army when the president died.

The children had opened up a whole new series of pedagogical questions for me. When was government supposed to be taught? How much should sixth-graders be expected to know about the way the society works? What should I do to help them learn what they needed to know? What was the fit between my work, what children could reasonably be expected to know and needed to know, what the system set out for them, and what they did or didn't learn? This led to other troubling questions: How much curriculum making should an individual teacher or group of teachers undertake? What are your responsibilities as a teacher to what the system mandates versus what you conscientiously believe children ought to know? What do you do when students simply have not yet learned things that you are not mandated to teach them but that are necessary for their understanding of the world?

All of these questions revolve around the central question creative teachers in most schools face: how free is one to shape the learning environment and curriculum if one's best judgment runs directly in opposition to the demands of the administration or district policies? I believe from the day I decided to become an elementary school teacher my intent was to follow the lead of the children first, consider my conscience second, and weigh the demands of the system third. I learned to do this in high school when I was president of the New York City Inter-GO Council. I spent a lot of time at 110 Livingston Street in Brooklyn, the headquarters of the board of education, and did not emerge with much respect for the people who made and implemented educational policy. And I had learned from the few good teachers I had as a student in the New York City public schools that the most important thing was to help children become sensitive and intelligent adults, the set curriculum be damned. My few rebel teachers were the ones who helped me get into Bronx Science and Harvard.

The problems that were highlighted on November 23, 1963, have remained with me, and the responsibilities of a caring teacher in an uncaring system constitute a central theme of my writing about school and education as well as of my current work with schools and teachers. At that time, for that class, I added to the list of things I intended to do with my students a mini-course on the structure of the U.S. government, the Constitution, and the Bill of Rights. I planned to use newspaper articles on the passing of power to Lyndon Johnson as my textbook. However, events moved so quickly that I didn't get to do the research or the teaching until ten years later, in another state, at another historical moment.

Another event occurred about the same time that put me in opposition to both the teachers' union and the system as a whole. Along with Roger, a respected fourth-grade teacher and gym instructor, I volunteered to do lunch duty. The job was to monitor the line of about 1,400 students as they waited for lunch. Until Roger and I took over, the lunch line was violent, disorderly, loud, and thoroughly unpleasant. Most teachers took their classes to the end of the line and ran. The kids knew that there was no adult control, so they behaved as if they had to divide up the power among themselves. Fights and food wars were normal events, ignored by most of the food-service workers because they didn't have the power to discipline the children. Roger and I decided to make the line a civil place where kids could chat and joke while they waited for lunch. We had to work to establish an acceptable decibel level that wouldn't make eating and digesting food a physiological nightmare.

Roger and I agreed to walk continuously up and down the line, chatting with students, breaking up fights if necessary, maybe jumping some students to the end of the line, and doing this with humor and not a touch of hostility on our parts. For a month or two we were in perpetual motion on the line, and it paid off. I loved to joke with the children and gossip with them. The goal, which we achieved, was to change the waiting time into a pleasant social event.

However, lunch duty meant that Roger and I got the first forty-five minutes of the teaching afternoon off for our own lunch. At first I didn't want to miss that time with my class, but so many of my students had been returning from lunch hungry and angry that I felt working on the lunchroom problem would be of educational benefit both to the students and to me. It was exhausting and unproductive to take the beginning of the afternoon to settle students down from an unpleasant lunch.

During my lunch break, after the rest of the school had finished lunch and returned to class, my students were to have an enrichment class in music. It was the fight over a music teacher that led me to confront the educational irresponsibility of those who had power in the school system. As I have mentioned, P.S. 103/79 was lucky enough to have two teachers who were professional classical musicians and also happened to be African American. In other words, the school had an abundance of riches when it came to selecting a music teacher; when such a position opened up for the first time, I wondered which of them would get the job. There were no other logical or pedagogically responsible choices.

As it turned out, neither man was even in the running. The main criterion for the position turned out to be seniority. Any teacher who had taken or was willing to take a course in teaching music and was willing to try to teach introductory recorder was qualified to apply. The one with the most years in the system automatically won.

The music teacher turned out to be someone near the end of her career, who was fed up with the classroom and angry as hell at just about every child at the school. I protested the decision to both the principal and the union delegate and was told it was none of my business. I tried to share my anger and frustration with Joseph and Joshua, the musicians, but they just shrugged: that was another confirmation of how little the system cared about the children.

For about six weeks the music teacher covered my class during my brief lunch. After a congenial start, things got tense between her and some of the boys in the class, most notably Ronnie, Allan, Harold, and Paul. She wasn't even trying to teach music; she just brought some worksheets with her to keep the students busy. I found the four boys breaking away from participation for the rest of the afternoon, disrupting the tenuous unity of our learning community, and I sensed an imminent explosion. After a while, deciding I could do without lunch, I arranged with the so-called music teacher that she not come to my class. I got a warning from the union delegate, but nothing ever came of it. I've never forgotten the missed music opportunity, or the fact that between them the administration and the union didn't even try to find a way to make the educationally most sensible decision about choosing a music teacher.

Christmas vacation provided a welcome rest. My several tasks for the holidays were to work on integrating the many strands of my curriculum, to figure out what to do about the upcoming school boycott, and to check in on as many former students and their families as possible. Judy and I made the rounds, visiting with the Rodriguezes, with Jaime and his family, and with about a third of the children from 6-1. Though it was wonderful to see everybody it was also depressing. Many of the children were having a difficult time, clearly the victims of indifferent teaching and chaotic schools.

One teacher, one good class, though it may be inspirational and redeeming for a few children, is not adequate. Children need wonderful school careers—not just wonderful teachers.

I began thinking about how I could do more than be effective in my classroom for one year of my students' lives. Several things were clear: I needed to cooperate with other teachers, and we needed to share our students and our ideas. Perhaps we could pass our students on to each other, setting up a stream within a school where the students would have caring teachers throughout their elementary education. We could even begin in kindergarten; by the time the first students reached sixth grade, we might be able to get junior high teachers to join in with us, and maybe after that high school teachers.

I let my imagination go and could almost feel what it would be like to have a mini-school in which everyone centered his or her concern around the students and the community. We could involve the parents, get our friends to come in and help the children, set up apprenticeships and one-on-one tutorial situations. It would take no more money than our salaries and the money the board of education claimed it spent per student on supplies.

Taking the idea a bit further, I conceived of teaching kindergarten the next year and asking for permission to keep the students through the first grade. There was a new second-grade teacher at the school; she, Judy, and I had become close, and it was likely that she would join in during the second year.

One of my New Year's resolutions was to observe the five- and six-year-olds at the school more carefully and get to know some of them. Lunch duty provided a natural and unobtrusive way to do this; I began the day after vacation. I also began to visit kindergarten and first-grade classes when I had time off.

My idea grew all that semester; I finally raised it when new class assignments first came up at a faculty meeting. The assistant principal in charge of kindergarten through second grade dismissed the idea out of hand. She said there was a board of education policy against men teaching kindergartners and first-graders, and that moreover it didn't look good for a man to be in charge of disciplining such young children. I don't know whether there was such a policy, but to this day I regret not having that opportunity in 1964 in New York City. I might still be there.*

Over the 1963 winter holidays, I also began to think of how to integrate cultural studies into my central theme of work and vocation. I began to look for Puerto Ricans and African Americans who had succeeded in doing interesting things and could serve my students as role models. I knew, through Rob, Joshua Robbins, and other friends, and through the Puerto Rican organization ASPIRA, that I could

---

* Almost ten years later, in Berkeley, California, I spent several years teaching a combined kindergarten and first-grade class and loved every minute. My two daughters and their friends, who were in the class, agree that it was a wonderful growing experience.

find people to talk to the children. I could also call upon some Puerto Rican and African American college students I had met through Jaime's cousin Nelly. My students could take people's pictures, tape interviews with them, maybe even produce a jobs magazine.

The push given me by Joseph and Joshua helped me begin to understand how to integrate cultural studies into every aspect of the curriculum and how to move beyond opposition to racism into positive programs that confirmed and enhanced children's cultural and personal identity. This seemed a natural way to enrich what I was doing, a deepening of my students' encounter with history and ideas. It was possible to design math problems with cultural and historical content, to find science history that integrated the personalities of scientists and their working habits. There were work songs, poems, biographies, and fiction about the tasks people had to do to get by in life, and the things they loved to do as well. There were also tales and legends from all over the world that illustrated people's work. I began to play with integrating math, science, literature, and social studies into the theme of work. I could take the process only so far that semester, but it was striking that as the students became more involved in learning and began to articulate their own interests and preferences there was so much material outside of educational texts I could draw on. Once I freed myself of the boundary between subject areas, everything could be put to use in the classroom when the occasion, the students' interests, and my perception of what was needed converged.

Reorganizing the curriculum this way also meant restructuring the classroom, making it a living museum with continual visual interest for the children. I wanted the walls to let the students know what we were studying and to display their contribution to their learning. I posted students' writing and photos of people at work that they had taken out of magazines and collaged into images of themselves in the future. We had our own classified-ads section; students wrote the ads or cut them out of the newspaper and added them to our running list of available jobs. If the students learned nothing else that year, they learned how to read the classifieds, write one for themselves, and play-act the process of getting the job. We did the same thing with the college admission process. Even though the students were only in the sixth grade I wanted them to take away from that year a knowledge of where to go in the future.

In addition I put up puzzles, riddles, fables, a whole variety of intellectual challenges that the children could discuss and think about whether or not they ever came up formally in the curriculum. My goal, increasingly, was to make the physical space of that classroom a combination toy store and laboratory where learning took place as a matter of course, not as a matter of compulsion.

I implemented my ideas during January, centering the class even more on discussion and group reading on the one hand and small group and individual work on the other. I moved slowly, so that I would not lose control and the students would not be disoriented. It wasn't so much that I had thought out the pace of change as that I refused to give up that sense of order in which learning can happen. During that month I found myself once again fully absorbed in the magical substance and practice of classroom teaching.

In late January 1964 the board of education finally came up with a plan for the integration of the New York City public schools. It was inadequate and insulting, and a several-day boycott was scheduled by the Harlem Parents Committee and the NAACP, to begin February 3.

I was one of the few people who came to school that day. This was not an easy decision, but at that moment I couldn't see how any educational benefit would result from the boycott if it succeeded only in putting more power in the hands of teachers who were already failing with the children, or if it resulted in some bogus integration plan that would move children out of the community into an even more racist environment without dealing with qualitative educational issues.

Only three or four of my students came to class, about the same percentage as showed up throughout the school. Perhaps I should have gone out, but when it comes to militancy I am a slow and cautious learner though a tenacious fighter once I make a moral commitment to a struggle. The moral dilemma posed by the boycott was very difficult for me; staying in made me look like a conservative, uncaring person to some members of the community. But I just could not see how the children would benefit.

After the boycott I asked the children to write what they thought it was about and what they did during it. Here are the responses that have survived. I believe they are representative of the whole class.

Why I Was Absent

Roberta

I was absent yesterday because my mother told me to stay out of school because in the paper it said not to send your children to school sorry mother didn't send me to school yesterday.

A Boycott

John A

The reason I didn't come to school because the boycott

My mother wouldn't let me come to school she wanted me to stay home that day because she thought it will start a fight that howcome she wanted me to stay home for that day. My sister stay home from school that day to because of the boycott she thought that it will be a fight they was marching for civil rights and better education.

Feb. 4, 1964 Boycott

Maria

Monday Feb. (3), 1964. There were picket. People were with big sign. It was a revolution of the Puerto Ricans and Megrols of the U.S.A. The board of Education had to at least sent one police man in each school. because maybe it was going to be like troble but it was a suecess.

Boycott Why Absent

Sarah

Belinda was absent because her mother thought they was going to beat her up. Her mother said that when Wonde go to the door to get thought they would hit her with a rock or a stick.

Some other children stay out because they want better work like the white children there learning more than us. When they be in or the six grade they be reading a 8th or 9th grade book and they out for better education.

Why I Was Absent

Felicia

I saw absent yesterday because my mother not to come to school because the radio said not to send children to school because of the boycott that maybe there will be trouble that children will be hurt that people work if they have to sent teachers to there house they will but don't send children to school.

I think that the boycott was good because some schools got more book than other and that not fair to other schools.

Why I Was Absent

Debby

I was absent yesterday because my mother took my sister and me to the hospital to take out my sisters tooth and I went for my finger.

WHAT I FEEL ABOUT THE BOYCOTT

I feel about the boycott because we need more books and the board of education doesn't want to give us anymore books. We don't mind of interrogation because we want our school interrogated. We don't want our school to only have Puerto Ricans and negro children only we want all kinds of children in the school.

Boycott

Richard

The boycott was go for me
I was in the boycott going
I saw the boycott march on Board of education
I did not come to school yesterday because I was in boycott
I saw the Boycott in Brooklyn
I saw a program about the boycott
The boycott was about the civilrights and better education

After reading the children's papers and talking to people in the community I felt ashamed of my resistance to the boycott. I should have taken the boycott as an educational opportunity and been in the community teaching rather than staying in my classroom. Nobody brought up the issue if I didn't ask, but I often did. The result of the boycott was certainly not the desegregation of the New York City school system, which will doubtless continue its segregated way well into the next several millennia. In their papers, the children made it clear that they were aware of the issues involved. I told them I had been wrong to stay in school and Rosy, speaking for the rest, told me that it was okay, I was a good teacher anyway. Many of the parents I spoke with also told me not to worry, but I didn't know what they actually felt and was very uncomfortable with myself for a while.

The boycott certainly did energize the community. When I visited people's homes they were much more willing to talk about what was wrong with the schools. There was a sense that they could be involved in group action and could improve the schools by speaking out. There also developed a strong sentiment that school improvement did not need to wait upon the false promise of desegregation. The boycott and Freedom Schools reaffirmed, for many of the parents at P.S. 103/79, the intelligence and worth of their children, which they had begun to doubt because of the demoralized atmosphere of that place.

I quickly joined many community discussions on what to do about the schools and began to attend meetings of the Harlem Parents Committee. I told people in that group of my reluctance to join the boycott, and I remember being told that there were many people in the HPC leadership who knew that integration was not on the minds of whites in New York. But it was an issue with national focus that could lead to mobilization in the Black (the word "Negro" dropped out of people's vocabulary at just about this time) and Puerto Rican communities. The struggle was over the education of children, and anything that forced people to act was worth trying. Some members of the group had observed my classroom and told me that judging by what they saw, I was more than welcome to join the struggle. The issue of my staying in school during the boycott never came up again.

Several events that began in my classroom and spread from there made me participate even more actively. As I tried to integrate science, math, and literature into the curriculum I found the lack of resources distressing. Judy and I had been able to scrape up enough money to buy used books for my reading program. But science materials, math texts, maps, and the other resources even a moderately well equipped school had to work with were beyond our means. One day in the lunchroom I complained about how that lack of materials starved our children's minds the way lack of food could starve their bodies. One of the teacher aides, Bernice, suggested we meet after school in the aides' lounge.

Bernice and I had become friends. She worked with me on the lunchroom line, coordinating the children's passage from the hall to the serving tables. I had also seen her in the neighborhood; we had coffee a few times and chatted about the children. Once she saw me pick up a first-grader who had fallen and scraped her leg on the playground. I carried the girl inside, bandaged her leg, then carried her back to the playground and set her free to run with her friends. It felt like releasing a wounded bird whose wing had been healed. I was smiling at the beautiful running child when Bernice came up and told me that she and several of the other aides wanted to ask me a question: "Are you passing?" At first I wasn't sure what she meant, but she made herself clear. "No white man can love one of our children that way." I said no, but she just smiled and told me she understood the complexities of my position.

What I had done was just what many teachers do every day as part of yard duty. And my expression of joy at being among children is shared by caring educators everywhere. But Bernice's comment indicated, by making an exception of me, her perception of the emotional chasm that yawns between many white teachers and their African American students. Parents, other members of the community, and many students are aware of that distance but it is often invisible to the teachers themselves. Over the years I have become convinced that this unspoken separation between student and teacher, which begins for too many African American children as soon as they start kindergarten, is one of the major causes of school failure. However, whenever I raise the issue among teachers there is silence and even hostility. Discussion of the subtle manifestations of racism that lead to school failure is off-limits in respectable educational circles. But Bernice was right: unless you can love your students as your own children and fight for their lives and learning the way you fight for your own children's, you give them less than they are entitled to—which is, at the very least, the affection and honor of the society whose future they will shape.

The day Bernice and I met in the aides' lounge she suggested we take a tour of the school's basement. I had never been down there. A bit puzzled, I followed her down the stairs past the boilers to the storage rooms. There she showed me a room full of science equipment, most of it still in unopened boxes; another room with unused audiovisual equipment; and a third and fourth room with brand-new textbooks and library books: resources for an elementary school the size of 103/79.

I couldn't sleep that night. At first I thought maybe I should ask Bernice to help me liberate the material for my classroom, but I didn't know how she would respond. Moreover, those books and equipment were meant not just for my students but for all the children. Should I tell other teachers, confront the principal, go to the union? I wanted to consider all possibilities.

One of the first things I did was ask the Harlem Parents Committee for advice. They suggested I inform the principal first, and then the union delegate. I began with the delegate and was told to speak to the principal, since this was not a personnel matter or a grievance (though I certainly felt the situation was grievous). The principal informed me that he was perfectly aware of the situation, but that there was no point in letting the children use any of new supplies because they would wreck them. I tried to counter that one of the reasons the children were so angry was that they were deprived of adequate resources for learning. He replied that the discussion was over and the situation would remain unchanged.

Before talking with the Harlem Parents Committee again, I mentioned my discovery to a group of parents representing children from both 6-1 and 6-7. They suggested we hold meetings at their homes, inviting other parents, and organize some strategy for getting the supplies to the children. I mentioned the Harlem Parents Committee and they told me to go ahead and ask for help, so some HPC leaders attended our meetings.

It was decided that we would bring the issue up at the next school PTA meeting. I provided the HPC with a school mailing list, and they sent every parent a notice of the meeting. That included a dsescription of the unused material. Some of the parents made posters and put them up in coffee shops, bars, barbershops, and beauty parlors. The glow from the successful boycott had not worn off, and people felt empowered to change the school.

The plan was to have someone from HPC bring up the issue at the meeting; then I and one of the aides would verify the existence of the resources and several parents would demand specific action to get the supplies to the children. I confided this plan to several fellow teachers, two of whom promised to attend the meeting although they were not sure whether they wanted to speak out. We would all wait and hope that the turnout was as large as the boycott indicated it might be.

Usually PTA meetings attracted about a half dozen people. An assistant principal would represent the administration, and a teacher would represent the staff and the union. Generally nothing much happened. The usual topic was how the parents could raise money for a trip or for graduation, or how they could help a teacher with a project. There was no politics other than the politics of acquiescence.

The night of this particular meeting Judy and I, along with one of the other teachers, arrived early with some representatives of HPC. The principal had obviously gotten a copy of the mailer, for the entire administration had shown up even earlier, along with a representative from the district office. Also present were about half a dozen teachers, the ones most loyal to the principal. The PTA was represented by its officers. All these people were gathered in front of the room. It was the largest staff attendance at any parents' meeting in my brief history at the school.

Not one parent came. The agenda item never came up, and we left in disarray. The next day I was greeted with the silent treatment from most of the staff. The aides and those teachers I was close to were still friendly, though somewhat awkward, and my life at the school became uncomfortable despite the joys of the classroom.

Afterward, the parents who had been instrumental in organizing the meeting told me two things. First, they were sure that when the principal heard about the meeting he called people from the welfare department: many parents got calls from their social workers warning them that if they got involved in political action they could lose their welfare payments. Second, in deciding whether to come to the meeting, most parents were swayed by the fear that their children would be singled out for punishment by teachers loyal to the administration. These parents probably weren't completely wrong. In any case they were sure in their knowledge that the system punishes people who try to change it; when it came to this issue, they didn't believe there was enough strength behind it to be worth taking a major risk.

I spoke to Isaiah Robinson, a leader of the Harlem Parents Committee, about the parents' response and he told me that it would be a long struggle. He knew. As a member of the Tuskegee Airmen and a lifelong activist he understood that taking risks, experiencing defeat, and then going on went with the territory. But I was just learning and therefore much more devastated and discouraged. My classroom work was still rewarding, and I threw myself even more into discovering ways to help students get the tools they would need to survive. But the next step in survival for my students meant junior high school, not the world of work or college, and it wasn't so easy. Some were doing quite well, but Larry and Phillip weren't, nor were many other children from 6-1. The chaotic junior high made elementary school seem like a calm, orderly, and effective place of learning.

As summer approached, Judy and I had to figure out what to do the next year. I wasn't allowed to teach kindergarten and didn't want to take another sixth grade. I felt as if I were preparing lambs for the slaughter. No matter how much the children progressed or how hopeful things seemed for them at the end of the sixth grade, junior high was, for most of them, a disaster. The early adolescent years are tumultuous at best. But in a disorderly, demoralized school dominated by the control of violence, learning took second place to sheer survival. The few good teachers I knew at the junior high were always on the verge of exhaustion. Nothing negative I could say about my school could approximate their critique of the conditions under which they worked. (The situation hasn't changed much; the conversations I had with caring, worn-out teachers in 1963 were not dissimilar from some of those I have today.)

In addition, things were heating up on the streets in New York. Kennedy was dead; there was a general feeling that violence was the only and inevitable result of current racial struggles, and a growing sense that Judy and I were no longer welcome in the community. Several parents had called me and said that they were sorry but that, because of community pressure and for our safety, it would be best for Judy and me not to come by in the evening. Our adult education program ended because Richie's parents were afraid for our safety. Ann's mother, whom we saw a lot, told me: "Caring people and racists, if they are white and you don't know them, look alike." She suggested that if we did meet, we do so downtown.

By this time I had come to realize two things that in the context of P.S. 103/79 were contradictory: I was going to be a lifer as a teacher; I was not going to put up with teaching under conditions that destroyed children's minds and spirits. So what to do? Judy had come to a similar conclusion after a year of substitute teaching in schools that were often worse than mine. Having reached a politically and socially untenable place at P.S. 103/79 and not being sure whether another year of the silent treatment would be worth it, we decided to take a year off to regroup.

Judy and I visited all of the parents and as many of the children as we could, to let everyone know we had decided to take a year off. Those farewell dinners made me even more painfully aware of the distance between the options I had in life and those of the people I served as an educator. On the way home from the last dinner we headed west on 120th street from Madison Avenue. When we reached Lenox Avenue we found the streets transformed. Garbage cans were falling from the roofs, fires were burning everywhere, the streets were full of people running and screaming, and our terrified cabdriver headed straight for anyone in the way, miraculously avoiding a collision and eventually making it to safety on the West Side. Harlem had exploded, as almost everyone in the community had predicted it would, and Judy and I, shaken and confused, were on our way to a small town in Catalonia which we had never heard of.

There, for a year, I tried to teach myself how to write well and consider how to reenter the struggle for equity and justice for our children.

Chapter 3

TEACHING BEYOND SCHOOL

Yes it was the prince's kiss.
But the way was prepared for the prince.
It had to be.

When the attendants carrying the woman
—dead they thought her lying on the litter—
stumbled over the root of a tree
the bit of deathly apple in her throat
jolted free.

Not strangled, not poisoned!
She
can come alive.

It was an "accident" they hardly noticed.

The threshold here comes when they stumble.
The jolt. And better if we notice.
However, their noticing is not
Essential to the story.

A miracle has even deeper roots,
Something like error, some profound defeat.
Stumbled over, the startle, the arousal,
Something never perceived till now, the taproot.

—Muriel Rukeyser, "Fable"
For Herbert Kohl

TEACHING AGAIN—WITH A DIFFERENCE

During our year in Spain, from August 1964 to August 1965, I corresponded with about half a dozen of my former students and with several members of Jaime's family. By the grace of the BBC, Voice of America, and Armed Forces Radio we kept up with events in the United States. My students' letters were often troubling. Junior high was difficult, there were problems on the streets, and despite a few academic and personal successes the racial climate in New York was tense and the children (now young adolescents) were bewildered about their futures. I felt guilty about my happiness, about being able to afford time to grow when they were consumed by the fast and hostile demands of life in their community.

In their last batch of letters my former students said they were looking forward to our return to New York. It became clear that there were important things to do back home and that there was no moral excuse not to return. We arrived in August of 1965. I didn't have the slightest idea of how to pick up where I had left off and was confused about the kind of role I could play to help the children and the community.

As soon as Judy and I returned we visited some former students who lived on 119th Street, a block from where I had taught. The Vietnam War was still going on, and we joined the escalating protests against it. Malcolm X had been murdered. Watts had burned that summer, just as Harlem was burning the summer we left. In a positive vein Lyndon Johnson's Great Society programs were beginning to be felt in the neighborhoods of New York. The antipoverty program MEND had opened a number of small offices throughout East Harlem and many of the people I knew were now involved in organizing community-based projects. There was hope in the air, and Judy and

I joined in. The riots and violence had not yet led to the burning out of communities. Instead of the despair and depression I see in the late 1990s there was a sense that all this struggle would lead to a better life. My uncles returning from fighting in World War II felt the same way people in Harlem felt in 1965: despite all the horrors of war, they believed, a finer life would emerge from what they had risked in battle.

One night, while we were having dinner with my 6-1 student Ann and her family, Ann's older sister Janine asked me if I was interested in helping her, her boyfriend, Allan, who was also at dinner, and some other high school students in the neighborhood with their writing and classwork. Ann's mother, Janice, said we could use their living room a few evenings a week; several days later we began.

I needed that opportunity to begin to work with young people again. After a year away, I missed the dialogue and the magic of watching young people discover things about the world that they had never imagined before. I also missed the sense of being useful, which I seem to need.

Seven students came to the first session—not counting Ann and her younger brother, who sat in, somewhat to Janine's annoyance. Unsure of how to prepare, I had brought some writing exercises, poems, and diagnostic tests; however, on the way across town I decided to leave all that in the car. I came in with a pen and an empty notebook. Since Janine and Allan had asked me to teach a class, maybe it would be best for them and the other students to tell me what they wanted, and for me to listen. Why not shape a class around what they wanted to learn, rather than what the school system wanted them to learn and what I thought they should learn? After all, we were free of the constraints of the system and could do anything we wanted to do.

We settled into the living room and Janice provided tea, coffee, and cookies. I suggested that the young people tell me what they wanted to learn. Janine, who was never shy about speaking her mind, plunged right in. The problem, she said, was that she didn't know what there was to learn or how well she was doing. Teachers just told her what to do and then graded her. She was confused, angry, and frustrated. The others agreed. Janine then told me my question was not at all helpful. How could she know what she wanted to learn without my telling her what was out there to learn and what she needed to know to do better? She was sick of either obeying teachers or teaching them. She wondered if there wasn't another way to go about learning.

Janine had gone to the heart of one of the great dilemmas of teaching: how to get beyond the opposition between learning based on teacher demands and learning based on students' interests. At Teachers College I had learned the difference between teacher-centered and student-centered learning and participated in debates about which was the better approach. In the classroom, and most dramatically in Ann's living room, I learned that neither would do.

I answered that if the students helped me learn what they could presently do in terms of school-based skills, I'd help them explore the relationship between their interests and what people do in the world. The group was small enough to enable for me to search out people who would share what they knew and how they worked and lived.

To make practical use of that first session, I selected about ten books from around the apartment. Several were easy children's books that Janine and Ann had read when they were younger. A few were junior high and high school history, biology, and general science textbooks. I also borrowed several of Janice's romance and mystery novels. With these items I made up a reading diagnostic test based not on a preprinted set of questions, but on what was available at that moment and on the knowledge about reading I had gained in the classroom. The test didn't have to be quantitative or sophisticated; it just had to let me know where to begin with these students, so that I could avoid assignments that they simply could not do and that therefore would humiliate them.

My test was simply to have each person pick a book and read to me. If the book was easy, they'd pick another one, until they reached the level where they began to have trouble. If they could handle all the books, they didn't need to worry about reading so much as about what they read and how they understood it.

With the information their reading provided I would be able to design a program that was challenging, but not humiliating to anyone who had skills problems. The idea was to shape the class so that we would begin with sophisticated content that respected the students' age and intelligence, then reach a point, over a period of time, at which everyone could deal with complex reading material commensurate with that content.

However, before anyone read in front of the group we had to deal with feelings of failure and shame at displaying in public what one didn't know. I noticed that Charles and Mel were getting nervous and might tell us all that the whole venture was crap and walk out. So I picked up one of the simplest books on the table and began reading in a hesitant and frightened voice, deliberately making common mistakes such as reading "throw" instead of "through" and "breed" instead of "bread," until the meaning of the text was garbled and couldn't be guessed through the mistakes. At that point I threw the book on the floor and said, "I quit."

After a pause I asked the kids what had happened with my reading. This opened up a personal discussion of the struggle to make sense of what one reads. Willie said that he wouldn't have trouble with the simple book I was reading, but he might throw the high school texts. He confessed that reading at school often frustrated him; he often pretended to be attentive and prayed the teacher would never call on him. Mel had another strategy: whenever reading came up he put his head on the desk and pretended he was asleep. If the teacher called on him he made up some story about having a hard night and was usually left alone. Once a persistent teacher insisted he respond, and he did—by throwing the book across the room.

Almost everyone had developed some repertoire of responses to deal with texts they couldn't read. Janine and Allan, who were successful students, had learned a few tricks to help them take control of a difficult text, such as looking at the questions at the end of the chapter before reading it or looking at picture captions before attacking the text. The others felt failure when they faced complex reading; instead, they developed strategies to avoid reading altogether.

Our conversation seemed to loosen people up and everyone volunteered to read so long as we wouldn't make fun of them. It clearly took courage for Charles, the first reader, to try even the simple book he chose. After a few words he began to sweat and stammer; Mel started giggling and imitating Charles's voice. Charles took it for a little while and then threw down the book and challenged Mel. He stopped when Janice, who usually spoke quietly, came out with a stern and unambiguous "Not in my living room."

Everyone froze. Was this meeting going to turn Ann and Janine's home into an urban classroom, with all of its disrespect, violence, and failure? For a second I wished I were back in 103, where at least I could establish my own kind of order. But Charles immediately responded with profuse apologies to Janice, as did Mel. They seemed shocked at themselves, ashamed of overstepping the boundaries of Janice's hospitality, appalled by what the rude manners of school had done to their sense of home and community.

Then they turned to me and, in a tone I had never heard in a classroom, asked me not to quit on them. I suggested that Charles continue, only with everyone attending to the specifics of Charles's mistakes; each person was to come up with a suggestion to help Charles improve his reading.

This worked. Mel suggested Charles take a breath and think about the meaning of what he was reading, Janine suggested he look at the pictures, and Allan, who had written down the words Charles had missed, suggested he begin a vocabulary notebook. This slow beginning, with its orientation toward solving an educational problem rather than turning it into a humiliating failure, was the beginning of the foundation of the reading community I hoped to develop with this group of youngsters. Clearly, respect for Janice and for her hospitality contributed as much to making this possible as any of my educational expertise. The place of learning was no small part of the quality of learning that developed.

After this we met at Janice's several times a week. The sessions were informal. I chose readings from school textbooks or newspapers, and after a while the students took over the agenda, bringing up issues that were on their minds. My job was to provide reading skills, discover reading material related to their interests, and keep the conversation going.

The small learning community we established in Janice's living room was a blessing for me. It reconnected me to what was going on in the community in which I had taught. I could have returned to my old school, P.S. 103/79, if I'd wanted to, but it was clear I wasn't welcome and I didn't want the system to involuntarily transfer me again and find myself having to begin in a new community once again. When I called in the Harlem Parents Committee in the spring of 1964, I had alienated myself from the administration and most of the staff; I knew that the trouble would only get worse, since I had not changed my mind on one central issue: that the school had to change fundamentally for the children to be well educated. So, instead of returning to the school I was determined to get to know people in the community better and to learn from their experiences with the schools and their sense of how their children should learn.

Furthermore, I didn't think enough other people at 103/79 were willing to take the risks needed to make significant changes; battling from within the school, I decided, was a no-win situation. I didn't feel that I could teach well under the social pressure I'd surely feel, and I didn't know how to continue to work within the public schools in a way consistent with my conscience and judgment as an educator. Other people have solved the problem of surviving within the New York City public school system while remaining faithful to their values, but I just couldn't figure out how to do it.

On the other hand, working in the community was a constant source of hope and joy, so I embraced it. I also enrolled in the department of special education at Teachers College, where I had received my master's degree and teaching credential, and managed to scare up enough scholarship money to pay tuition and have a little left for rent. Judy had found a teaching job she loved, at the Manhattan School for the Severely Disturbed; and that, too, made it possible for us to support ourselves and for me to continue working in East Harlem.

One of my classes at Teachers College led to an educational adventure that helped shape my understanding of what it means to teach well. During a session of my informal reading group, Allan asked me about my classes at Columbia. I described them, and the class on counseling psychology intrigued everyone. Allan, I believe, said that he had always wanted to study psychology; he wondered if it would help him dealing with his life and troubles. Having been through analysis myself and having found my psychiatrist, if not all of her theories, very helpful, I shared some of my own journey with the students and suggested that we might study psychology together if I could persuade my professor to let me do so as part of the class. Allan and Janine were made uneasy by my suggestion; Ann said such a class might cause trouble. The others agreed and I pursued the issue: Why? What kind of trouble could it cause? Reluctantly and slowly it came out that students wanted to discuss sexual, gender, and family relationships as well as sensitive issues of race, and the males and females didn't feel they could deal with these issues in a mixed group.

I was willing to go with the students and have separate male and female groups. One of the things I've learned about myself is that I am not afraid to move away from a place where I am comfortable if it holds the promise of leading to an interesting learning adventure. So this new class took the place of our meetings at Janice's. I suggested that we take the implication of separate groups seriously and that I find a woman to run the female group. Everyone agreed, on condition that they like the woman. As it happened, one of my classmates was a brilliant African American woman who was a doctoral student in counseling and knew a great deal more about the subject than I did. The separate classes could provide a great opportunity for Betty Rawls and me to work together and would give me a chance to learn from her. I promised the kids that I would ask Betty to come by the next week.

I could easily have done the psychology class on an informal basis, just as I was doing the literacy class; I'm sure Betty would have volunteered as well. But I saw a bonus in connecting the class with Teachers College. We could ask for a room and meet at the college. That way I could get the students to be part of a college environment and to see themselves as being in that place in the future. We could introduce them to professors and in general socialize them to the world of higher education. Teachers College as an institution would be their teacher as much as we would.

The kids loved Betty, and it didn't take much persuading for our professor to let our classes become a joint term project. I asked Janine to set up a girls' group for Betty, and for the boys' group I also invited Roberto Colon, a former student from P.S. 145. I was a bit concerned about Roberto coming from across town and not being part of the other kids' neighborhood, but he told me he was game for a learning adventure. I also invited Larry and Phillip, former students from 6-1, and Harold, who was in 6-7.

Larry had moved to Brooklyn; Phillip to upper Manhattan. Harold was attending Columbus High School in the Bronx and playing varsity basketball. At the third meeting, Allan and Ronnie invited their good friend Akmir to join the group. Akmir was a member of the 5%ers, a militant Muslim group dedicated to Black separatism and violent opposition of white oppression. As Ronnie mentioned, they respected Akmir and believed he would keep me honest. He was indeed my challenge, and he became, for the rest of his short life, a good friend.

The male group began meeting first. Betty and I taught the first three or four sessions together; then she took over the girls' class. The two groups met together once during the semester.

All together there were ten students. The main theme of the class was not the subject of psychology so much as the use of psychological theories to help understand your own life. The emphasis was on understanding normal, not pathological, lives and on ideas that could help the students understand and manage their behavior. This was the first time I had an opportunity to shape a curriculum from scratch while trying to match it with educational needs that students had articulated. Betty and I worked on the curriculum, teaching it and testing it as we created it.

Going through my papers recently, I discovered a report I wrote on the project for my own class at Columbia. I said of the curriculum that it

> was not designed to treat psychological concepts historically or in depth. Nor was it designed to be a general survey of the field. The essential focus was on the individual and social conflict. There was no effort to present an image of how one should be. The entire emphasis of the course was on how to analyze and understand what one chose to be.
>
> A specific example of a situation that was analyzed was one in which a boss in a job interview said without even looking at the interviewee, "You know, everybody who works here works hard," with no little hostility in his voice. The boss's remarks were analyzed in terms of his defensiveness, his social position, and the image he was trying to project of himself. The range of responses available to the interviewee was also analyzed, and the differences his psychological understanding of the dynamics of the situation could make were discussed. Finally we talked about the general topic of putting up with crap and when it could no longer be done. . . . Usually discussions in the group ended when there was no more to say and the kids wanted to think about the issues at greater length and in privacy. They didn't want to be fed conclusions.

After the second week of class Roberto told me he was dropping out. He felt very uncomfortable being the only Puerto Rican student, and in particular, he told me, being with so many intelligent Black students bothered him. He wasn't sure why that made him feel angry and powerless. He was used to going to school with Blacks, he told me, but they were all cutups, bad students, people he could joke around with but didn't respect. Something in him was frightened by intelligent Black students who were able to discuss serious issues with sensitivity and sophistication.

I talked to him about this, suggesting that, as I believed, the other students in the class were just like the people he went to school with, except that they cared in our class, while they didn't care in school. Roberto didn't want to discuss the issue. He told me that his family and friends had trouble with Blacks who made it hard for them to get jobs, and he simply did not want to rethink his feelings about race. He seemed to feel he had too much to lose by giving up his ideas about Blacks being stupid.

At first I couldn't believe what I was hearing. None of my liberal pieties about fairness and about how racism would be overcome when people got to know each other personally worked with Roberto. He didn't want to like Blacks as a group, and that was that. I gave up, and though we remained close the relationship was strained from then on. I don't know what Roberto learned, but *I* learned how devious and deep-seated racism can turn poor people against each other and can fragment and distort otherwise sensitive minds. I also realized that I would have to learn to deal directly with racism in the future and be much more sensitive to its insinuations and nuances.

During the third session, the first one Akmir attended, I mentioned that Roberto had dropped out; Ronnie, speaking for the rest, said no one was surprised. Before I could bring up the issue of racism Allan told me not to worry about Roberto's attitude; they were all used to it, and there was no point in worrying about racism since it was everywhere. At that point Akmir challenged me, a white person facing a now all-Black class, and asked me to justify myself as a so-called expert. I responded that the class had been initiated by Ronnie, that I was responding, that he was welcome to stay, or to leave if nothing of interest occurred—and that, most of all, he was welcome to challenge everything as long as he listened and took the class seriously. He accepted the bargain in a way that deepened all of our learning. He did question everything, but in the spirit of inquiry rather than the spirit of the war that, it turned out, he had previously waged in high school.

Psychology was of passionate interest to the students. They wanted to understand and analyze their experiences, talk about what was happening to them, and get control, when possible, of their destinies. This sounds metaphysical, and it is; people under siege are constantly confronted with metaphysical problems, with ultimate questions about survival and meaning, about when to fight and when to retreat, and most of all, about what is worth giving your life to defend or create. In that class Freud, Jung, Erving Goffman, and Jean-Paul Sartre became weapons my students could use in the service of their own survival.

Betty's and my approach to the content of the male class was to mix original source material with examples drawn from the students' lives, and to concentrate on the development of a vocabulary the students could use to analyze their own experience. The case of Anna O. was used to illustrate the concepts of the ego, id, and superego and to discuss conflicts within the self. It was not our intent to advocate Freud, Jung, or Sartre so much as to expose the students to ways in which people thought about the self and the mind. The image of the soul in conflict made sense to them and they were able to extrapolate from Anna O. to themselves.

There was remarkably little resistance from the students to seeing themselves as individuals with psychic conflict. One concept that they did have trouble with was that of the unconscious. They could not accept the validity of denial and repression or the insidious workings of the unconscious. They said that they felt that there was one unitary self, which knew what it was denying, and they took a strong stand against the notion of repressed memory. Ronnie and Allan in particular insisted that when people messed up they knew it even if they tried to lie about. Larry said there was always a chance of lying to oneself, which Phillip denied. He claimed you always knew what had happened, even if you pretended to be ignorant. The psychological problem, as most of the class saw it, was how to accept responsibility for what you did and work your way out of trouble once you got into it.

Our discussion of the Oedipus complex was very lively; we talked about overcoming infantile wishes. The discussion, which turned not so much on father envy as on father absence, was very painful, dealing specifically with what it was like to grow up without a father or with too many people who claimed to treat you like a son. None of the students' natural fathers lived with them; most were not around at all. The question was not how to replace your father in the affections of your mother—you were already closer to her, in most cases. The question was how not to be like your father, how not to duplicate his mistakes.

We talked about neurotic and self-defeating behavior, and the students' hunger for a vocabulary with which to express the complexity and seriousness of their concerns became apparent. The students wanted to know the proper words for conditions that they knew perfectly well. Allan, for instance, described the behavior of a person he knew and worried about and I was able to tell him that it seemed obsessive-compulsive. "Obsessive" and "compulsive" were new words for familiar phenomena; as we studied these and other concepts in greater depth, I found myself surrounded by sophisticated psychological thinkers. It reminded me of how my use of Greek vocabulary with 6-1 had enabled the children to speak critically and well about life and literature. This was just one more experience that convinced me of the power of words to strengthen people's ability to transform their reality.

As the class went on, psychological naming almost became a game, though I was careful to introduce words and concepts in a way designed to avoid the students' substituting labels for understanding. The students would think of a situation that embodied a concept, and usually there was a word, often a whole literature, about it. Some of the words that emerged from the situations they described were "ambiguity," "regression," "sadist," and "masochist."

We also spent time considering the nature of learning and frustration, and in particular the confrontation of teacher and student as two complex human beings, each with his own difficulties. Everyone in the class had problems in school, but this was the first time they had tried to humanize the teacher and understand the dynamics of the teaching situation from a distance. We talked of ways of handling a situation to avoid frustration and facilitate learning. We talked of coping and defending and of how attitudes are conveyed and understood. I tried to talk about how unconscious attitudes are communicated. Once again the students resisted the notion of the unconscious, instead speaking, I believe intelligently, about hidden intention. Their challenge to my use of the concept of the unconscious led me to rethink the question of motivation and awareness;

since then, though I still worry about the nature and meaning of the unconscious, I never use the word if I can think of another way to describe what is happening.

One of the most refreshing things about the class was that I felt free to be challenged by my students and to stumble, to try to figure out how to respond to their provocations without having to worry about a preset curriculum, a bell that might interrupt the process, or an unexpected visit from a suspicious administrator.

Toward the end of the class we tackled problems of personal and cultural identity and the problem of roots in America. I tried to distinguish between neurotic reactions, culture-bound reactions, and normal defiant ones. The kids found my distinctions too simple; they talked about the difficulty of not reacting in an exaggerated way in a hostile and neurotic world. They began, slowly, bringing up the question of growing up Black in America, shifting my more generic discussion of growing up to the specifics of their life. Akmir jokingly said they had decided that I was ready for what they knew about the wilderness of North America.

As the students began to trust me not to grade or humiliate them, our conversations became more intimate and painful. Up to this point we had been tape-recording the sessions, but once we started discussing racism the students refused to be taped. As much as they had begun to trust me, they were sure that someone—a teacher, a cop, or a social worker—would use their taped words to harm them. It was not safe, in their view, to speak the truth about racism in mixed company.

I had brought up existentialism and Jean-Paul Sartre because his ideas were dear to me and I felt he might speak to them the way he spoke to me. He didn't. I talked about the subtle movement between hope and despair, neurosis and defiance that we all experience, and about aloneness and being human. Essentially I was trying to get at the notion that every person is ultimately alone and must make cultural and personal decisions in this aloneness. More, we must learn to take responsibility for decisions, since these decisions define us as people.

The kids found this idea of aloneness strange. They had the church, their community, the neighborhood, their friends, and the extended families that nurtured them. They agreed that life was hard, that the human condition was characterized by absurdity and alienation, but aloneness, no. They acknowledged moments when they felt vulnerable and isolated from everyone else, but around all that was a sense of belonging, belonging to the Black community, which would not and could not throw them out. I distinctly remember how adamantly the students refused to accept my idea that people stand alone. I have come to agree with them, and I see this class as a major step in my own growth toward understanding the importance of community and the need to create it when it does not exist.

One of the most interesting discussions we had was about caste, for which the students insisted on making an exception to the no-taping rule. They were prepared to make statements about race in America "for the record," meaning for the professor who supervised the course and for Betty and my final paper. We talked about India and then about America and the strangeness of caste in America. One of the boys asked me why the child of a Black person and a white person was automatically called Black. I said it reflected the whole bizarre definition of race in the United States, which protects white privilege. I made no attempt whatever to conceal my own disgust and despair over the racial situation in America.

The conversation turned to Black attitudes toward whites. The kids agreed that these attitudes were ambivalent and class bound, but felt that the intensity and ambivalence of these attitudes were normal reactions to an abnormal group of people. They then had a sophisticated discussion of the abnormality white Americans manifested on issues of race and provided me with a dramatic example of what it means to be watched while one assumes one is doing the watching.

Rage bubbled up to the surface as the conversation continued; once or twice Akmir turned to me and asked if I could take it. He assured me they would stop the discussion if I felt too uncomfortable, a remarkable concern for my sensitivities when the issue was the horrors whites visited on Blacks. The kids talked about the difficulty of accepting whites, any whites, and of working with them on issues of equality. They had no sympathy for the "weakness" of Martin Luther King, for what they considered his refusal to directly oppose white power with Black power. They had no hope for integration and thought that King was deceived in his dreams of one nation without racism. The man they admired was Malcolm X, "the truth teller" who was willing to change when he saw that some of his preconceptions were wrong. I tried to talk about how crazy and self-destructive it was to hate any people as a whole but there was no dissuading the kids from their view of the white man as a devil.

I did bring up the irony of what seemed to me to be our close and trusting relationship in the class, where though I was white I did not feel hated. They laughed and Allan said I was okay for now but that you never could tell what a white person might do in the future. I told them that was fair enough and suggested that I might be the devil in disguise. That was considered an appropriate estimate of the situation.

The class lasted for a semester. After the boys' and girls' groups met together, Betty and I began to toy with the idea of a pre-university for these and other youngsters. It seemed to us that setting the class at Columbia and basing it in a combination of the students' own experience and the academic world of psychology might be a model for a transitional learning experience that could help the students with their life problems and at the same time prepare them for college.

The privilege of teaching a small number of high school students a serious subject that they want to learn about, even if done just once a week, is invaluable. I believe all high schools should provide such opportunities for their teachers and students. This can be done in every school, if only for one period a week with one group of students. Just to be together and converse, without grades, with exciting material to read and think about, and with the ability to get to know one another as thinkers, as people who together can consider and challenge ideas and measure them against experience, is bound to enrich everyone's life and to keep teachers in love with the magic of well-crafted personalized teaching. The class I taught at Teachers College remained a guiding image when I designed a public high school and taught in it, when I taught college, and even when, in my kindergarten and first-grade classes at Hillside School in Berkeley, we had daily discussion groups using children's literature and the students' experience as starting points for discussions of important issues and ideas.

SERENDIPITY STRIKES

During my days at Teachers College in 1964 and 1965 I stayed in contact with friends who were still teaching in the New York City public schools and became close to other teachers who were also discovering the educational power of simply letting students write about what they saw, felt, wished, and dreamed. This was a time when people were confident that, with federal support, programs could be established that would move poor people—especially people of color—out of poverty and into the mainstream.

One day Larry or maybe Phillip showed me a copy of a magazine called *What's Happening,* which announced itself as "a newspaper in which the teenagers of today express their views." That issue, which is among the many I've saved, contained poems and stories about life in Harlem, about being young and Black or Puerto Rican, and about being awakened to a sense that teenagers can act to change their world. There was also an article about a rent strike led by Jesse Grey and the Harlem Tenants Committee on 117th Street. That was in P.S. 79/103's neighborhood, and I knew Grey. In fact, some of the parents of my students were members of the committee; I remembered how they had held the World's Worst Fair in 1962 during the World's Fair in Queens as a protest against all of the resources spent on new buildings at the fair site while the buildings around 117th Street were neglected and violations of housing regulations went uncorrected.

What's Happening, which was loosely affiliated with Haryou, an antipoverty youth program in Harlem, excited me, so I called the adviser, Elaine Avidon, who taught at Cooper Junior High School, across the street from 103/79. Through Elaine I got to know Sonny Jameson, who taught at Spofford Youth House, a maximum-security jail for young offenders in the Bronx. Though I became reacquainted with Sonny through Elaine, I had known him when I was in junior high and he was on the same City College basketball team as my cousins Lionel and Paul Malamud. It was an honor to visit his classes at Spofford; I was moved by his students' poems, and it was both a revelation and an affirmation to find him doing things there that I had discovered for myself at 103/79. We, and other teachers I met in those days, had learned from listening to our students that their problems in school had more to do with the silencing of their voices and the marginalization of their cultures than with any personal problems they had with learning skills or techniques.

Another teacher I met through Elaine was Ira Landes, who taught at a "600" school, a high school for "difficult" youngsters. He, too, had found a way to, as Homer Lane put it, "[turn] the energy occupied in destructive activities . . . into social service."

Elaine, Sonny, Ira, and I had each discovered independently that through imaginative writing, speech, and a heavy dose of what some people have come to call tough love it was possible to provide our students paths to significant learning and to have them become actively engaged in their own education.

It was wonderful to be part of a group of educators with the same passionate commitment to students' success. No matter how messed up the schools are, or how indifferent, cynical, burned out, or racist many teachers are, I have always found and been nurtured by fellow teachers who invent ways to be effective within the worst of systems and under the most difficult of circumstances. This fellowship of teaching, as well as the magic of seeing children grow, has sustained me as a person and kept me teaching and supporting the potential of public education over the years.

When I was given an office at Teachers College and hired to do some research on student opinions, I offered Elaine and *What's Happening* the use of the office and our ditto machine. For three years the magazine was published from the basement of Teachers College, without the official knowledge or permission of anyone at the college. This gave me an opportunity to test out writing ideas with some of the kids and to provide a place where Larry, Akmir, and other students of mine could be published. Through this relationship with *What's Happening* I began to understand how important writing for an audience was in helping students develop writing skills and the ability to shape ideas so that people they cared about would be moved by their opinions and passions.

All the time I was attending classes and working informally with the kids, I was looking for a more permanent and effective way to become involved with the schools in New York. My chance to do that came in an unexpected form and from a totally unanticipated direction. In March 1966, Nelson Aldrich, an old friend from Harvard who had also taught at P.S. 103/79 for a year, invited me to lunch at the Columbia faculty club. He asked me to bring along some of my students' writing, which was easy since I always had student work with me. Nelson was with a friend who turned out to be Robert Silvers, editor of *The New York Review of Books,* which had just been started to review books during the *New York Times* newspaper strike. Nelson and Robert were attending a meeting of writers and university teachers of writing sponsored by the Tufts Conferences.

The Tufts Conferences, a series convened by the White House Office of Science and Technology, were part of an attempt, initiated by the Kennedy administration and continued through the Johnson years, to totally change how curriculum was structured in all subjects from kindergarten through high school. The initial impetus for this sweeping project was *Sputnik* and the race to produce students able to keep the United States ahead in technology, a not unfamiliar tune today. The main idea was to bypass the educational establishment, especially the U.S. Office of Education, and instead initiate change through the National Science Foundation, the Office of Science and Technology, and other new organizations that were directly controlled by the White House's Executive Branch. Instead of using educators—or, worse yet, according to the planners of these reforms, practicing teachers—university experts in each field would be the ones to revise the curriculum in that field.

These top-down, university-based curriculum projects produced what came to be known as the new math, new physics, new biology, and new social studies. As intellectually sophisticated as they were, they were developed with little attention to how children actually learned in public school classrooms and less attention to the needs and craft knowledge of the teachers themselves. None of these curriculum reforms have survived, despite the many good ideas they contained and the millions of dollars spent on their development. Without the active support and involvement of the teaching community they were bound to be ineffectual, and they were.

While scientists and social scientists jumped into curriculum reform, the writers and professors of writing chosen to attend the Tufts Conferences on the Teaching of English continued having conferences and talking about it. The meeting Nelson and Silvers invited me to was to be the last or next-to-last one, as the Tufts money was about to run out.

That afternoon at lunch, I didn't know any of this background, so I was a bit puzzled when asked to read from my students' writing and talk about my teaching. Nonetheless I was game. This was my first opportunity to speak about the children's work and the kind of education that elicited it. At Teachers College, though many of us had been teachers before coming to graduate school, no one talked about what went on in actual classrooms.

What the writers and professors at the conference were saying about teaching and what they knew about teaching writing to children were in complete contrast to their honed and sensitive literary skills and intelligence. They had little idea of what kind of reading pleased children or of the information and experience children brought to literature. They had no experience reading young people's writing and had somehow forgotten that five-year-olds and adolescents are not necessarily interested in the same things. I remember jumping up at one point and saying that they didn't understand children or children's writing. Someone challenged my credentials, but instead of responding with a speech I read my students' work. The people in the room listened intently, moved by the work. I was practically in tears as I read. This serious response to the children's voices was beyond anything I had ever expected.

Afterward I said that if writers wanted to contribute, they should work directly with kids in the classroom and with teachers who were already doing creative work. I insisted that teachers had to be at the center of change in the classroom—not just teachers in general, but those whose work could stand up to the highest and most sensitive scrutiny.

At the end of the session I was asked to coordinate a meeting whose goal was to create an organization that would work to change the way writing was taught in the schools. It seemed surreal to me, going from boredom and despair at Teachers College, my hope barely sustained by my continual contact with kids from the community, to being asked to put together a conference to change all the schools in America. I figured there was nothing to lose by going along. However, I had conditions. The last thing I wanted to become involved in was an academic discussion of children's writing and educational theory. My concerns were to find ways to give power to the teachers I knew were already doing a good job in a bad system, and to help the kids and nurture their voices through writing.

My specific demands, which I presented much more softly than I had anticipated, were these: I would write an essay on the kind of education I believed in as a way of setting an agenda for the meeting; and all my teacher friends would be invited to the conference as full participants, not merely as guests from the school system. The goal was to have teachers intimately and essentially involved in the remaking of the curriculum.

To my astonishment the planning committee agreed, so I wrote a short essay called "An Exploration of Children's Writing," which was later published in expanded form in *The New York Review of Books* as "Teaching the 'Unteachable.'" (This was the first time I had tried to write about what I had learned from my students.) I remember typing out the essay and getting it copied at a local shop. Then one night in my apartment Larry, Akmir, Judy, and I collated and stapled the booklet and mailed it to the participants in the Tufts Conference with a cover letter inviting them to a final conference at the Huntting Inne in East Hampton, Long Island, from June 22 to June 29, 1966.

Beginning with a document that expressed specific educational ideas and reprinted children's writing turned out to be very effective. People arrived at the conference ready to talk about schools, writing, and the role of children's own voices in education. I had invited Elaine Avidon, Ira Landes, Sonny Jameson, and Debby Meier. Having these creative teachers present set up a context in which the participants, most of whom were writers or university professors, could hear about what actually went on in a creative classroom.

My naiveté about the politics of publishing and writing, combined with my obsession with teaching, students, and issues of social justice helped move the meeting from gossip and jockeying for federal support to a specific focus on what worked in the schools. I was sure that *somehow* I could use whatever developed out of this extraordinary combination of people for the benefit of the kids. That was the first consideration. Bringing writers and teachers together and changing the writing curriculum was secondary. I was willing to devote myself to the project, however—to write proposals, organize, and administer a program—because it was central to the collaborative vision of learning that would work for my students and I felt the organization might become a vehicle to realize it. Graduate school and Teachers College simply would not do.

The Huntting Conference was amazing. The teachers I had invited were excited about sharing their students' work. None of us had a natural audience or a forum where we could share what we thought about education or celebrate and analyze what our students did. Nor did we connect our students' work with contemporary writing—which most of us had simply not encountered, being occupied with the mechanics of teaching every day and then, in response to our students' writing, spending nights and weekends recreating the curriculum. We were isolated individuals, tinkering away at making good education; and this was a coming together beyond any of our expectations. When we read our students' works to the writers, they responded with sensitivity and compassion not just to the writing but to the voices and lives behind the words.

After spending a few days listening to the teachers read student works, the writers invited us to a reading of their work as thanks. I think Denise Levertov and Grace Paley orchestrated the reading, which was not on the agenda. It was revelatory for me. Mark Mirsky, Jonathan Baumbach, and Seymour Simches read selections from novels in progress; Grace Paley read new short stories; and Denise Levertov, Muriel Rukeyser, and Anne Sexton read poetry. I was drawn into the world of contemporary writing and writers' sensibility that my obsession with the everydayness of teaching had neglected. The writers spoke to us in the spirit of community and through the reading made their work alive and accessible. When I returned to the city I bought as many of their books as possible and had an orgy of reading, the inflections of their voices and the energy in their faces still in my mind. Above and beyond the Teachers and Writers Collaborative, which developed out of that week, what I learned of writers and writing had a profound effect on my teaching.

Every time I learn something I have a passion to share it, teach it, and test it by finding out what children can do to transform it. The new voices I heard pushed contemporary writing, and especially poetry, closer to the center of my work with children. Over the last thirty years I have been teaching a class that was inspired by the Huntting Conference and that began during the planning phase of the Teachers and Writers Collaborative. Though the students differ from year to year and the meeting place has been everything from a storefront to a classroom to my living room to the library at our home and educational center in Point Arena, California, there are some commonalities. Participation is voluntary and there are no prerequisites. There are no grades; there is no homework. The format is simple: I pick out some poems that move me (or, later in the class, the students pick out poems they like) and we read them out loud together and talk about what we have read. Sometimes we take turns, reading a line each; other times we might read and reread the poem until everyone in the group has had a chance to say it out loud. Then we talk about the poem—what the poet seems to be saying; how the poem affects us; the personal, social, and political issues the poem addresses; and a bit about craft, if that comes up. What we try to do is enter into conversation with the poem and the poet, knowing full well that we are projecting our own place, time, and desires onto the poet's work. Since we are a small temporary community of readers and writers there is no need to worry about the "correctness" of our analysis or taste.

After reading the poem and talking about it comes writing. Sometimes I suggest a topic for us to write about. At other times, a topic comes up in the discussion. However, the topic for writing also relates to the poem, so that the writing we do is also in dialogue with the poem and the poet.

If someone doesn't want to write, that's okay; if they want to write about another topic, that, too, is part of our reason for gathering. After writing we go around the circle and read out loud. Anyone too shy or embarrassed to read can pass. Finally we talk about our writings, and then we go home.

People are there to be there, and they take different things away from the class. Simply wanting to be in the group is sufficient. There is no evaluation, follow-up, or testing. Hoped-for among the outcomes are friendship and a continuing love of poetry. The class ends when the group feels it's time or when I move to another community. Of course, class members are free to continue meeting, and anyone can lead a group. There are several offshoots of this class that so far as I know are still alive.

Let me give two brief examples of recent versions of the class. One developed when I was a visiting professor at a small urban college. During my stay I got to speak to a number of English classes at the local high school. For visits like this, I always bring "stuff" with me—things to provoke the students' interest, to get their attention away from their interaction with me and distract them from the power games that go along with it so that we can get on with learning. On this occasion I was carrying a barnacle I had removed from the skin of a whale that had beached on the shore near my house, the vertebra of a dolphin that washed up on the same shore a year later, and an assortment of short poems. I began with the poems, and read Louise Erdrich's "Indian Boarding School: The Runaways" although the teacher had warned me that it would be too difficult for the students. My experience has been that important content overrides school-based skills deficiencies, and the first line of the poem proved this once again. "Indian Boarding School" begins, "Home's the place we head for in our sleep," and goes on to speak of the injuries created by boarding schools and the longings of the children to be home and whole. There were a few Native American children in the class, and many more East Asian children. In addition several of the white children had just moved to the city because industry in their small town had closed down. I chose the poem because it spoke of home and the pain of social dislocation, and I wanted to show the students how poetry can address them, not from a foreign literary country, but from the heart of the poet.

After class several of the students asked me if there were any more poems like that. I said hundreds, more than I knew or we could imagine. Then they asked if it was possible to read poems together a few times, so the class continued for the semester. We met once a week in the teacher's living room and read poems by Li-Young Lee, W. H. Auden, Marge Piercy, Victor Hernandez Cruz, and many others. Reading out loud made many of the poems accessible for the students, and taking poems a line or a few lines at a time, letting the readers pace the poem as we entered it, helped. In this class, writing was minimized. The students were hungry to read and talk, and that, for the most part, is what we did.

A teacher who sat in on one of the sessions asked me why everyone talked so much when we could have gotten more writing done and read the poems more critically. My response was that this was *our* class, not the system's, and what it became was up to us and not to be determined by some outside measures of efficiency or achievement.

A second, more recent version of the class took place in 1991 at our home library and learning center. Initiated by the parents of several high school students of mine, it included high school students, a few people in their early twenties, and some others in their thirties and late forties. The poetry couldn't have been more different from that we read in the other class I've described. And this class had an emphasis on writing. Everyone in the class wanted to write songs and to use the reading and studying of poetry to develop their songwriting skills.

I had never written a song, nor had I ever thought of teaching a class on songwriting. I agreed to do it, figuring I'd learn a lot along the way. That's the beauty of a class that has no institutional basis or cost—it can open the way to explore new ground, free of the academic and social judgments that inhibit learning. This kind of learning is more akin to the classes immigrant workers developed for themselves in the early twentieth century, the kinds of classes my grandfather attended, in which laborers and bricklayers read Yiddish poetry and discussed politics. People have forgotten how to organize learning for themselves; they look to experts and critics to show them how to learn. However, there is an old tradition in our society, dating at least as far back as the self-improvement groups Benjamin Franklin participated in, a tradition in which people were not afraid to read poetry, politics, or science for their own edification and without the help of so-called experts. Reading circles and circles of conversation nurtured the intellectual, cultural, and social health of the society, and we need them now more than ever. We need to find ways to help people learn for themselves and with their friends so that they can make informed decisions on major issues that affect their lives rather than shift responsibility to politicians, "experts," gurus, and charlatans whom they end up hating.

In the songwriting incarnation of my class, we had as many members as could comfortably fit around the table in the library, about a dozen on a crowded day. I have to admit that before the first session I was panicked; though I love music, teaching it is not something I could responsibly do. Usually when I needed music for one of the plays I directed, or for a political protest, I could call on my son, Josh, who is a skilled musician and sensitive teacher. But Josh was off at college and I was on my own. So I came up with the idea of chanting and comparing the use of silences in poetry with the use of rests in music. Fortunately, everyone knew I was reaching beyond my comfort zone and had agreed to go along on the adventure. Since for me doing education is a bit like inventing or improvising a fugue, it's a privilege to have students who want to set out on a voyage of discovery.

I brought a few rhythm instruments to class and found a wonderful Native American chant that would allow us to speak and read in many voices—Frank Mitchell's "War God's Horse Song II," translated by David P. McAllester. Each verse of the chant ended "With their voices they are calling me."

After we read the poem a few times, one group became the chorus, chanting "With their voices they are calling me" while we took turns reading the rest of the verses. Then we added instruments and set up a series of rhythms, creating alternative performances of the text. After that I suggested we set up our own choral line and create verses. The chorus was simple, as our community was undergoing outrageous and irresponsible logging: "Where are the redwoods now?"

I don't have a record of the improvised verses, but I remember feeling a sense of connection between poetry and place that reminded me of Walt Whitman. For the next class I brought in Whitman's "Song of Myself," and to my thorough astonishment everyone in the class found it new and exciting. No one had ever read Whitman before, except for "O Captain! My Captain!" in high school; his voice was an inspiration and a revelation of their own longings for connection and grounding. The rest of the class consisted of reading Whitman's poem out loud many times and then creating songs in many different modes out of Whitman's song.

I am now choosing poetry for the next version of the class, which I hope will take place in San Francisco next fall.

TEACHING CLOSE UP

For me the late sixties and early seventies were a creative time. Though I was involved in the civil rights and anti–Vietnam War movements, my life was centered on teaching challenges. Upon returning from the Huntting Conference, in July 1966 I was offered an office at Teachers College and wrote a $1.2 million proposal to the U.S. Office of Education that called for the establishment of a Teachers and Writers Collaborative whose charge was to change the way writing was taught in schools throughout the country. A few months later, the Office of Education released some provisional money. I had already begun to act as if the Collaborative were funded. This was a habit I'd developed in the public schools. If you waited around for permission to do what made sense for students, you'd lose them in the process.

Several writers who had attended the Huntting Conference were anxious to get to work in schools, and they made it clear that money was not the issue for them. Being of use to children was the prime motivation. Anne Sexton called me a week after the conference to ask me to encourage her to co-teach writing in a local high school class. She wanted my support, wanted to know that I would be available to talk with her about all the problems she was sure she would have with the students. Anne phrased her desires in negative form and preceded every one of our many conversations with a litany of the failures she was confident would take place. Somehow she intuited that I could talk her out of this attitude and focus her untutored passion to teach. I agreed to talk her through this educational adventure, which eventually led to the wonderful work produced on the record *Anne Sexton and Her Kind.*

Muriel Rukeyser wanted students and I recruited members of the psychology class—Ronnie, Janine, and their friends—for a poetry class, which Muriel could participate in whenever she had time.

The novelist and poet Ishmael Reed, whom I had come to know and whose work I admired, also came over one day with a young man whom he presented as a new student of *mine.* This was Victor Hernandez Cruz, then barely hanging on at Benjamin Franklin High School in East Harlem though he was a published and respected poet. Akmir, Ronnie, Janine, Larry, and Phillip joined us, as did other former students. Victor brought some friends and we had a full class. This was the first of my poetry and writing classes.

I remember that first day of class, which began with my asking everyone to write a poem and then read it to the class. I wrote too. My poem was mediocre, as one could expect from a first effort at writing to a set theme. The same was true of all of the other poems, with the exception of Victor's. I don't have a copy of the exact poem but it could have been this one, which Victor wrote during that time in New York:

After the Dancing

(for Pamela)
we move
to the whispering
after the dancing

do you dare
for all your dreams
for your sometimes stupid head
dug in the air
passing like cars
from one room to another
for what's left in you
after the dancing
do you sometimes wonder
your skin stretching
your head turning
your ass pushing
your arms flying
do you sometimes wonder
if you let go
if the walls move
if the floor cracks
if the ceiling lights up
& you be there
do you sometimes wonder
if the people cheer
if you get busted
for illegal steps
if the Judge say
your boo-ga-loo is ammunition
do you sometimes wonder

we move
the whispering
after the dancing.

My initial response was, Here's a kid with a good memory. It was clear that a "poet" had written the poem, not one of my students. Despite having taught for several years and witnessed the brilliance of my students' writing, I was still bound by my expectations that students' writing would be expressive and sometimes brilliant but not crafted and shaped—that is, not literature. I thought Victor had memorized the poem and that it probably was written by one of Ishmael's friends. So I tried again and again and each time Victor confounded me with a *poem*, not a personal outpouring. Finally I realized I was in the presence of a young person who knew more about how to write poetry than I ever would. After class I asked Victor if he would co-teach the class with me.

There was still a lot I could offer Victor. I could give him poetry books he had not encountered before, show him a bit about teaching, introduce him to other writers, and introduce him to some more academic learning in fields such as philosophy and sociology. As a teacher, I could be a resource and provide opportunities for him to teach that he could not discover alone. His knowledge and mastery of poetry being more advanced than mine, I could not tutor his brilliance. But I could encourage and support it.

During my teaching career I have met other students who knew more than I did about what they loved. These students have been, among other things, computer wizards, musicians, athletes, pool players, actors, inventors, and entrepreneurs. I have learned from them, but have also learned that there are things I can teach them: the traditions of their crafts, where they can work, what people they can speak to, and psychological and political awareness that will help them place their work in the larger moral context of society. For these students, I have been more of a resource and guide than an instructor. These are two roles teachers play; but it is a major mistake, often made by school reformers who like to think of teachers as resources and coaches, that these are a teacher's *only* roles.

Teaching is a multifaceted vocation. These days I work with one youngster who has a good chance to play pro baseball, another who wants to be a professional skateboarder, and a third who thinks she can make it as a singer. What all three share is that they have trouble reading and want to know how they can read with ease. My job is straight-ahead reading teaching; giving advice and providing resources are a bonus.

Back in East Harlem, Victor Hernandez Cruz never resisted any offer of resources, nor have many of the other young people I have taught over the years who, in the areas of their obsession, know more than I do. Often these gifted people had learned their craft on their own or were born with gifts out of the ordinary. My job as a teacher is to nurture those gifts; to be encouraging and supportive despite the pressure my students will feel to conform or to temper their interests; and to add to the depth, perspective, and context in which they develop. I have encountered teachers who, jealous of their students, try to contain their gifts and make them fit into the ordinary round of school life. I do the opposite: go with the gifts, support the students as people, provide resources, and, as Langston Hughes said in his poem that begins "what do you do with a genius child," "let them go wild." Besides, if you are open to it you never know what unexpected genius you might help to unfold.

Having Victor in class shifted my attention to the quality of student work and helped me concentrate my teaching on the craft of writing as well as on student expression. To get children to write honestly and openly was a wonderful first step. To tutor that writing was another challenge, which I had to learn more about—and what better way to learn than from the writers involved in Teachers and Writers?

I held the writing class in a seminar room across from our office at Teachers College and also began a curriculum development class with teachers I knew. *What's Happening* moved into the office and for a while I loved the place. It was full of kids who knew and cared about each other; teaching and learning were going on and people of all ages mixed casually over poetry and curriculum. You could walk in and find six members of the editorial board arguing over what position to take on the Black Muslims, three or four teachers talking with a group of poets about reorganizing their writing curriculum, a small group of parents from East Harlem working on school reorganization proposals. It was like my classroom at its best, humming with creative activity going on in many different places separately and simultaneously, full of excitement about literature, ideas, politics, all held together by a sense that we were making the world better. Hope was the mortar. I loved being in the midst of all of this, wandering from group to group, sometimes participating, sometimes directing, sometimes just listening. It was like recreating my classroom as a larger community of learning that approximated my ideal of what school could be.

It got crowded in my small and isolated office at Teachers College; besides, I wanted to move closer to the community the kids lived in. So I suggested Teachers College rent a storefront for Teachers and Writers. They didn't do that, but they were willing to rent one that would serve a project they wanted my help on: the reorganization of Benjamin Franklin High School, where Victor, Janine, Ronnie, and many of the *What's Happening* kids went.

Benjamin Franklin High School was built in 1932 by Mayor Fiorello LaGuardia with the help of Congressman Vito Marcantonio for their friend and teacher Leonard Covello, one of the leading progressive educators in the country. There was a long struggle to build a school in East Harlem, the largest and poorest Italian ghetto in the nation; it took the election of an Italian American mayor and congressman to get the political muscle necessary to fund the school.

Covello's Ben Franklin was a school for the community and considered its mission nothing less than the nurturance of the whole lives of the people it served. Covello lived a block from the school when he ran it; he was still in the neighborhood when I was working in Harlem. Activists and educators visited him, and he was as generous with, and as respected by, the African American and Puerto Rican communities as he had been by the Italian and Jewish communities during the flowering of the school in the 1930s and 1940s.

But by the time I became involved in the reorganization of Franklin, it was considered one of the worst high schools in the city. The community programs had been killed and many of the best teachers had been red-baited out of their profession during the McCarthy era. Though there were a few wonderful teachers, most of the current staff and administration felt no organic connection either to the school's history or to the community it served. If you could reorganize and redeem Franklin you would have a model for the reconstruction of high school education in urban America—or at least, that's how people from Bobby Kennedy's office, Teachers College, and what was left of the John Kennedy Office of Education felt. I was recruited by some people in the administration of Teachers College to work with their program and use my connections in the community to help them establish credibility as they developed plans to change the school. It took me a while, and cost me considerable grief, to discover that they had plans for me that I didn't know anything about.

My role was to convince people in the community around Franklin that Teachers College wanted their input in the planning process.

I met with parent activists, many of whom worked for the antipoverty program MEND and whom I knew through the Harlem Parents Committee and my struggles at P.S. 79. We discussed the high school they might like to see for their children; I talked about the Teachers and Writers Collaborative and the idea of bringing people from outside into the process of designing school programs. We even came up with a plan for Benjamin Franklin High School, based on replacing the departmental structure of the school with a series of scholar-parent-student collaboratives in each subject area. We proposed developing Puerto Rican studies and African American studies collaboratives as well.

Many people in the community became committed to working with the school and bringing the ideas for reorganizing the high school to parents and local organizations. During this time, in 1966, I met David Spencer, a father, community activist, storyteller, person of courage, and, for me, a sorely needed mentor. David was and is a wild man, someone who has lived through so much that the only things that impress him are qualities of the heart. He is currently a minister; his ministry grew out of his experience in the gangs in Harlem in the 1930s, the time he spent around Birdland in the 1950s, and his work with the prison system. When I first met him in 1965 he worked with the East Harlem Triangle antipoverty program and had five children in the local public schools.

Dave was known to everyone in the East Harlem community. I say this without exaggeration: it used to take us an hour to walk one block. Everyone on the streets stopped to share gossip with him or ask his advice or just listen to his latest story, which he would tell over and over, with variations that made everyone feel that it was crafted specifically for them. I was one of Dave's listeners and whenever possible would walk with him or have lunch with him and ask a question or two. It never took more than that to set him off on tirades, stories, local history, and most of all his dream of schools controlled by the community. In his dream, parents would have a major say in the education of their children and poor people would feel that the schools were their schools, not controlled by outsiders with no personal stake in the well-being of the children they taught. I believe Dave did more community education about the nature of schooling in one week of walks than the schools attempted in a year.

I remember asking Dave how he got involved in education in the first place and he told me that he hadn't planned to; he'd wanted to work on housing and jobs. But one day his son Darren, who at that time was in kindergarten, did not come home on time. Dave and his wife, Deedee, were worried. Dave went to the school and asked Darren's teacher whether his son had been in school that day and whether anything had happened that would have made him so late coming home. The teacher looked at Dave and said she couldn't remember whether Darren had come to school. What did he look like? Dave was stunned. It was May; Darren had been in the class since September and the teacher, who was white, didn't know what he looked like and didn't have the slightest idea whether he had been in class that day. She couldn't, as Dave told me, pick him out of all the other Black faces. At that point Dave made up his mind to pay attention to what was happening in the schools, not merely for his own children, but for all the children in the neighborhood.

Dave and other members of the community began looking closely at the schools, going into classrooms when possible. What they saw appalled them—and educated them as well. Many adults in the community had not done well in school themselves; when they found their children failing, too, they initially thought it was their fault. They also accepted teachers' judgments of their children's progress. I had seen teachers telling parents that their children had done well when the children had no skills. The teachers' expectations of the children of East Harlem were so low that to "do well" meant, for most teachers, to be quiet and make some effort to learn.

Dave and others in the community began to realize that it was the schools and the people who worked there that were failing. The failure was institutional and not to be blamed on parents and children.

As Dave and I got to know each other, he explained how reluctant people in the community were to talk about their feelings about school in front of white teachers. He also told me about the history of the school I taught in, 103/79, which he had watched for twenty years, and about the fears parents had that their children would be hurt by school authorities if the parents objected to the way schools were run. He said that what had happened to me at 103/79, when none of the parents had shown up for the meeting concerning undistributed school material, was not a reflection on me so much as a manifestation of the belief that white teachers, no matter how liberal, could always find another job, whereas the parents and children would be left behind to suffer the consequences of defying authority.

Dave gently, and sometimes not so gently, led me to understand the intelligence of the people in the community I worked in. I knew this about my students but didn't live in the community and didn't know its institutions, stories, and rituals well enough to see where informal leadership was, how communication took place, and how problems were solved informally.

Dave said—and this is still true of our friendship—that as long as I would listen and respond sincerely rather than retreat into my whiteness, we would always have a lot to talk about. I am lucky to have had him as a mentor over the past thirty years.

It was through our friendship that I first became involved in community education struggles outside the classroom. Dave was part of a group of parents who wanted to develop community control of schools in East Harlem, and he was at the center of the 1966–1970 struggles over community control that led to the decentralization of the New York City public school system. This conflict was a far cry from the boycott to speed integration. After the failure of the boycotts to achieve results, integration had ceased to be an issue in New York City; the struggle shifted to control of the schools.

Back in 1966, as I was waiting to hear whether there would be any money for the Teachers and Writers Collaborative, people who were central to Teachers College's involvement in the Franklin project asked me to inform community members that there were no a priori plans for the school; this was not to be another case of outside experts coming in to tell a community what to do. They assured me that what local groups came up with would be honored and that they just wanted to be resources. Like a fool, I believed them—until I discovered that there was indeed a plan, and that my role in it was to cool out the parents. Nothing we did or said was ever taken seriously. The people at Teachers College, along with their advisers from Robert Kennedy's office, had specific notions of how to change the school; those plans didn't include community or any kind of outside governance or input. I told Dave and a few other parents what was happening; there were a number of tense, almost violent meetings, in which I took the parents' side. This was just one of many deceits that provoked parents and community activists to occupy some schools in 1967 and agitate for complete control of the education of their children.

Meanwhile, my July 1966 proposal had not been funded by the end of October, and my antagonistic role at TC began to threaten the funding. One day, distracted by the hostility developing at Teachers College, I did what no native-born New Yorker does: I crossed the street with the light but without looking for oncoming traffic. I missed being killed by a car that ran the light at 120th Street and Amsterdam Avenue only because at the last instant I saw something coming at me and I jumped. The impact shattered my left femur without even breaking the skin.

When I got out of the hospital, a few weeks before Christmas, I found myself in a wheelchair, still waiting for funding for Teachers and Writers, without mobility or a place to teach, but with a lot of time to write. During the next month I finished *36 Children.*

It turned out I was wrong about having no place to teach: there was always our apartment, wheelchair or no. I learned then that teaching can take place wherever people gather for learning. Over the years I have held school in a park, out of the trunk of my car, in a barn, at a county fairgrounds, around a table at a garden restaurant, in churches and community meeting halls, and in motels. So teaching in my apartment in a wheelchair during 1966 and early 1967 was really not the big thing it seemed to me then.

I got back to teaching because the doctor who had nurtured me through the pain of my broken hip called asking for help for another patient. Laura, who was in the sixth grade at the time, had smashed her head against the dashboard when her family car was broadsided. She had suffered severe headaches ever since and had forgotten how to read, though her verbal and mathematical abilities were completely intact. Before the accident she had been an exceptional student for whom reading sophisticated books had been no problem.

All the neurological labs and remedial programs at the hospital had failed her. Experts on post-traumatic effects were confounded and felt they could do no more to help her. Would I work with her?

When I first saw Laura and her mother, Laura was thoroughly demoralized and her mother depressed and frightened for her future. Laura had recently scored 2.7 on a reading test; she had to score at least 5.0 to be promoted to the seventh grade and go on to junior high school with her friends. She was sure she would be left behind in the elementary school, and put in a "dumb" class to boot. That was what her guidance counselor had told her. I asked Laura to read Maurice Sendak's *Where the Wild Things Are*. The language is simple; the story is sophisticated and not insulting to a twelve-year-old; the pictures are interesting and a bit menacing.

Laura read the first few pages with no trouble. On about the fifth page she made a simple mistake, reading "mild" for "wild," a word she had previously had no trouble with. Immediately she panicked and read every other word on the page incorrectly. I noticed she looked away from the page, wrinkled her brow, and began to make sound associations that had nothing to do with the story. For example, she read "more" as "four," then said, "door," "boor," and "coor," and finally trailed off into some indistinguishable sounds. I asked her to stop for a while and rest. She did, then began again, and was fine until she made another mistake. Then the same flight from the written page occurred.

Laura didn't have any problem with phonics. She knew how to read in a technical sense. But she could not sustain herself for more than a few sentences. She had no stamina and didn't know how to help herself when she made a mistake.

I spoke to Laura about my observations, and she was surprised. She was used to going to remedial reading clinics, getting a "workup," and then being given a reading treatment. No one had ever spoken to her about the process of reading, or about what they saw as her difficulties. She had been treated like a sick child, incapable of understanding her own problems, and was usually told to do exercises that made no sense to her.

I worked with Laura for two hours a week over a period of three months. She wanted to learn to read again, and I saw no reason she couldn't. For the first few weeks we talked about her problems and I listened to her explanation of them. Every time she made a mistake we stopped and talked about how she could check herself. My goal was to make her familiar with her own problems so she could sense them in advance and anticipate a solution before she panicked, lost a sense of the meaning of what she was reading, and took flight into word salad. After a while she could stop when she made a mistake and start again. She found, too, that slowly counting to five helped calm her down after a flight of sound associations.

There was nothing mystical about her problem, or "professional" about its resolution. I didn't depend upon any medical explanation to help me determine what to do. For me to be effective I had to look at her as a particular child, at a particular moment in her life, with particular habits of learning, and, with her help, reconstruct her reading skills. My strategy was to take her educational problem as just that and come up with a pedagogical solution. I wanted to stay within the realm of learning and away from all the extraneous paraphernalia of medical models and the learning-disability profession. This meant using my skills as a teacher, and specifically using what I had learned watching students as they approached new learning challenges.

It turned out that Laura had a problem focusing her eyes on the written word. I didn't need a test of perceptual skills to see that; it was only necessary to watch her squint and contort her face to know that she had to make an uncommon effort to keep print in focus. I suggested that she follow along on the page with her finger, and this seemed to work both during the lessons and at home. Her finger on the page seemed to track her eyes and pace them. She had greater control over the pace of reading with her finger in control of her eyes.

The finger strategy created serious problems at school. Laura's teacher refused to let her use it, having picked up the notion somewhere that it was a bad thing to do. The school's remedial reading specialist agreed. I spoke to both of them about it on the phone, but neither could give me any reason why reading with a finger on the page was wrong or harmful. They referred me to the school reading specialist, who took the same position in the same irrational way. Finally, I had to get a note from Laura's physician and have him threaten a lawsuit to enable Laura to read in school in a way that was obviously helping her. When the doctors and lawyers entered the situation the educators retreated.

I am sure that those teachers had in mind some research about how children learn to read, but they were paying no attention to what helped Laura. I learned years ago that educational research, at its best, produces approximations and guesses about how some children learn; you have to go with the leads children give you, not with the theories or the research results. The entire debate between whole-language and phonics-based reading instruction, for instance, is foolish. Children learn in both ways; as long as you keep in mind that the goal of teaching reading is to create intelligent readers, the methods that get you there are simply strategies to pick and choose among, not theories to waste time arguing about.

I also noticed that Laura tired after a few pages of reading, so we did a lot of stamina training. What I did resembled what I would do if I were coaching a runner. It was as if Laura wanted to train for a marathon but only did well at a thousand yards. There was a simple explanation for her panic and word salad when she tried to read a long selection: she had lost her conditioning. She had to build stamina; her skills fell apart because she tired easily. I don't know what that means in physiological or neurological terms, but in educational terms it means addressing the specific problem of stamina and not transforming it into anything more complex. We practiced the equivalent of wind sprints, with her reading several passages quickly three or four times. Then we sat together and read slowly through longer and longer selections. And I showed her how to practice stamina development at home.

Laura was one of the most motivated students I had ever taught and recovering, for her, like was recovering from a sports injury, then reaching and surpassing a former level of competency. I teased her along and supported her through the process of relearning to read, which was not very different from the process of relearning to walk that I was going through at that time.

After three months Laura could read again and could also understand what reading problems were all about. There was nothing magical about what happened, but seeing it so close up taught me how to listen more carefully and be infinitely patient with young people's individual ways of learning. More than anything else, I learned the value of talking to students about their own learning and bringing them into the process of designing learning programs for themselves.

In June I felt Laura was on grade level again and ready for a reading test that would assure that she went on with her class to junior high school. She scored on a sixth-grade level. Instead of being congratulated, Laura and her mother were called to a conference with her teacher and the reading specialist. They refused to accept the results. They said progress could not be made that quickly and therefore Laura and I must have cheated. They retested her, and she scored at the same level. They refused to accept the second test results. They gave her a third test, and this time Laura scored on the fifth-grade level. Some of her nervous habits had begun to return. The school was beginning to create a new reading problem for her. With the help of a doctor and another threat of a lawsuit, we got the school to accept the results of a *fourth* test, on which Laura managed to score on the border between fifth and sixth grade.

Laura was promoted to junior high, and I lost a student. I never saw her again, though her mother called me over the years to tell me that she had gone to high school, graduated from college; the last I heard, she was about to enter an M.B.A. program.

Laura wasn't my only wheelchair student. Bobby Torres lived at Ninety-third Street and Columbus Avenue, a few blocks from our apartment. Roberto, Jaime, and a few other former students of mine brought me flowers when they learned of my accident. They brought Bobby with them, too. Roberto suggested that since I wasn't going out much maybe I could teach their friend to read. Once again a former student led me to a new teaching and learning adventure.

Bobby's situation was completely different from Laura's. He had never learned to read and therefore didn't, strictly speaking, have any remedial reading problems. I had to start from scratch with him, treat him as a first-time reading student, and be careful not to duplicate his prior experiences of failure.

When we met, Bobby was fourteen and lived with his mother, three brothers, and two sisters. He had stopped going to school the year before; instead, he told me, he stayed on the roof of his apartment building from nine in the morning until three in the afternoon, taking care of his flock of pigeons and flying them. Only after three, when school was out, did he hit the streets and spend time with his friends.

After chatting for a while that first afternoon, and with some urging and nudging from Roberto and Jaime, Bobby agreed to be my pupil. From December 1966 through June of 1967 he came to my apartment punctually at four o'clock every Monday and Friday afternoon. (We both pretended for the first few months that he couldn't have lessons any earlier than four because he was in school every day until three.)

About the time Bobby became my pupil I began to notice the

word "Bolita" scrawled across the elevator doors and halls in my apartment building. Under each inscription of the name was a date. It took me over a month to figure out that all the dates were Mondays and Fridays. I mentioned my discovery to Bobby and asked him to stop documenting his visits since my neighbors didn't appreciate it. He erased the graffiti without my pressing the issue any further.

One week he came to the lesson with "Bobby Bolita" written boldly across the cover of his notebook and "Bolita 2-10-67" scrawled in ballpoint on his left palm. *Bolita* is Spanish for "little ball." Johnny explained to me that his mother gave him that nickname because he was so small and full of energy and mischief.

I forgot about the matter until several weeks later, when I noticed Bobby's handwriting on a wall several blocks from my building. The wall was layered with names and nicknames, declarations of love and hate, boasts and insults. On one corner was "Bolita as Bobby Cool."

I looked at the wall more closely and was able to find other signs of Bobby under the coats of graffiti. I could discern the worn-out declaration "Bobby and Anita—Don't Mess!" and an acrostic:

> *BolitA*
>   *Nestor*
>   *G*
> *JamiE*
>   *Larry*

Next to it was another one:

> *MariA*
>   *N*
>   *Tito*
>   *T*
> *AnnA*

Between the two were the initials "T.L.F.E." scratched into the brick on the wall and then carefully traced over in blue and yellow Magic Marker.

That wall fascinated me and I often returned to search for new additions or unravel the layers of writing. There were many things that were puzzling:

Golden Boy as Anthony Cool
Edgar as Jose
Gilbert as Fire Box [an obsession?]
Anna as Brillo [her hair?]
Willie as Papo

Other things began to fit into patterns:

Bobby of 93
Jaime of 89 as Batman
Maria the Black Queen of 89th

The more I attended to that wall, the more I felt like a voyeur, peering in on the lives of strangers. I found myself looking closely at the young people in the neighborhood, identifying their faces with names and nicknames from the wall, manufacturing intrigues and adventures for them. Bobby's friends were special targets for my imagination—Maria the Black Queen, Jaime Batman . . .

Bobby appeared in a different perspective to me because of the way he was described on the wall. During reading lessons he was shy, and ashamed because he couldn't read. At the same time he was a serious and persevering student who, despite his shame, was willing to start from the very beginning and learn the alphabet and elementary phonics even though he was over fourteen. He arrived punctually and was always polite and considerate.

"Bobby Cool"; I watched Bobby more closely on the street after discovering his nickname. It was easy, since he was a delivery boy for a tailor across the street from my house. I saw him bopping down the street with plastic bags full of clean clothes swinging over his shoulder. He would stop and rap with some girls for a while, then continue on, followed by at least one of them. In fifteen minutes he would return, his arm, empty of cleaning, hanging casually about the girl's shoulders or waist. They would be chatting away, laughing. Bobby seemed like another person on the streets—or perhaps it would be more appropriate to say that he was another person with me during lessons.

My discovery of Bobby's other aspects led to a change in our relationship. I told him about finding "Bolita as Bobby Cool" written on a wall and he blushed, yet began to talk about it and other nicknames. He told me that some kids had as many as four—one from their parents, a second from their friends, a third from their teachers, and a fourth they chose for themselves. I mentioned "Jaime as Batman" and Bobby said laughingly that it was Jaime's fantasy about himself. Maria was called the Black Queen because of her attitude, and he was called Bobby Cool because he had nice vines and a good rap.

As we grew closer, Bobby became more relaxed during lessons. He seemed more like the Bobby I'd observed on the streets, which was in obvious contrast to his school persona. Often we spent lessons talking about writing on the walls and what it tells of the life of young adolescents. When I mentioned that I was thinking of writing a book on graffiti he offered to help. He enjoyed thinking about things he had until then done without much thought. Once I asked him why he put his names on the walls of buildings in his neighborhood. He replied, "Because all the kids do," and when I pressed him he had no response. But when he'd thought more about it, he talked of the joy of knowing that other people see one's name and the sense of satisfaction he felt in seeing his own name next to those of his friends.

One day, in despair that our lessons, though interesting and informative for me, were not helping him learn to read, I asked Bobby to write down all the names he knew by heart and could spell. He produced this impressive list:

Nestor	Maria	Freddie	Lydia
Angel	Titi	Hector	Julie
Jaime	Anna	Betty	Wanda
Larry	Anita	Cookie	Roberto
Johnny	Victor	Bewitch	Joseph
Milta	Letty	Nora	Louie
Tito	Slim	Millie	Fernando
Miguel	Lefty	Joseph	Marta

Bobby could read and write those names, and probably others that hadn't occurred to him at that moment. Yet he was still reading on a first-grade level.

First-graders are supposed to have mastered a reading vocabulary of approximately one hundred words. In addition to his friends' names, Bobby could read without trouble the following:

Buick	Coca-Cola	Black Jack
Ford	Newport	dry cleaning
Cadillac	Salem	Yankees
Thunderbird	Marlboro	Giants
Pontiac	Pall Mall	Willie Mays
Falcon	Chesterfield	Joe Torre
Lincoln	Budweiser	Luis Rodriguez
Mercury	Ballantine	Joe Cuba
Oldsmobile	Knickerbocker	Puerto Rico
Ajax	Rheingold	San Juan
Mr. Clean	Gypsy Rose	Cassius Clay
Crest	Chiclets	Muhammad Ali
Colgate	Juicy Fruit	the *Daily News*
Pepsi-Cola	Cafe Bustelo	United States

He could also handle with ease:

mother (as in motherfucker)	pants	parking
fuck	suit	walking
shit	shoes	talking
dick	kill	trespassing
pussy	love	power
cop	hate	soul
cap	father	brother
price	pig	sister
sale	no	stop
discount	smoking	dog
shirt	spitting	

Bobby also new many Spanish words and could read all of the song titles printed on the more than 200 45-rpm records that made up his personal collection. Yet none of this knowledge did him any good in school. Many of the words he could read were prohibited in the classroom. I managed to discover his reading vocabulary only by talking with him about his life on the streets, listening to records with him, and showing an interest in his world. I became able to help him learn to read using what he already knew but did not validate as "real" reading. He was surrounded by the written word and had developed an organic reading vocabulary simply by living in an urban environment.

We began to use this vocabulary during lessons, with me providing the connecting words he didn't know how to read—"through," "before," "beyond." He began to write his own textbooks. He wrote about the cigarette brands he preferred, about drinking and partying and listening to music. He wrote about pigeons and with my prompting produced an interesting book on raising and training pigeons. Before long he got bored with simply writing about what he already knew and began to explore the world beyond his block. I provided books on sports, on bird life, on anything he asked for. And I added to his vocabulary, providing him with concepts and ideas that enabled him to express his feelings and opinions.

By the time I was walking again and ready to return to work full-time Bobby was able to read on his own. He could read the *Daily News* and even make his way through a few articles in the *New York Times* (though this was still a chore). I had him join the public library and he enjoyed hanging out in the reading room when he was trying to escape the streets. He told me there were always interesting new books there and looking through them was a good way to relax.

I still enjoy the challenge of close-up teaching, which I began to do with Laura and Bobby. It enriches my experience and to my work with groups of children adds an eye for the particular. It's a delight to see someone learn to read, forget about the mechanics of reading, and grab at the substance of a book.

Each child I've worked with in such an intimate way has produced new challenges and insights into how learning takes place, so I try to make time for one-on-one teaching whatever else I may be doing. Figuring out how to teach someone to read is like working out a jigsaw puzzle when you don't know the larger picture you're working toward. You have to get hints and clues from the student and use all the techniques and skills your craft provides in new constellations for each child. Once you get a fuller picture of how the child learns, you're on your way.

Today, along with my other educational commitments, I also work individually with four youngsters. Each has been brought to me because he or she experienced trouble learning to read in school. However, having trouble learning to read is not a generic condition. Knowing that a child has struggled with print tells you nothing. That's why most remedial reading programs don't work. They're based on the assumption that there is one way to not learn how to read, and therefore one fix for the problem. I've found the opposite to be the case: there are as many variants on failure as there are children. In fact, it may be that a version of the first line of *Anna Karenina*—"All happy families are alike, and each unhappy family is unhappy in its own way"—applies to educational misery as well: all readers learn to read in similar ways, and each failed reader fails in her or his own way.

One of my current students hates the printed word. Sal treats books as his enemy; my job is to get him to hold a book with affection. Sometimes we play baseball and then read; sometimes I force the issue and read to him and make him read back to me. My strategy is dual: convince him that he can learn to read with me, and then provide no experiences of failure to feed into his expectations.

April, by contrast, wants to learn to read but somehow just doesn't get the relationship between print and spoken language. I have to quiet her down. She's charming and a master of evasion. We could gossip for hours about other kids in town, or talk about the movies she's seen or her favorite TV shows. I have to get her to the book, to print, and then get her to rest her mind there for a while. So far I've been doing it through illuminated manuscripts, which fascinate her. She loves the Persian miniatures and books of hours I've shown her, and we've chosen texts for her to copy and illustrate. The slow activity of copying, not mechanically but with an eye to making the page look beautiful, seems to have settled her down; she's been making phonic discoveries every day.

My third student is silent and unresponsive. Initially I took this for resistance and rejection, but her grandfather, who is Native American, told me that watching was a way of learning she had been taught from early childhood. School moved too fast for her and forced her to respond in ways that humiliated her. He assured me that if I explained what reading was all about she would listen and practice it in private. When she was ready, she would show me what she had learned. He was right. So teaching Delsie, who quickly learned how to read, consisted of reading to her slowly, talking about what and how I read, and talking about sounds and print. I asked nothing of her, and the absence of testing and forced responses gave her the ease she needed to be able to understand and master reading.

My fourth student, Marcie, had a severe health problem in early childhood and looks five years old, though she is ten. People treat her like a precocious five-year-old when in fact she's a precocious ten-year-old. She is clever, and can fake any number of accents, create faux-Shakespeare monologues in her version of the King's English, and charm me into forgetting that she is with me to learn how to read, not how to act.

Marcie was ill during what would have been the first few years of school, so early reading passed her by. She has too much pride to show she can't read; with the help of her mother, she has memorized books and appears to read. I noticed this the first day we met. She read me a fairly complex book—but her eyes were on my face, not on the page. I had to gently bring her back to the page and let her know, indirectly, that I knew she wasn't reading.

She and I agreed that she had to start from scratch and learn the way adult learners do: from "hard" texts that I would help her sound out and understand. She has an enormous vocabulary, and her skills are the opposite of those of most children who have problems with reading: her comprehension is sophisticated and her simple phonic skills nonexistent. She agreed to start from scratch on the condition that neither her mother nor anyone else know what we are doing. I agreed to let her show me in private what she didn't know, and with the help of her mom, she is certainly coming along quickly.

When I tell tales like these, the first question people ask me is "Don't you ever fail?" Well, I spend a lot of effort keeping "failure" out of my list of possibilities and like to think of someone I'm having trouble helping learn to read as simply a person who has not yet learned to read. I want to stay with the child for as long as it takes. There is never a point at which I'm willing to say someone will never learn how to read. This may be absurd, but to teach well you sometimes have to make absurd assumptions in favor of your students. This summer, for example, I'm working on reading with a twenty-year-old I've been helping since he was five. He still has genuine problems reading but we agreed to have another go at it, and as long as he has the courage and strength to want to continue I'm here for him.

There is, however, one meaning of failure for me. If I ever find that I have caused a student to hate learning more than he or she did before, I have truly failed as a teacher. It has happened several times in my career, either because of some personal incompatibility between the student and me or because I was distracted or exhausted, lost the patience and ability to focus outside myself, and therefore neglected my student. These few cases still trouble me.

The joys of individual work with students aside, at the beginning of 1967 I was out of the classroom and missing it terribly. Teachers and Writers presented a wonderful opportunity to bring creative writing into the schools. Also, it was a privilege to struggle alongside parents and community activists to control and remake schools in Harlem. The possibility of assuming educational roles other than teaching opened up for me and I had to decide whether to return to working directly with children, or to become an administrator, director, or program developer.

Early in the year the Teachers and Writers Collaborative received $78,000 and I officially became its first director. I was also hired part-time as an educational consultant and proposal writer by the community board of Intermediate School 201 in Harlem after they had taken control of the school and received a grant from the Ford Foundation as an experimental decentralized school district.

During the takeover I had to make one of the most difficult moral decisions of my life. I knew how terrible things were in the schools and, through Dave Spencer and other members of the community as well as my own work with the children, how much promise there was if the schools could change. So, when the United Federation of Teachers threw up a picket line around I.S. 201 protesting the community's takeover of the school I had to choose whether to cross a picket line and continue my work with the community, or show my loyalty to the union.

I come from a union family; my grandfather was an active member of the Carpenter and Joiners Union for most of his life. I had also been a member of the United Federation of Teachers, a delegate to the union assembly, and a picket captain during the 1962 teachers' strike. At this moment it was the children and the community on one side, the union on the other. For me the issue was whether to oppose what I saw as racism and neglect in the schools or show solidarity with a teachers' organization that had become an agent of business as usual—that is, of continued failure in the schools. After much agonizing, I chose the children and the community and crossed the UFT picket lines. Eventually I worked for the parent board, writing proposals and developing curriculum and bringing it into the schools, which were kept open using community volunteers. (Among the volunteers were many of the writers involved in Teachers and Writers.)

If I was clear about anything after my first six years of being a teacher and an educational activist, it was that my first priority had to be the children. Loyalty to any idea, institution, or organization was secondary. If the children are nurtured, are learning, are treated with dignity and affection; if their voices are honored and their thoughts respected; if their culture and language are welcomed; and if they are acquiring skills and learning about the world and themselves, then I am willing to be loyal to the learning community. A teachers' union has to be judged on the quality of its members' work. When the union tries to blame children, parents—anything but its members—for failure, I refuse to go along. If humiliation, incompetence, and dread of learning characterize an institution, then I oppose it and am willing to take the consequences of speaking out against it. The issue was not too different from my stance in refusing to go along with the boycott. In one case I acted in opposition to the community, in the other with it. At the heart of both decisions, however, was my conviction that if something is not working for children I simply can't support it, no matter what the personal risks might be.

The continuing need to teach kept me from feeling rooted either at I.S. 201 or at the Collaborative. And New York was wearing me out. In July Judy and I had our first child, Tonia. I was still physically tired from the accident and from jumping back into work so quickly. And Akmir, whom Judy and I had come to love, died of a heroin overdose. That was yet another loss of young life I still cannot fathom; it compelled me, over twenty-five years later, to write my essay "I Won't Learn from You."

Though there were positive things at I.S. 201 and in the Teachers and Writers Collaborative, there was so much continuing pain for the children, and so much temptation to give myself over to despair, that it was clearly time to step back and become renewed for what was obviously going to be a long and constant struggle. It was much harder to change things than I had ever imagined. So when Lazar Ziff, who had attended the Huntting Conference, called me one day and asked if I would like to be a visiting professor in the English department and at the education school of the University of California, Berkeley, for a semester, it seemed like an opportunity to rest and refocus on teaching.

In January 1968 Judy and I arrived in Berkeley for a semester of rest and recreation.

Chapter 4

TEACHING ON THE EDGE

For Poets

Stay beautiful
but don't stay down underground too long
Don't turn into a mole
or a worm
or a root
or a stone

Come out into the sunlight
Breathe in trees
Knock out mountains
Commune with snakes
& be the very hero of birds

Don't forget to poke your head up
& blink
Think
Walk all around
Swim upstream

Don't forget to fly

—Al Young

OTHER WAYS

After the school struggles in New York, Berkeley seemed calm. Of course there were antiwar demonstrations, student-initiated courses, and general ferment about how to change the university. But the focus of most activity at Berkeley in those days was inward, on the university itself. I taught two classes: one on education, the other on writing. For all their self-declared activism, the college students in my classes seemed passive compared to the high school students I was used to working with and to the activists in the I.S. 201 community. Nor did struggles on campus have the urgency of those in the I.S. 201 community, where children's education was at stake and people had everything to risk: their livelihoods, their freedom, and their hope.

A group of students asked me to teach an unpaid, student-initiated class. (Such classes had been instituted as a compromise offered to student activists during the Free Speech Movement.) I readily agreed. During the first session, a number of students were very vocal about wanting to set the curriculum, define the subject matter, and develop the pedagogy. They didn't want me to be an expert and lecture them. I said fine; it gave me an opportunity to learn from them and catch up on what was going on in California.

The first sessions were frustrating for the students. I sat and let them run the class, but it turned out they had only vague ideas about what they wanted to learn about schools and schooling. They spent most of the time caucusing. Sometimes the caucus groups were organized according to people's interests—early childhood education, high school humanities, student organizing, and so on. At other times the lines were drawn according to gender. As I remember, the class was all European American, so there were no ethnic caucuses. After about a month of this, several students dropped out.

I watched the process and participated when they asked. During the fourth week, the class met, at their request, without me and then invited me to come to the next meeting, when they presented a petition. That class met, not in a circle as was usual, but as if for a lecture, with me and the students' spokespeople sitting in front and everyone else, the audience, facing us. It felt more like a courthouse than a classroom.

I was presented a series of demands. (This seemed to be their mode of doing business.) In effect, the demands were that I lecture, set a series of readings and papers, and in general conduct a traditional class on radical and nontraditional education. I refused, because teaching about open education in an authoritarian way seemed contradictory to me. Besides, this was supposed to be *their* class, not mine; I was already teaching my class in the education department. However, I agreed to meet students over lunch at a restaurant on Telegraph Avenue and in their apartments, to talk about education issues and perhaps help them discover what self-motivated learning was all about.

About half the class dropped out. The rest of us met for the rest of the semester to talk about schools and learning. There was no reason to call what we did a formal class. We talked, shared dreams, and looked at the real world as well. I enjoyed those conversations and my formal classes at the university, but missed the kids and the excitement of working in the public schools.

A few weeks before Judy and I left for California I got a call from Margaret Mahoney, a project officer for the Carnegie Corporation of America, who wanted to talk to me about doing teacher training with a grant from Carnegie. We had lunch and I realized she wasn't kidding. The one condition she set—a curious one that it took me several years to figure out—was that I work with Allan Kaprow, the Happener. I knew of happenings and was intrigued by such wild events—many of the demonstrations I'd been involved in certainly resembled happenings. But to work with him? I couldn't understand it, but didn't give it much thought until Margaret contacted me again in Berkeley at the end of my semester there. She reiterated that the Carnegie Corporation would indeed give Kaprow and me a grant to conduct teacher-training seminars and to develop and print teacher-training and curriculum material. We would even have money to bring poets, artists, community organizers, scientists, and other skilled people into the schools to work with students and collaborate with them and teachers in developing sensible and humane forms of schooling.

I jumped at the opportunity and was delighted when Carnegie agreed to transfer the grant to the Berkeley Unified School District. Judy and I were not ready to return to New York and the Berkeley and Oakland communities that were not part of the university were beginning to intrigue me. I realized, for example, that Berkeley was a divided city, with a large African American population that was ignored by the university. The public schools had all the problems of New York schools, though on what seemed to be a more manageable scale. And Berkeley was actually trying to implement school integration. Clearly there was educational work to do, work in which my experience might be useful, so in the fall of 1968 I found myself back in the belly of the beast—and delighted to be there.

The Berkeley Unified School District located our project in a storefront on Grove Street (now Martin Luther King, Jr., Way), down the block from Berkeley High School and on the divide between academic, predominantly European American and upper-middle-class Berkeley, and the more middle-class and working-class African American and Asian communities. We couldn't have picked a better place to gather people concerned with children's learning.

It was clear that I would need help setting up the project, especially within a large school bureaucracy. One person I'd gotten to know and care about during my brief time at the University of California was the secretary assigned to me, Betsy Barker. She was sensitive to all the educational issues I tried to discuss and was involved in the social and political life of Berkeley as a whole, not just the university. So I asked her—actually, I had to work hard to persuade her—to become the secretary and administrator of the Carnegie project. This decision was definitely one of the wisest I made in those days. I have always worked best when there were other people around who cared about children and were willing to hang around after class and talk about the work. Betsy saw everything, said what was on her mind, and tried to temper my sometimes too-romantic enthusiasms with a hardheaded sense of what was doable with the resources we had.

During the summer of 1968 Allan Kaprow, who was a professor of art at the State University of New York at Stony Brook, came out to Berkeley a few times and we talked about the project. Before we met I began reading about the happenings, events, and multimedia arts he was involved in. It was not easy. I didn't understand much of what he was doing and I wondered why Maggie Mahoney had roped me into such an improbable partnership. Happenings are what my grandfather would call meshuggeneh events.

Allan Kaprow was formal in manner and dress and wild in ideas.

When we first met, during the summer of 1967, he talked about the happenings and other large-scale public events he had put on over the years, and about his deep disregard for boundaries in the arts and education. I was intrigued by the scope of his dreams. He thought nothing of taking giant blocks of ice and organizing an event that consisted of people watching them melt, or of having hundreds of people paint stripes down the middle of a two-mile dirt road and then erase them and paint them again. He parodied and celebrated small rituals in large ways and designed events that could be as much fun and as absurd as the be-ins and love-ins that younger, less academic, and less wealthy people enjoyed.

Though I was intrigued by Allan's work, I wasn't sure what to make of it. Though I acknowledged that happenings could be fun, these events manifested an ignorance of the everyday needs of the poor; they seemed like indulgences for people with time and money on their hands. Still, something about them fascinated me. The public enactment of daily rituals could lead to a reconsideration of those rituals, could create political and social statements about equity and justice, could be used as much to educate as to amuse. Maybe there was a reason for me to hang around with Kaprow, after all. As open as I was in the context of school, the world he played in was much larger than mine. I owe him thanks for getting my thinking out of the confines of the classroom and helping me see the world as a stage for learning.

Kaprow and I had one fundamental agreement: neither of us wanted to project the idea that we knew *the* way to learn or live; rather, we imagined ourselves opening people up to possibilities, to options, to the creation of new social and personal forms of learning, communicating, and living. We came up with the name "Other Ways" for our joint work to emphasize that we were not a program with a set way of doing things, but a project whose goal was to explore ways of doing things. These days, I suppose, our approach would be called postmodern, but for me then it was simply an acknowledgment that if you follow a single rigid path in education you are going to lose too many students, have a long, lonely, boring journey, and end up on the margins of hope, wondering about the value of your work. If you consider yourself an inventor, a craftsperson, even an artist, then education is a constant challenge and no child is ever thought of as permanently lost to learning.

Speaking with Allan during his visits that summer was important for my development as an educator. I began to understand how close teaching was to artistic performance and how lesson plans might be conceived of as scores or scenarios for semi-improvisational performances. When Kaprow described how he and his friends thought about their audience, about ways of moving them, perhaps infuriating them, usually puzzling them, and bringing them to new perceptions of their own lives and pleasures, it occurred to me that this was analogous to much of what I attempted as a teacher. In a nonclassroom context, happenings were a form of education; I began to understand that broadening my thinking about alternative spaces where learning could take place might be more effective than thinking about learning within the confines of the walls, desks, doors, windows, and single door of a classroom.

Until then I had moved in the stream with students and their community, inventing things that made sense at the time and responding to interests, to student needs, to structuring what I felt was worth learning. I was also continually responding to demands created by current social struggles. It was time to take a step out of the water and think about the ecology of the stream, time to begin to articulate a tentative theory of my own work that would guide future teaching. Reflecting on education with Allan, who had no desire to be a public school teacher but was definitely an educator, let the specifics of schooling and the particulars of politics fade into the background for a while as I refocused on the larger question of how learning takes place.

Allan and I talked about ways of presenting ourselves and Other Ways to the artistic and educational communities in Berkeley. This exercise in self-definition brought us to an initial common agreement on our work. Even though this initial harmony didn't last, many of the ideas Allan and I discussed became central in the work of Other Ways during its first year.

From working in people's apartments, devising curricula on a daily basis during the struggle at I.S. 201, and simply improvising with whatever I could get hold of in my own classrooms, I had learned that the major resource for learning had to be the teachers' and students' imaginations. The materials for learning had to be crafted out of what was at hand and out of the primary sources of tradition—music, poetry, theater, history, the stuff of scientific experiments. The indissoluble unity of learning and teaching was, after all, a form of magic consisting of creating something out of nothing, of seeing new powers and skills emerge where there was previously only frustration, desire, and possibility. Packaged educational material, predigested and overstructured learning programs, workbooks and textbooks all inhibited the free play of the imagination. Given the freedom provided by the Carnegie grant, I did not want to spend one penny on anything we couldn't devise, invent, or develop ourselves. In fact, the idea that you can create your own learning environment and construct a physical place for learning that had the unmistakable signature of you and the learning community of which you were a part was central to my vision of what Other Ways could be.

Allan agreed, since his work used the most common substances —such as boulders or ice—in interesting metaphoric ways or took the waste products of industrialization and transformed their meanings. He was not antitechnological, and I'm confident he would have thought nothing of taking thousands of pictures of a simple event and covering a basketball court with them.

We wanted the people we worked with in Berkeley to understand that we did not have a set program, that we were about to embark on the educational equivalent of what scientists call messing about. Messing about in science takes place when people are looking for the right questions or trying to tease hints about the nature and structure of a problem from a wide variety of sources without knowing exactly what they are looking for. For me messing about in reading means throwing books, poems, plays, and dozens of other forms of print at a youngster as we come together, to find that delicate balance of sensibility, will, and intelligence that will result in the skill of reading with ease and delight.

We decided to use a simple white poster with the word "Suppose" in bold print at the center with radiating arms of suppositions emanating from it to announce the project to the Berkeley community:

Suppose . . .

   you could find architecture in a junkyard
   you had to make music only with a rubber band

you were given the elements of a game and had to create the rules
you had to write your own *Dick and Jane*
you discovered the mythology of everyday life
you used graffiti as a textbook
you saw hot rods and dragsters as moving sculpture
you couldn't write and could only take pictures
you saw basketball as a dance

These questions covered the whole curriculum from reading, writing, math, and science to the arts, social studies, and history. We drew the net as wide as we could and kept things as open as possible.

The storefront we were assigned had been used by school administrators for planning the desegregation of the Berkeley schools, which was scheduled to begin at the same time Other Ways was to formally open, September 1968. Dozens of maps of Berkeley had been left behind, including a giant population map on the wall, with purple areas for whites, blue for Blacks, green for Asians, and pink for Latinos. Nobody was their own color, though it was immediately obvious what stood for whom. There was even a legend at the bottom, in case you needed it. This reminded me of the silly disguises I faced in junior high school in the Bronx where, in order to avoid the stigma of homogenous grouping (where students are assigned to classes on the basis of their achievement scores) class numbers were chosen at random. It was a joke among the students that we attended a school where 7–1, the so-called gifted class, was labeled 7–7, and 7–12, which contained students in trouble, was labeled 7–2, and none of the teachers could count. All the students knew that the classes were grouped homogeneously, and most of us felt that the grown-ups weren't fooling anyone but themselves.

The Other Ways storefront consisted of a large room off the street, several small offices, a toilet, and a large storeroom at the back. There were dozens of chairs, a few desks, some corporate couches, a large meeting table, and a miscellany of abandoned stationery and art supplies. My immediate thought was, We have the makings of a school here. However, our mandate from Carnegie was teacher education, so we planned weekly teacher education seminars. We invited people through the Berkeley schools, by an announcement we attached to some of the "Suppose" posters, on radio station KPFA, and through Allan's artistic connections in the community. There were no fees, no requirements, no academic credits—just conversation about how to make the schools work for all children.

In September 1968 the storefront opened. Betsy set up an office and reception desk at the door and I began to clean up the storefront, distribute the furniture and put things in some semblance of order. Because the funding did not cover Allan's whole salary, he commuted from New York and set aside one room as a place to stay during his visits. During most of the first weeks Betsy and I were the only ones at the storefront—with a few major exceptions. The "Suppose" poster had unexpected consequences. The first responses came not from teachers but from students, who had absented themselves from Berkeley High School.

In those days there was a very active anti–Vietnam War movement on the campus of Berkeley High School. A number of students had raised the Vietcong flag on campus; others walked out of school on a regular basis to participate in community-based political activity or join the many different communes and crafts collectives that had sprung up. Most of these students did well in school; they came from university families or were part of the substantial interracial and interfaith progressive community. Our poster provoked the interest of a number of these students, and they were the first to visit the storefront.

There wasn't much to see: Betsy, me, occasionally Allan, lots of furniture, and, fortunately, dozens of maps of the city. One of the first students to drop in was Frederick Douglass Perry. Fred was big boned, about six feet two inches tall plus another four to six inches for his ample Afro. He seemed the image of the black militant of the sixties until you looked into his gentle eyes and experienced his delightful, slightly wicked smile. To be sure, he was angry and militant, but to me he projected intelligence and joy. From our first meeting, we became friends, and twenty-eight years later we still are.

Fred was unlike Akmir in many ways, less severe and much more politically sophisticated. He grew up in a middle-class family and lived with his mother, who was Italian American. His father, who had died in the fifties, was a distinguished writer and progressive political figure. Fred had Akmir's inquiring and probing mind and was willing to test his ideas and beliefs in action as well as conversation.

Fred brought several friends with him, and for a while we did "map poetry" as a way of talking about the character and politics of Berkeley. We cut up maps; wrote, painted, and drew all over them; and made them into visual and verbal statements about life in Berkeley. It was a wonderful way of learning about life outside the university, so I pushed the students to tell me more and more about their experiences and their knowledge of the community. We also discussed the statements on the poster and then did what it suggested: transform and recycle what was given to us. We discussed imaginary Berkeleys, redrew the maps, wrote poetry on the maps, made resource inventories, drew route maps representing where different members of the community walked, drew ethnic boundary maps, and made map sculptures and map paper airplanes, until we'd run maps into the ground but had begun to know each other and think about learning projects we could do together.

Fred introduced me to his sister-in-law, who was a kindergarten teacher in the Berkeley school district. Susie invited me to come with Fred and play with her class. Over the year I made a number of visits, bringing maybe a bag of paper scraps, some odds and ends from a lumberyard or plastics plant, maybe some paints and discarded billboards, and played with the children. I listened to their stories and made up some stories myself, wild tales largely derived from stories my students in Harlem had written or shared with the class. I even ventured into the Bronx of my childhood, making up stories about mythical characters who lived in sewers and played stickball after midnight.

Playing with Susie's class gave me the taste of kindergarten and first-grade teaching, and once again I resolved to spend several years doing that full-time. However, 1968 was my time to push teaching to the edge with junior high and high school students, teachers, and community members instead of returning to the joys and challenges of a self-contained classroom.

The educational climate was right for experimentation. My books *36 Children* and *The Open Classroom* had just been published. Through my writing I had the opportunity to meet teachers throughout the country and talk about ways of transforming the schools. What later was called the open classroom movement was just beginning; teachers, primarily those working with poor and African American children, were restructuring their teaching to allow for more student input, a multicultural curriculum, and in particular an emphasis on imaginative writing and learning that honored the voices and experience of young people.

In addition to my books, John Holt's *How Children Fail,* Jim Herndon's *The Way It 'Spozed to Be,* and Jonathan Kozol's *Death at an Early Age* were part of a national conversation on education that, at its root, expressed faith and joy in children and their intelligence while at the same time hitting hard at authoritarian schooling as a main cause of failure and alienation. *Time* published an article—in 1969, I believe—drawing all of us, along with the sociologist Edgar Freidenberg and the essayist, poet, and thinker Paul Goodman together as part of a new open education movement, a conspiracy against the schools.

I remember reading the article in Berkeley and feeling delighted to be part of a movement and a conspiracy, especially since I didn't know most of its members. I remember calling and introducing myself to Herndon, Goodman, and a few other people named in the article. I had met John Holt briefly, but thanks to that *Time* article I began to read his work.

I even invited everyone to get together in Berkeley during the academic year of 1968–1969 so that we could figure out if indeed there were common threads in our work that could lead to a movement to change the schools. We had a series of three conferences, sponsored by the University of California, Berkeley, and held at Berkeley High School and our storefront. Over 500 people showed up for every one of them. Though there was no movement developed and there was a great variety of educational ideas and solutions among us, there was a sense on the part of teachers and parents who attended the meetings that things could be done to change the schools and enrich children's lives, and that the time to do it was now. This was not just a Berkeley attitude, either; I encountered it all across the country on my book tours and at conferences I attended throughout the late sixties and into the mid-seventies.

Despite my excitement, I was a bit overwhelmed—after all, at thirty, with only eight years of educational experience, I could hardly claim to be an experienced veteran. Nevertheless, I did have a clear sense of what *didn't* work in the schools, and since more established educational authorities and experts were passive in the face of student failure, those of us who felt our work was successful took the initiative and entered the national dialogue on education.

At the same time, I did not want only to be part of a national movement. I needed to work directly with children. When you remove yourself from the process, it's easy to forget what everyday life in the classroom is like, or how truly challenging it is to teach young children. I had seen good educators become boring experts who had nothing to offer practicing teachers, and I didn't want to fall into that role. Besides, my whole reason for being a teacher and writing about teaching was to teach.

The idea that change can come from the action of small groups of caring people willing to take risks and act in the service of children is profoundly different from the attitudes I currently sense. Faith in children's abilities and intelligence has eroded; there is a push to force rigid standards upon children, to shut them up in boxes and twist them to fit into the economic structure of a society with diminished expectations. As a consequence, trying to change schools is quite a different matter now. Hope and support for children have to be mobilized, whereas at Other Ways in 1969 we had to prove that *we,* as educators, were adequate to realize in our everyday practice the hope and faith in children that were common. It was a daunting but exciting task; I believe that during those days being an educator was as exciting a vocational choice for many young people as being an astronaut. There was a sense that we were pioneers, helping make a new and more just world through work with children, particularly the children of the poor.

In retrospect, it was naive to assume that working with children could change all of society. But the underlying belief that children would benefit from our struggles and become the compassionate, democratic leaders of the future is worthy of our democracy and should not be dismissed lightly, even in these cynical technological times.

It was in that late-1960s context of high hopes that our weekly teacher-education seminars began at Other Ways. Throughout the school year, from thirty to fifty people showed up every week on a voluntary basis; many of them had attended the meetings sponsored by the University of California. Fred and several of his friends also came to the teacher-education sessions, adding wonderful energy and insight. Their presence was welcomed by the teachers, and I'm sure that the responsibility they took for what happened at Other Ways as we evolved into a school grew out of the way they participated as equals from the very beginning.

Using the Carnegie Corporation grant, we were able to invite people from New York to work with the teachers for a few days. Allan Kaprow would give a presentation on happenings and do some with the teachers. Some of his artist friends brought in multimedia work; the storefront itself began to look like a work of art in process. Hoping to maintain educational continuity between my work in New York and the evolving work in California, I brought in people I had worked with in New York. Victor Hernandez Cruz read poetry and conducted writing workshops for teachers and students. Elaine Avidon visited, along with the whole staff of *What's Happening,* including my former student Larry. They succeeded in getting many teachers to emphasize their students' voices and, in particular, African American literature and culture. Even in Berkeley, this was pushing the envelope, though many teachers welcomed the idea that their students' writing and ideas could make creative contributions to the shaping of curriculum and the development of learning programs.

During one session, the environmental architect Sim van der Ryn brought an inflatable classroom to the storefront. We all sat in a circle, leaning back on the air cushions, talking about the reconstruction of learning environments while sitting in one attempt to do it. This was a continuation of my concern for the physical nature of learning environments and the importance of shaping learning places so that students feel both welcome and provoked to learn.

Our visitors also inspired the Berkeley High School students, who began to take more clearly defined leadership roles among their friends and brought more students to join in the sessions.

I ran the teacher-education sessions rather loosely. The teachers we had attracted were very creative and didn't need much pushing or cajoling. What they needed was each other and a time and place to explore ideas without worrying about being judged, something I still see as a major need to nurture effective school reform. I knew that students needed safe learning places; those seminars convinced me that teachers needed them just as much. As the sessions developed and a group of regulars emerged some of the teachers took the place of outside visitors. Mike Spino, who at that time was teaching in

Richmond, California, began to bring ideas about integrating poetry, meditation, and athletics into a single subject in high school. Mike, a world-class runner, demonstrated ways of using meditation to improve athletic performance. One day we all went out to the basketball courts near Berkeley High, meditated, wrote basketball poetry, and played basketball. I grudgingly admitted that there was as much pleasure in that total experience as in playground basketball, which I loved. It was clear that everyone could be involved, not just the most aggressive and skillful players.

We provided Mike a place to do the things he passionately cared about that were not part of the curriculum he was required to teach. Interestingly enough, out of those beginning experiences Mike has built a career as a track coach who integrates meditation, visualization, and the arts into training. This is no longer considered crazy; it's practiced by many world-class athletes. Our contribution at Other Ways was to give Mike a laboratory where he could experiment with how mental and spiritual discipline contribute to the health of the body and to enhanced athletic performance.

The sessions with teachers were not enough to satisfy my desire to teach, so in mid-October I asked one of the teachers in the seminar if there was any way I could have a group of her junior high school students come to the storefront a few times a week for a writing class. We had money for a bus, and she or any other teacher was welcome to join them. After some complex political maneuvering the first group of twenty-five students came to the storefront late one Tuesday morning. As with every new encounter with students, I overprepared and was nervous as hell. And I didn't want to repeat myself. Here was a chance to break some new ground in teaching writing. I knew how to get students started, knew how to help them through the first statements and begin to do sensible revision. This time I wanted, first, to help them read each other's work with sensitivity, to develop a sense of quality and be able to analyze each other's writing without being destructive or vindictive. This was a further step in the development of a community of learners. My second goal was poetry performance—the integration of music, poetry, and movement. I had seen people developing performance out of their poetry in New York; it excited me, so I wanted to explore it with my students and perhaps take it a step further.

The class was not at all what I had expected. Most of the students were female—and all were white, at a time when about half the students in the Berkeley school district were African American. The "gifted" group that was allowed to come to the storefront reflected the segregation through tracking that existed throughout the Berkeley secondary schools. But setting aside the structural problems of the school system, the students were wonderful. They were sensitive, creative, full of life and curiosity. Many of them became core leaders at Other Ways over the next few years.

At the beginning we had only a few hours a week, so we started writing in the first session. I find it best to begin with a challenge that draws directly on experiences that everyone has. The idea is to keep the circle as wide as possible at the beginning and then home in on the students' interests and skills and relate them to the subject you want to teach. Every class I teach begins this way: the goal of the first class is to be sure not to lose students but rather begin to get to know them. A creative writing class is closer to performance than other classes and an enticement to stay engaged while making them feel comfortable enough to reveal some things about themselves that could help shape their learning.

The subject I chose was garbage—the garbage on the street, in the cans, in the media, and on your mind. Perhaps that came from the fact that at that time I was janitor as well as educator at our storefront. I still have a few of the poems; this one, Jena's, has the other students' comments and criticisms handwritten on it:

> sharp silver blade
> slicing little red seeds
> crunch
> I heard every seed scream
> but I ate them all
> I shoved them one by one
> through my teeth
> they were tangy
> & succulent
> they were sweet
> & juicy
> and I ate them all
> I left a trail of
> organic garbage
> behind me,

everywhere garbage
I went to the park
to get some water
for my garbage
I turned on the hose
& started to drink
I drank & drank
my toes looked like
hippos feet
my stomach grew huge
& I burst
into little spurts
of green
I shared my green
with yellow
together we made
green/gold
& we felt high

The comments on Jena's paper were "I like it" and "I don't think it is good." These were what I expected, but were of no use to Jena or to the rest of us if we wanted to discuss how the poem might be revised. The second session began with a discussion of what a useful comment on writing might be like. Jena could and couldn't take criticism. She was intense about her work and was delighted to talk about it even in the most critical of terms, but she would not put up with any attacks on herself. She was a hippie and proud of it, dressed in a long granny dress with beads, flowers in her hair, and a small hand-painted flower on her cheek.

With Jena's permission, we went back to her poem and the comments "I like it" and "I don't think it is good." I set ground rules for the discussion, explaining that our challenge was to translate "like" and "don't like" into specifics that could be found directly within the poem. We began by hearing Jena read the poem out loud, an act of courage for young people. She pulled it off beautifully but changed some words in the process and apologized for the changes when one of the students laughed at her. I jumped in at that moment with a story, my way of refocusing and, I hoped, deepening the conversation.

I told the students that as an undergraduate at Harvard I'd had the privilege of hosting a Robert Frost reading. Frost was very old at the time; as he read from his work, I followed along with a printed copy of the poems. He changed phrases and added lines; sometimes he paused and thought his way to a new way of saying what had become for all of us canonical poetry.

At the reception after the reading, I asked Frost whether he usually improvised on the texts of his own poems, and he said he was always working and reworking them, rethinking words and phrases, always looking for another twist in a line or a slight readjustment of an image.

I concluded that if it was good enough for Frost it was good enough for Jena. Then I turned the conversation from the personal to the critical and asked Paul, who'd written that he didn't think the poem was good, what specific line or lines he thought were problems. He said he didn't remember and I asked Jena for permission to put her poem up for critical scrutiny once again. My intuition was that she, more than the others in the class, would have the courage to expose her work that way and I wasn't wrong. I suggested we all reread the poem and then had Paul comment.

Paul said that he felt the last line was a copout: ending a poem with "& we felt high" was like ending a short story you couldn't quite figure out with "and then I woke up." Everyone, including Jena, agreed. This led to a discussion of how the poem might be ended, which required the students to ask Jena what she had in mind. She tried to provide an exposition of her meaning but finally laughed and said the poem was just an assignment, that a lot of it just came out, and added that she'd rather bring a poem she had worked on to class for such a detailed consideration. I was delighted, for it was precisely this desire to share and critique work that I hoped would be at the heart of this class.

As the class developed, it was joined by Larry, my former student from P.S. 103, who was staying with Judy and me for a while. Larry's work had developed since the sixth grade; he was experimenting with performing his poetry as songs backed by drums. He and a number of other young poets at Other Ways were transforming personal rhymed poetry into the rhythms of the blues and of the dozens, a traditional African American form consisting of improvised rhymed insults thrown back and forth from person to person as a contest. This was a precursor of what is now rap music and Larry's performances excited the students in the writing class. They began to use

African American forms, folk music, and protest music as well as early San Francisco rock to set their poems. Some of the students began to bring flutes and guitars to class, and one brought conga drums. We began to experiment with transforming poems into performances and songs. In addition, revision groups were set up in which students read their work out loud to a group of student critics they chose and trusted.

Several of the junior high students also began coming around to the storefront after school. It turned out that Jena was a friend of Peter and Eric, and as the word spread around the community new students arrived. Ron and Karmie came because their father, a teacher at the Continuation school, had come to our seminars and they liked what they heard from him. Bobby came at Jena's invitation, and so did Sky. I found myself involved in dozens of little projects ranging from photography and super-8 film making to writing and even reading philosophy (mostly Sartre on existentialism). We were doing the high school equivalent of teach-ins. A subject that students wanted to learn about would come up, I'd research it and prepare material, and then we'd consider it for a few sessions and move on to the next challenge. Without having planned in that way, we began moving toward becoming a school. We were not developing an imitation of Berkeley High School or a substitute for it, but a learning community in which everyone was a willing participant, where the lines between required curriculum and personal interest and between teachers, students, and community resources were blurred. The community allowed for everyone who chose to be a responsible member to participate in a number of ways: as student, teacher, resource, and citizen.

THEATER AND THE MAKING
OF A LEARNING COMMUNITY

Most of the students who first dropped in to Other Ways had experience in theater and music. Some were street kids whose parents were involved in the arts and crafts community. Some had performance experience in jazz and rock or at church. Others knew how to organize a rally or a demonstration. An incredible number of unexpected skills not learned in school emerged among high school age students in Berkeley then. With few exceptions our students were actively engaged in political, social, and cultural events in the community. They willingly brought those skills to our small high school.

Many high school students bring similar and even more complex skills, from music to creative computing, to school with them now. Yet usually no one at the school bothers to ask what students already know, and all the knowledge residing in the student community is wasted as a potential resource for learning. Often students have the solution to problems they are blamed for, and the skills to help redeem a failing educational program from disaster. It's just that teachers are not experienced in the craft of involving students in their own learning and helping them take responsibility for the quality of life during their time in school.

As wild as the Other Ways students could be, they were much more confident of the importance of their own ideas and of the arts than the students I had been used to working with in New York. When these youngsters, many of whom were from academic or professional families, were rejected by the authorities at Berkeley High School—who responded not to their skills and dreams but to their defiance of schooling-as-usual—they didn't have the same sense of defeat and failure that most of my former students had. The Berkeley kids had proved to themselves, the school authorities, and their parents that they could make it—and, in fact, excel—if they chose. And when they chose to reject school it was with the full knowledge that school learning was easy and life much more challenging.

Playing with maps, talking about Berkeley, and conducting focused teach-ins were only a beginning. Peter, Mark, Johnny, Cathy, Jena, Tovia, and a number of the other kids who had begun hanging around talked about wanting to make statements to the high school and the Berkeley community at large about their feelings on education and the Vietnam War. They wanted to demonstrate alternatives to a world they considered unreasonably and arbitrarily authoritarian. That was what had attracted them to the name Other Ways and the questions on the poster.

Theater seemed a logical focus for their desire. The students were inspired not by the staged plays done at Berkeley High School but by the park performances of the San Francisco Mime Troupe, the Bread and Puppet Theater, and the Teatro Campesino. All these troupes performed in the streets; dealt with social, political, and cultural ideas as well as personal struggles; and, most of all, used improvisation as a way to respond to the passions of their audiences.

Challenge was the mode of the day, and I was not immune. I had mentioned to the kids that Other Ways could become what they made it. Peter and Julie said Other Ways should do some theater and suggested I show them how.

Though I love theater, I had never thought of teaching it or taken a course on anything remotely connected to teaching it. So when I was challenged to do theater in Berkeley all I had to draw on was my confidence that, in an educational vacuum, jumping into something new myself made more sense than doing nothing.

I asked Peter where we should begin, and he told me the best place in town was the costume and prop room of the Berkeley Community Theater, which was located on the Berkeley High School campus. I bought a book on improvisation and managed to get permission to use the room, and we set up a theater class. Learning how to teach as we went along, I found myself looking to the students for ideas and techniques.

This was neither the first nor the last time I had to figure out what to do in midstream. One consequence of believing that every child can learn is that as a teacher you have to become a good improviser, adjusting, changing direction, and feeling your way—while maintaining order and projecting confidence when you may still be unsure of the direction you want to take with a particular group of students. The craft of teaching requires the habit of innovation. One of the most troubling aspects of many educational situations these days, especially those that claim to be innovative, is that craft is reduced to a set of abstract principles of learning or techniques for student management when it is a question of the personal development of teachers. You learn to carve wood by carving with the help of a master craftsperson; you learn to teach through direct contact with children and the support of people who care about them and have succeeded in teaching them. If teacher-education programs were designed with this in mind they would, for example, never place student teachers in classrooms that are disaster zones. Unfortunately, this is a common practice in teacher education; it is one reason why so many motivated young people enter teaching having experienced only bad models, which they tend to reproduce unless they either quit teaching altogether or become rebels within the system. The neglect of the craft of teaching makes it easier to fail students, to come to believe that not everybody can learn, and to look anywhere except at the quality of one's own work for the reason for student failure. Until a major reexamination of the nature of the craft of teaching and the kind of continual creative intervention in the learning process it implies takes place, educators will continue to look in the wrong places to find out why schools don't work, and gravitate to simplistic formulas for change and to mechanical answers to complex pedagogical questions.

I wasn't looking for a simple fix for educational problems with my students in Berkeley, but was delighted to be struggling with the development of my craft. I still remember the first session we had in the costume room. The night before, I had heard a short radio feature about a mime who was hired to work at a wax museum. Dressed like one of the wax figures, he made slight changes in his position to create the eerie sensation that the denizens of the wax museum might be alive.

The costume room was like a wax museum without the figures. There were hundreds of costumes and props from every historical period, culture, and fantasy world. I told the students what I'd heard on the radio, and before I finished they started dressing up and freezing in place. What had started out as a raucous adventure suddenly became focused and disciplined. I found myself surrounded by a dozen frozen figures, among whom were a king pointing a John Dillinger submachine gun, a cross-dressed fairytale princess holding a Greek warrior's shield, a ballerina in a medieval helmet, and a World War II veteran wearing a German helmet, a U.S. pilot's leather jacket, and six-inch heels.

Two of the students, Laurie and Jon, couldn't find costumes they liked, so they became the visitors to the museum. The rule for the improvisation was that the "statues" could change positions only when the visitors weren't looking. As Laurie and Jon walked through the wax museum it began to change subtly. They couldn't see all the characters at the same time, so they couldn't anticipate the changes happening behind their backs or to the side or in the corner. Soon all the wax figures began to move closer and closer to the spectators until they were surrounded, almost trapped. At that point someone screamed and they fell laughing on the floor. The wax museum improvisation had become a hunt, turning the witnesses into the witnessed.

We all agreed that it was worth trying the scene again, with different costumes and slight differences in the rules. We did the same improvisation about six or seven times before our time was up and we had to clean. The same students who had talked about destroying the high school because of the way they were treated there had no problem understanding how to nurture it. By the time we left, no one would have known we had ever been there. They demonstrated respect for the high school when it gave them something that they found meaningful.

Our experience in the costume room was the beginning of the Other Ways Demolition Squad, our resident theater troupe, which was willing to (and often did) perform anywhere and for all audiences, expected and unexpected. It was also the beginning of my attempt to understand and use the power of drama to deal with sensitive social and personal issues.

This first experience was only one of many I had in which young people found themselves coming together as a community through theater. I always try to make a time and a space available for theater where I teach, because it is a way of bonding the most disparate people, of letting them show something of their inner selves without feeling threatened or revealing aspects of their experience that they want to keep private. I have found that theater creates a model of communal work that often leads to a vision of a convivial learning community. I've done theater in the most diverse and potentially explosive teaching situations and always found that it led to intelligent discussion, critical analysis, and, perhaps most important of all, communication among people who would otherwise never look each other directly in the eyes without turning the encounter into a battle.

Throughout my involvement with Other Ways I continued to teach theater and to grow as a teacher of theater, thanks often to the boldness and sensitivity of the students. Berkeley *was* theater in those days—hippie theater, antiwar theater, police and National Guard theater, and media frenzy theater. My high school students were involved in all the street activities and in a lot of political activities as well, and they were often able to act with abandon, sometimes on the edge of craziness. I was the conservative in the group, insisting that our improvisations and street performances include an intellectual component. I was sure that knowing other people's plays, reading and studying Beckett, Ionesco, the Noh plays of Japan, Shakespeare —a wide range of theater dealing with themes that were on the students' minds—would allow us to explore character and history in greater depth than we could do if we depended solely upon our own imaginations. I argued, for example, that *The Tempest* was wilder than any play we could invent, that *The Bald Soprano* could lead us into a hilarious surreal world that parodied ordinary life as the students were attempting to do in their own improvisations. Eventually most of the students concurred, so one of our four weekly meetings consisted of play reading in a group.

We did one particular improvisation that became public theater: *Worship in the Temple of Science. Worship* was Becky and Eric's idea.

The original magnet from the first cyclotron is mounted in front of Berkeley's Lawrence Hall of Science as a monumental sculpture. I wasn't opposed to the students' idea, but I resisted all of their early ideas, which were confrontational, or might deface the magnet, or might end up hurting some innocent museumgoers and getting the kids arrested. So we went to visit the magnet and get a feel for it as an object, to see how people who came to the museum related to it. We read about its history and construction. Then we talked to guides and scientists at the Hall to find out what the magnet represented to them. The conversations were revealing. For a number of the staff, the magnet was a symbol of the university's investment in war science. Others celebrated it as a major scientific breakthrough. A few people talked about it in worshipful, almost sensuous terms as if it were a holy object.

The nature of the group's thinking and improvisations changed as we did the research. Theater became the vehicle for serious research and intense critical conversation. The insistence upon site analysis, research, and development rather than uninformed protest was my contribution to the event. The students designed a dance, accompanied by flute and sax, in which people stroked the magnet's sides as if they were a lover's thighs and placed votive offerings of candles, vials of what looked like blood, and bloodied war toys at the base of the monument. The students also designed mourning robes. They developed chants about the love affair between Science and

War and created leaflets to leave behind that included specific information on why people should oppose the Vietnam War. I was determined that if they were to make a protest—which they would have no matter what I did or said—I hoped it would be done with the maximum possibility of persuading people rather than offending them.

The event came off very well. It was covered in the newspaper, and when the students ended their performance people came over to talk with them about the moral dilemmas created by the war. Afterward the students felt that what they had done would not, to be sure, end the war, but might contribute to its end and was certainly an expression of deeply felt moral convictions.

I still use theater as one way to introduce children to discussion of important issues that is rooted not merely in their own experience but in literature. Over the last dozen years I've done, among other works, *A Midsummer Night's Dream, Macbeth, Antigone,* and *Tartuffe* with seven- to thirteen-year-olds and Thorton Wilder's *The Skin of Our Teeth* and Eugene Ionesco's *The Lesson* and *The Bald Soprano* with high school students. Each of these productions involved students reading the text to the degree they could, discussing the central issues in the play, and collectively deciding how to render the text. The production was just part of a larger learning experience in which meaning, language, structure, and gesture were all discussed and played out. As an educator, I loved the preliminaries as much as the performance—and have been able to build upon both in my subsequent work with the same youngsters.

One of the productions that delighted me most as a teacher was one I directed in 1984 at the Acorn School in Point Arena, California. The Acorn School was a public alternative one-room schoolhouse for about forty children from the ages of four to nine. Deborah Ages, a friend, was the person central to the school's founding and early nurturing. She and I were "new time"–"old time" teachers in the school. By "new time" I mean that we developed integrated learning themes; that our curriculum related to our local community and was strongly oriented to the arts, the environment, and experience; that students of different ages were grouped together; that we offered qualitative evaluations instead of standardized tests; and that we had the freedom to shape our program though we received some funds from the public school system. By "old time" I mean that none of these innovations were new; we did what creative one-room school-houses have been doing for over a hundred years.

Right after lunch we had story time; during the early spring we read the children *Alice in Wonderland.* In conjunction with reading the book, we embarked on a simple puppet-theater project. I made a very crude posterboard puppet of the Mock Turtle, modeled on Thai stick puppets, and suggested that the children make their own puppets with the characters from *Alice.*

During free time and art class the kids made puppets—Alice after Alice after Alice, with one March Hare, a few White Rabbits, and an occasional Mock Turtle, Carpenter, Mad Hatter, Duchess, or Queen. Then we did improvisations with the puppets.

During one of these sessions, a girl in the class said that the puppets were boring. She wanted to *be* Alice, not just play with an Alice puppet. Everyone in the class agreed, so I asked the children who would like to be Alice. There were four volunteers. Rebecca— our school's Pippi Longstocking, who at the age of nine drove a two-ton truck down Highway One for her father, could use a chain saw, and lived by herself in an old trailer in the woods—Rebecca, who was the most likely Alice, remained silent. I knew something was up but had to turn to the problems of the four Alices.

It was up to me to decide who would be Alice. The more I thought about it, the less I could choose and the less I wanted to. With *A Midsummer Night's Dream* I'd had twelve Pucks: most of the seven- and eight-year-olds wanted to be Puck, and by dividing up the role I gave each of them an opportunity to speak a few lines of Shakespeare. Besides, Puck is everywhere, and in the spirit of Puck there was no reason why he couldn't have twelve faces. In *Macbeth* we'd had six or seven witches—after all, what was one witch more or less to the spirit world? So why not four Alices? Any book that has magic mushrooms, talking rabbits, and an entire monarchy con-sisting of a deck of playing cards is perfect for fantasy and elabora-tion.

The next day in class I suggested that we have four Alices. The kids were disappointed—they wanted to experience the competition among the four girls who wanted the role—but I had no intention of yielding to their will. The whole question of choice, beauty, and competition emerges whenever you do theater. I use it as an opportunity to create an antic and collective sense that we can make the world more rather than less compassionate by making some adjustments in received reality. That doesn't mean that other people shouldn't do plays straight from the text, or that actors are all equally skilled. But I do theater for pedagogical purposes, not to go to Broadway.

So we were going to have four Alices. The challenge was to pull this off in a way that would be convincing and exciting for the children. I discussed that problem with the whole group. We agreed that Alice, like any other person, has many aspects, and that there was no reason why four of the parts of Alice couldn't be onstage at the same time. In other words, the children didn't want to take turns being Alice, or split up the role. They all wanted to be fully present as Alice, and that's how we decided to do it.

However, there was still the matter of Rebecca. Though she hadn't said a word, I knew something was working in her powerful and wild mind. After we solved the Alice problem it came: Rebecca informed us, as we entered our first improvisation with the four Alices, that they were all too young and tender to go to Wonderland by themselves. They needed an older sister—Susie was her name— who could show them around. In Rebecca's view, there was no reason that Alice's older sister, who in the book falls asleep and misses the whole adventure, couldn't stay awake and lead the journey. Rebecca was our school leader, and out of either affection or deference every- one agreed that Susie should be the tour guide to Wonderland.

But this wasn't enough for Rebecca. She had been thinking about Susie and felt that it would be good for the production if Susie was a blues singer, wore high heels, stockings, and a long fancy dress, and sang a few songs. That almost threw me completely, but I have learned to stay composed, at least temporarily, in most circumstances with children, and listen carefully to their thoughts. Besides, it is precisely this boldness and creativity on the part of children that makes teaching so wonderful. What might initially seem far-fetched or outright impossible often turns out to be the germ of wonderful learning opportunities. So a blues singer Susie would apparently be. However, I didn't give in that easily. I told Rebecca that she could play Susie as a blues diva if she could write the blues songs herself, find someone to transcribe and orchestrate them, and get a band to perform them. After all, if she could drive a truck and use a chain saw better than I could, why couldn't she assemble a band? And my role as a teacher was to take her ideas and add some content and challenge to them.

That night Rebecca called my son Josh, who at the time was the lead guitarist and a songwriter for a local reggae band, and set up an appointment for him to write the music to her blues song. She convinced him and the rest of the band, as well as some other community musicians she rounded up, to play for the performance. So we were on our way to a production of *The Four Alices and Their Sister Susie in Wonderland: A Musical Version of Alice in Wonderland.*

During the next weeks I had to struggle with how far to take the play, how much time to spend on it, and where to fit it into what was already a very full educational program. The first thing I decided, after talking with Deborah, was that the play could not completely take over our work at the school, even though I was tempted to drop everything else and do Alice exclusively. I compromised and spent a half-hour to an hour a day rehearsing for about three weeks, then an hour or two a day for a week, and finally two full days just before the performance.

We held two performances, one for the school and one for the community. Rebecca's blues rendition of Susie, with high heels and long silky gown, was a hit. And, after the performance we had a wonderful cast party—which, in a funny way, was the point of the whole production. If any student had been miserable at the party I would have failed. My goal was that all of the students should participate in and feel good about their role in creating something both larger than themselves and delightful. If a student is part of something big once, he or she may get the idea of doing it again, at a time and in a place where it might be more serious. As a teacher, I let the children lead me on this wild adventure. And I loved every minute of it.

GROWING A SCHOOL

Theater and writing were not the only subjects I taught at Other Ways from 1968 through 1971. In fact, much of what I did emerged out of the painful organic growth from a project to a school. Mike Spino began coming to the storefront after school and eventually worked with Other Ways full-time. Victor Hernandez Cruz decided to remain in California and began working with the students at the storefront. A few other credentialed teachers joined us, including Arnold Perkins, who was teaching at the local Continuation school. Allan Kaprow spent less time at the storefront and more with the artistic community in Berkeley, so I had the freedom to take the project in a more educational direction. There we were, with willing and motivated students, an interesting faculty with enough creden- tials to qualify for a public school, and a storefront. And everyone cared about the students; that was the central factor that made Other Ways possible. We had a common interest in seeing all of our stu- dents succeed and were focused on doing whatever was necessary to make that happen. By the end of the first year we were, in all but name and formal approval, a half-day, afternoon, and evening school —an early version of a charter school, though without the theory or political support such schools have been able to mobilize in recent years. Our problem was to convince the public school system to grant us—with no more than fifty students and about ten adults, mostly part-time—the status and per-pupil funding of a public school.

Fortunately, the superintendent was not entirely opposed to what we were doing; he even sent us some students from an experimental high school in his previous district. (As soon as he moved to Berkeley, the experiment had been closed down, leaving these students, seniors in high school, without credits or a school.)

At the end of the year we were granted provisional status as an experiment in education; I was made a member of the school district Principals' Council (a council of all the principals in the district); and the union agreed to look the other way as we proceeded. These events led to my being able to talk with other educators throughout the country about autonomous schools within public education sys- tems and to encourage teachers and community people to create options within public education rather than just criticize the schools. In the Twin Cities; Chicago; San Antonio; San Francisco; Portland, Oregon; and many other places I was fortunate enough to meet with other educators who felt the same way. They did succeed in creating teacher learning centers similar to Other Ways, as well as in devel- oping teacher-created curriculum and establishing small schools within larger ones, where teachers, parents, and often students shaped the nature and process of learning. The central responsibility

of people directly involved with children to control educational innovation seems to me a key to effective change, as relevant today as it
was in the sixties and seventies.

Support for new ways of organizing schooling and the acceptance
of people who take nontraditional routes to certification as teachers
are currently major problems for teachers' unions as well as for government and university-based educators. The unions in particular
must either embrace change or face the privatization of schools and
the deunionization of the teaching profession. Many union leaders
refuse to acknowledge that there are many schools which, like Other
Ways, generate parent support and need public funds for survival.
The idea that one system and one way of teaching and learning suits
all children is not viable in our society, where education is a local
and state function and where people want a say in their children's
education. If teachers' unions continue to support schools that are
failing and continue to neglect the specific needs of local communities, I have little doubt that public education will atrophy. It is likely
to be replaced by a system of schooling that resembles a free and
unregulated market: the poor will have to fend for themselves, and
people will be forced to accept the kind of education they can afford
rather than receive quality education as a right. The implications of
this for a democratic society are frightening; the dream of equal
opportunity and equity through education will be dissipated, and
with this another source of hope for poor children will be closed off.

Late in 1969 the Berkeley school board, after a few cantankerous
meetings, granted us status as a public school for seventy students.
However, the lease on the storefront was up and the owner refused
to renew it. Thus began three years' wandering around the Berkeley
community in search of a permanent home and funding. I was determined to work twenty-four hours a day as teacher, administrator, and
fund-raiser for as long as it took to get a permanent building, faculty,
and program.

During my three years at Other Ways we were in many locations.
After our first storefront, now a real estate office, we found another
storefront, which is now a Thai restaurant. It was across the street
from the District's tenth-grade school and we picked up a number of
tenth-grade students who otherwise would have wandered the streets
looking for something to do during the school day. For a while we
were on the second floor of a stained-glass studio, next door to a

garage; during that time we set up stained-glass and car-repair classes. For some students, this was an important grounding of their desires to do things that were engaging, physical, and artistic and also had the potential to produce income in the future.

We also rented the Finnish Meeting Hall in West Berkeley, which we could use from seven in the morning until four-thirty in the afternoon. All of the staff and many of the students became very good part-time janitors, since we had to leave the hall every day as we had found it in the morning and the Finns were meticulous in maintaining their building. We became adept at packing the entire physical apparatus of the school into the trunks of our cars, a skill that came in handy a few years later when I was working helping migrant communities design mobile schools that traveled with them.

The most challenging move, the one that shaped the way we did education, came during the Berkeley protests for People's Park and against the bombing of Laos and the U.S. incursions into Cambodia. At that time we were located on the second floor of an abandoned school right behind Cody's Books, a few steps from Telegraph Avenue and half a block from People's Park—in other words, ground zero in the Berkeley war zone. We shared the building with the RAP Center, which cared for people with emotional and drug problems, and with the Free Clinic, which took care of wounded and tear-gassed demonstrators and people who had overdosed on drugs or had other medical emergencies. It was an uneasy mix, since we were trying to run a school in the midst of the continual confusion of anger, exuberance, trauma, and joy that reigned around Telegraph Avenue those days. I tried, for example, to teach math and reading and writing and make them exciting while it seemed to many of the students that the world was undergoing a major rapid transformation. Noticing that our students had many negative responses to the clinic and RAP Center clients, who were often hostile in return, I got students to visit the clinic and the center and get to know the staff. They were wonderful and began to recruit our students as interns and apprentices on an emergency basis. There never were enough people to provide for those who walked off the streets asking for help.

In the midst of this, on January 6, 1970, it seems that the unified police and military forces of Berkeley, Alameda County, and the California National Guard somehow decided that Other Ways was a bomb factory and that they should close the school down and perhaps arrest some of us. We got this information from the staff of the Free Clinic. My guess is that they came up with this pretext because they wanted our high school kids away from the protest zone.

One evening the police fingerprint van parked across the street from the school. I was out of town with some of the kids raising money, but one of the students or staff people called Judy and told her that we might be raided. The next morning Judy got another call: the paddy wagon had just driven up. With some friends, she went to the school and evacuated it—not a minute too soon. The police did arrive that afternoon; when we returned to the building a few days later we found all our books torn to pieces. The chalkboards were in fragments and some of the chairs and tables were smashed to pieces. Antihippie, racist, and prowar graffiti was scrawled on the wall. The windows were broken and the door was caved in.

We moved the school into our homes and never returned to that building. There was a bonus for me in the police raid: I decided to get off the road and get down to teaching full-time. I taught in the kitchen, living room, dining room, and study of our house in the Berkeley hills; it was one of the most creative times in my entire life of working with young people.

The Berkeley school district was very helpful in those days, not for educational reasons but because they had the onerous task of protecting their students during that wild time, when hundreds of students, even kids in elementary school, participated in street events, many of which were dangerous. The administration was delighted that we vouched for the safety of a combined total of eighty full-time students plus thirty-five part-time students who also attended Berkeley High for science and advanced math classes. So by the end of the year we succeeded in convincing the school district to rent an old factory for us. During the last month of the year classes were suspended and students and staff pitched in to renovate the new building.

One of my favorite classes emerged out of the fact that I was teaching at home. One day right after the move, I was sitting around the living room talking with Danny and with three John's: John F., who spent most of his time at Berkeley High School and intended to become a research chemist (which he succeeded in doing), and John H. and John L., both of whom were in my small philosophy and politics class, a subject they intended to pursue and later did, at the London School of Economics. This was the intellectual set of the school, Fred Perry having already graduated. The conversation got around to their dreams and aspirations and then, unexpectedly, to their deepest anxieties. The issue was this: how could they could live alone and take care of themselves away from the families that had nurtured them and that still did their laundry and cooked their food while they dreamed and talked of utopia? I suggested, offhandedly, that I teach an evening class in our kitchen one evening a week for about eight male students on cooking, furnishing an apartment, budgeting, and learning how to travel or how to get settled.

The wonderful thing about teaching in a place like Other Ways was that when demand for a class arose spontaneously the class could begin the next week. No elaborate proposals, no bureaucratic procedures. Just pure education. The class met on Wednesday evenings from seven to ten, which gave Judy and me time to feed our own children, read to them or tell them a story, and put them to bed —or pretend to, for Tonia and Erica would either be listening through their bedroom doors or coming in to taste the food we cooked. Judy insisted that she play no role in the class other than watching, which meant that I had to model what I hoped the students would learn. It was both harder and more delightful than I imagined.

I decided to start by showing the students how my grandmother cooked and having them inventory our kitchen. Then we would go to a kitchen store and a hardware store out to find out how much it cost to furnish a modest usable kitchen. Of course, this meant I had to reconstruct my grandmother's cooking from childhood memories, and that didn't always work. For example, I thought I remembered how she made latkes: grate some potatoes, mix them with eggs, add salt and pepper, throw some chicken fat into the frying pan, and cook. Only I didn't know how to get chicken fat, forgot about the bread crumbs or matzo meal, and had no idea about the proportions of the ingredients. My research for the class consisted of calling my aunts, reading a few cookbooks, and making a lot of tasteless practice latkes.

I discovered how to render chicken fat and make *gribenes* (I think that's how it's spelled) by slow-cooking fat cut off a fresh chicken with raisins, almonds, and other sweet things. One of my cousins explained that the jar of *gribenes* my grandmother had in her

Frigidaire, and which we used instead of butter on bread and matzos, was the secret to the flavor of Grandma's latkes. So, in Berkeley, with no sense of how to do it, I cooked and cooked gribenes until they smelled and tasted like what I recalled from childhood.

I certainly did not intend to make my students exclusively Yiddish cooks, so I invited friends to spend an evening cooking with us. Antusa Gautum, a consultant for Other Ways who was from Sri Lanka, spent an evening showing us how to prepare chicken curry, papadums, and various spice dishes that enhanced the curry. We had a vegetarian cook, a friend who cooked Mexican food, one who cooked soul food, and one who was intimate with Italian cuisine, as well as someone who specialized in eating on the run and making quick but tasty meals. We also had soups and stews and salads galore.

As homework, the students wrote recipe books; toward the end of the semester they had to purchase food for their own meals and cook them.

We priced each meal and noted how much it cost to feed one, two, four, and ten. We talked about cooking for yourself, about communal cooking, about saving and reusing leftovers. The students kept lists of the utensils needed to cook different dishes, with an eye to developing a complete inventory for a well-stocked multicultural kitchen. We wrote critical reviews of the food while we ate our way through the curriculum and also washed dishes and kept the kitchen clean.

This last didn't occur spontaneously. Initially, the kids wanted to cook, eat, and run. Some also wanted to bring their friends to taste food and then go off into the night together. Judy refused to touch the kitchen, and our agreement was that the kitchen would be clean before we went to bed. So I had to confront the students with their laziness, and my own, about doing the dirty work of cooking.

It was a long day, what with having no stable location for our school, a community under stress, and complicated lives with parents and friends and on the streets—but there were dirty dishes, too, and I figured a good way to deal with cleaning up was to make it seminar time. We washed dishes and talked about being male and nonaggressive in a hostile world, about how to deal with feminist critiques of traditional male roles, about trying to discover who you were when there were so many pressures to conform, pressures that came not merely from the left and right but also from the streets and the "counterculture."

Navigation was really the theme of the class—steering between all the perilous and delightful temptations provided by the freedom that the sixties promised, while still coming to a calm place in yourself where you felt morally centered and grounded in rewarding work and a caring community.

The things we discussed in class were not just on my students' minds. They were problems I faced as well in trying to figure out where I belonged in this culture and in the worlds of education and writing. It is never easy to follow your conscience instead of conforming to institutional demands. Throughout my teaching life I have wished to find a way to teach without the anxiety, both personal and financial, of being on the margins of security. I haven't found it, and sometimes the anxiety takes its toll: I get tired, and angry at myself and at the people in schools who are secure whether or not they're competent; every once in a while I withdraw from teaching altogether in order to rest. However, I am very lucky; my withdrawal is into writing, not depression, and the call of new children and teaching challenges has always drawn me back to the work. And Judy and my own children have always been there, too, so that my life has had a stable center that makes it possible for me to teach on the edge without falling off the planet and becoming bitter and impatient.

At Other Ways I also taught a small class on philosophy, called "The Individual and the Community." There were about twelve students in this class, which included the entire cooking class plus a number of female students. It was the closest Other Ways came to a college class and was, like the college prep classes at Berkeley High School, all European American with the exception of Eric. I simply couldn't recruit more than this small group of students to do an intensive reading of Plato's *Republic,* Engels's *Condition of the Working Class in England,* the introduction to Sartre's *Critique of Dialectical Reasoning,* and selections from other writers from Rousseau to C. Wright Mills. The group, all of whom clearly were headed to college and who have since graduated with distinction from fine universities, were part of all the other events and classes at the school. But they had a particular intellectual hunger for current ideas that I felt it would be irresponsible not to meet. Besides, being part of passionate yet abstract discussion of issues such as the relationship of individual freedom to communal responsibility, and the role of society in molding the person, was part of the reason I loved teaching. It was Harvard, high school, and social activism rolled into one. I always found myself rethinking old ideas and texts through the fresh and immediate questions my students raised.

Mathematics was another subject I taught at Other Ways, mostly by default. I love math and have written about it, but it was not what I wanted to teach in those days in Berkeley. However, no one else on the staff was willing to take responsibility for anything but elementary math, though we all thought more advanced math had to be covered if we were to be a responsible school. Besides, the students, knowing full well that the world was larger than Other Ways and that someday they might be held accountable for their math skills as well as the quality of their hearts and minds, demanded we "do something about math."

My first task was to find out what the students knew. The results of my inquiries presented a serious pedagogical problem. About 30 percent of the students did very well in math and were hungry for abstract math, advanced problem-solving challenges, technical and commercial math, and an introduction to mathematical thinking. About 30 percent couldn't have cared less about math and hovered on or about their grade level. They just wanted to be able to pass a test to get into college. Another 10 percent, what could be called the hippie core, wouldn't touch math and, at least for the moment, there was no point in trying to compel them to, unless an option such as chess or the creation of games was offered. That left the 30 percent of the students who had some informal knowledge of math and could deal with money and simple arithmetic but couldn't pass a fifth-grade math test. Unfortunately, but not surprisingly, the groups broke down by class and race, the most motivated mathematics students being predominantly European American and the ones most in need poor, African American, and male. We had inherited the consequences of the regular schools' and the society's diseases and incompetence.

The dilemma was how to meet everyone's needs while avoiding segregation. As a staff we decided that we had to focus on challenging all of the students, rather than put all of our energy into mixed groups that satisfied no one. Consequently I ended up teaching three sections in math.

One of my math sections was called—rather pompously, I now think—"Logic and the Abstract Theory of Form, Infinity, and the Imagination." I designed it as an introduction to basic concepts of higher mathematics, with an emphasis on the relationship between intuitive math and abstract math. Into this class, I put everything I'd learned studying math at Harvard; we did complex math including some calculus, group theory, and functional analysis.

In the second math section I taught cybernetics and systems theory and added a sociological component, which considered such questions as, Can mathematics and technology be value free? Who controls different systems and to what ends? Where do the scientist, the technologist, and the technocrat fit in our society? Finally, what is the role of mathematics in understanding and controlling the world? This section also covered probability and statistics, so that the work included both "hard" and "soft" components, as the parents of some of our students had insisted.

Here's a sample of the questions these two classes dealt with:

1. What is a transformation?
2. What do you need to know in order to predict completely the behavior of a finite-state machine?
3. What is feedback?
4. Write out rules for ticktacktoe. Develop a simple symbol system to describe these rules. Try to design a machine that could never lose at ticktacktoe.
5. Describe how a person grows from baby to kid to adult using some example involving a system of objects or a game or other process (e.g., the growth of a bee community, a game like Life, etc.)
6. What is a machine? Try several definitions. On the basis of your definitions, can a machine (including any computer you could imagine) think?

It was simple to understand what these questions were asking for, and very difficult to answer them—which, of course, was my intent.

The classes were built around developing strategies and doing research that would lead to answers that every one in the class could understand. The goal was not to have a few students understand all of the questions while others failed by not answering any of them. Rather it was to set up a learning community in which, by the end of the semester, each student could articulate in her or his own way an intelligent answer to each question.

The third section covered basic mathematics, approaching it through everyday transactions such as borrowing money, purchasing a car, running a small business, furnishing an apartment, and costing out a wedding. I incorporated the skills taught in junior high and basic high school math into an everyday-living class that dealt with adult numerical issues in a way that didn't insult the students. I believe this class worked better than the others, because I put more time into catching up the students in this section than into turning those in my abstract-math classes into competent graduate students.

This last section was eventually taken over by another staff member and I turned to the development of a schoolwide reading and writing program to deal with disparities in the reading skills students brought with them to Other Ways. I also taught a small class in beginning reading to the students who were in greatest need. Eight of them were African American; one was from El Salvador. All were male. As a group they were some of the toughest, most intelligent and articulate students at the school. Roger, Franklin, and Carlos were in the middle of all community discussions, made friends with just about everyone, and hung out at the school whenever an event was taking place. After school they were a terror; we had to work overtime to keep them out of fights, to convince them to stop ripping people off or shaking them down. I worried for them.

Luckily, the reading class had other members, like David, Alfred, Mark, and Rick; though equally tough, they were much more self-disciplined and had freed themselves of the streets. With the exception of David, who was on our student governing board, they didn't participate in classes as much as the others, though they were very vocal in school meetings and demanded a voice in shaping the content of our curriculum. Despite their self-consciousness about not being able to read and do math they insisted on having full voices in our deliberations as we tried to develop democratic forms of governance and deal with questions ranging from sexism and racism to the students' use of drugs.

However, the academic gaps within the school could not be completely overcome socially. They did create a deep-seated sense of imbalance which made the division of students into groups inevitable. If, even in a new high school based on small classrooms and innovative ideas—such as the New Visions high schools I currently work with in the New York City public school system—there is a radical gap in academic skills, with a class system dividing students into readers and nonreaders, and if that division also coincides with race and class divisions, so that the nonreaders are overwhelmingly African American and Latino and the readers European American, no amount of democratic governance or conversation will eliminate the internal friction and resentment. At Other Ways we created a wide variety of classes to meet all of our students' interests and were surprised, though we shouldn't have been, to find that all the classes that required math skills and sophisticated reading skills were overwhelmingly white. No matter how ingenious or motivating we were, the basic problem—that many students arrived in high school with dysfunctional skills—had to be faced directly. Until the skills gap is overcome we will not be able to eliminate racism, the idea that some people are inherently inferior to members of other groups.

The basic reading class was one of my most important educational challenges at Other Ways; I believed that if it succeeded the entire life of the school would change. There must be a democracy of skill and achievement if young people are to be able to participate in a learning community as equals. The goal of the class was to catch students up so that they could fully participate in the intellectual life of the school as well as in our political, artistic, and social life.

David told me that he liked the idea that all the students in the class were African American or Latino: they could get down to business without having to worry about what white students were thinking and could talk openly about the school experiences that had brought them to a very uncomfortable place in their minds. I asked David whether it was appropriate for me to teach the class; he said it was okay because I was Herb. I believe, after my experiences in Harlem, that it was clear that he meant he wasn't a racist; he just didn't like being around people who, he felt, didn't respect him but was perfectly comfortable with learning from anyone who did.

Most of the students in the basic reading class (especially David, Mark, Alfred, Rick, and Samuel) worked hard and by the end of the year had made genuine progress, going from being unable to read a fourth-grade reader to being comfortable with junior high textbooks, novels, and newspapers. Several of the students never really tried. Roger astounded me: in six months he went from reading on a third-grade level to being comfortable with high school reading.

With that class, I tried everything I had previously learned about teaching reading, and invented a few more things as well. Each student chose five words a week (echoes of Sylvia Ashton-Warner); these became our weekly vocabulary and spelling list—forty-five words a week, close to 200 a month. We took walks in the neighborhood, writing down lists of words the students already knew; I used these words in language games and exercises. For example, from "Lucky Strike" we generated words that ended in "-uck" and "-ike"; the students' names were anagramed and used as the basis for word ladders. Mark wrote a poem beginning with the word "son" called "From Son to Strain, Running in the Rain," which began with the words in his list and added new words the class helped him spell.

We did simple crossword puzzles. I got some old elementary school reading tests and we went through them together, analyzing the items for signs of racism and other forms of discrimination. The students learned to read and take the tests at the same time as we talked about the gatekeepers and test makers in society.

We also read and wrote poetry. Fortunately there was a flowering of powerful African American poetry being published at the time; with the help of writers involved in the Teachers and Writers Collaborative, I was able to keep up. Poems by Don L. Lee, Sonia Sanchez, June Jordan, and Amiri Baraka all spoke directly to these youngsters and got them to write poems. Here's one I saved:

i used to be a *junkie*
but now i'm *freed*
i used to shoot *junk*
but i know it wasn't *me*
i used to lie, cheat, *steal*
but i know i would be *killed*
used to be really cool
but i had to stop before i end froze and cold

The poem was inspired by Gwendolyn Brooks's "We Real Cool," which the class had read and discussed together. Roger's poem was a beginning—something to take pride in, to compare with more crafted work, to use as a basis for discussing sensitive and important issues.

We also read from school textbooks, and the students did a great deal of peer teaching. I had them take responsibility for each other's learning and even caught a few of them studying vocabulary in the hall when no one was looking. Ours was a fugitive class of sorts. The students didn't want any visitors, and we were all very evasive about the substance of the class. Pride and self-respect are so tied up in knowing how to read that the students didn't want their efforts at becoming literate to be a subject of public discussion.

I'm not sure why the kids showed up, but I was passionate about their learning and maybe that was infectious. My basic operating principles for the class were these: keep it adult; remediate nothing; repeat no prior school failure; and always remember that these people are learning to read for the first time. Earlier failure is irrelevant.

Recently Rich Coleman, a student from the poor Black community who did well academically and was involved in almost all of the school's activities, came to visit me in Point Arena. He told me that everyone at the school had wondered what the seret of our group was. My status at the school was enhanced because the reading students left my class determined to learn; this astonished the other students, who had anticipated chaos from such a volatile mix. It never occurred to me that the mix was a problem, and to this day I don't know what the cement was or why the "problem students" stayed to learn. My feeling is that there is a love of learning, however hidden, in everyone, and that a teacher who has respect, a sense of humor, well-crafted material, and passion for the students' learning can free that love.

These days one of my obsessions is trying to persuade people that high school–age youngsters are teachable no matter how resistant or educationally crippled some of them may seem, and that every high school teacher must be a basic-literacy teacher as well as a math, science, or English teacher. Rather than lament the lack of skills many students bring to high school, we have to take responsibility for teaching these skills while working to transform the earlier grades.

But we have to teach them as if we were teaching adults, not as if we were doing remedial work with ten-year-olds.

Perhaps the central and most pleasurable class I taught at Other Ways, one that lasted almost three years, was called "The Unconscious and Decision Making." Looking back, I see that it was an extension of the counseling psychology class Betty Rawls and I team-taught at Teachers College, though the immediate occasion for the Other Ways class was the drug crises that some of our students and their friends faced. One of them, Ruba, had joined in a party at Provo Park and shared a pitcher of what she told us she thought was punch. I'm not sure how candid she was being, but in any case the punch contained an unhealthy dose of LSD and Ruba ended up in the hospital hallucinating and close to a debilitating psychological crisis. The next weekend William, who attended Berkeley High School and hung out with some of our students, threw himself off the deck of his home while tripping and killed himself. Another young man (he later became a student of ours) got equally high, jumped off a telephone pole, and ended up a permanent cripple.

I was frightened for all the students and worried about how vulnerable they were at a time when half the wildness and defiance around them was healing and nurturing and the rest foolish and dangerous. The week after William died Nora, Siri, Becky, two of the three Johns, Mark, Alfred, and I were talking about how he had turned despair and confrontation with his parents into a terminal act. The students were clearly in shock; as for me, I had not (nor have I ever) recovered from Akmir's unnecessary death. As we talked, my teacher's impulse took over. I wanted the students to come to terms with their futures and decided to use other people's experience, literature, and the insights of social thinking to help them through hard times. As an educator, I have always found that my students responded as much to traditional wisdom, the insights of writers, and shared understanding as to personal confession and individual counseling. I do not consider this a matter of theory but of human temperament.

My intent in this class was to get students to explore questions that puzzled them or that they were unconscious of and needed to articulate. I focused on questions like these:

How do I figure out what is right and what is wrong, and act on the basis of conscience and conviction?

Why do I fall in love with one person rather than another?

How do I discover my own skills and talents and decide what to do with my life?

How do I deal with temptations that take me away from my innermost needs and desires?

How do I resist peer pressure when I know resistance will create social isolation?

How do I respond to the cultural pressures I get from home, the media, and society?

How do I choose a style, a way of presenting myself publicly? In other words, how do I decide how to dress, wear my hair, walk, talk, and in general shape my public self?

What resources can I use when I have to make decisions about problems with parents, friends, and authority figures?

How can I deal with anxiety, panic, despair, and depression?

What is my responsibility toward other people?

How do I learn how to step outside myself and become aware of the sources of my actions and feelings?

These are sensitive and personal questions, but I did not want to deal with them on an individual basis or mold the students' thinking. I wanted to provoke them into thinking about values and about the choices they made. With so much confrontation and rage being expressed on the streets and with psychedelics being dangerously romanticized, young people frequently went along with the "spirit" and often hurt themselves unintentionally. I wanted the kids to stop and think about what they were doing and how they felt, and somehow begin to articulate ideas about how to sustain a life based on their values. I chose to construct a curriculum consisting of writings and other explorations, such as improvisation, sculpture, painting, music, dance, sociological studies, polls, radio shows, and even happenings that spoke to these issues—the Allan Kaprow influence. I hoped that my students would see that their individual struggles were also universal ones that people have to confront across culture, space, and time. The issues implicit in these questions are as broad as tolerance and ways of managing difference; freedom and slavery; riches and poverty; violence and nonviolence. They also include the relationship between knowledge and ignorance, selfishness and compassion, integrity and exploitation, and individualism and collectivism. It is easy, as a youngster, to think that you (or you and your friends) have discovered for the first time the central problems human beings have faced throughout history in trying to build decent societies.

An educator's job is to take these abstract issues and translate them into the specifics of everyday learning. I was spending a lot of time worrying about how to discuss decision making with my Other Ways students when, during the first week of our second year—our first year as a school—I was suddenly confronted with an issue that convinced me to put aside my plans and get right to the question of tolerance.

A few days before school opened I got a call from a parent who explained that her daughter, Eve, "a sensitive white girl with artistic interests," had been beaten up by an African American girl at her junior high and was terrified to return to school. She had heard that we were starting a school and was confident that Eve would benefit from the environment we would create.

I met Eve and was very taken with her openness and sensitivity to the nuances of adult behavior, as well as with her determination to talk directly about her confrontation at school. She told me, without any preliminaries, that she had no desire to be racist like some of her friends and she did not want to run away from her problems. It was the violence of the attack that confused her. She said she couldn't imagine anything she had done wrong.

As Eve and her mother spoke to me, I realized we were going to have an interesting problem on our hands: Rhonda, the girl who had attacked Eve, was also going to be one of our new students. Her principal had asked me to take Rhonda into Other Ways. He explained that she was one of the brightest and toughest kids at the school; he hoped we could provide her with complex and interesting educational challenges and get her out of having to be tough and angry all the time.

We accepted both Eve and Rhonda, so it was clear that a very specific form of the universal problem of tolerance had to frame the first weeks of "The Unconscious and Decision Making." I talked to the girls separately and explained the situation to them. They agreed that they had never paid attention to each other before the fight and held no grudge or animosity. Eve confided that she was afraid of

Rhonda but said she was teaching herself to deal with things that frightened her.

Rhonda said she didn't go to school to cause trouble and welcomed the opportunity to get away from the junior high and its peer pressure. Only, she didn't want anyone to mess with her.

I brought them together, and they agreed that since they both wanted to be in the school they would tolerate each other. I left it at that. A decent and respectful school environment can command tolerance, but affection cannot be legislated. It has to come from the people. Though Eve and Rhonda attended Other Ways throughout high school they had little to do with each other and developed no relationship that even approximated friendship. However, we needed to build respect and tolerance at the school and simply leave the door open for affection and friendship to develop.

During those early days, our students were as segregated as those at the other Berkeley schools, even though we went out of our way to encourage students to participate in classes and other informal activities together. The struggle to create a coherent community of learners that was not afflicted with the disease of race was central to my work at Other Ways, but I do not feel we came far enough to claim general success, though we had many individual successes.

One of my projects involved Rhonda and Eve. I asked if I could raise in my decision-making class the coincidence of their coming to Other Ways at the same time and the challenges it made them face. They agreed, and Eve even enrolled in the class. I introduced the question of how one decided whom to tolerate. I wanted the initial discussion to stay focused on life at the school, but it was impossible. A number of the African American kids complained about how the hippie kids dressed and took care of their hair; they said it gave the school a bad name—and, Roger added, "a bad smell." That comment set a hostile tone. One of the hippie kids, Nonny, who was the smallest and feistiest student in the school, fought back with the comment that he didn't think looking like a pimp helped the school's image much either. We almost had a fight.

I had to work hard to defuse the situation, which I did by pulling out a color preference test I had devised and modifying it on the spot. The test was designed to allow the students to express and analyze personal and group preferences in a nonthreatening context. I pasted paint samples representing the colors of the rainbow on a sheet of paper and numbered them. The next step was usually for each student to fill out a questionnaire that asked such things as "Which color do you find friendliest? Most hostile? Most delicious? Warmest? Coldest? Most emotional?"

My intent was to take this questionnaire, which had no right or wrong answers, and analyze the results with the class to see whether any patterns emerged. We would—and later on in the semester did —analyze the results mathematically, like polling results. We looked for patterns and similarities associated with gender, race, social class, lifestyle preferences, and so on; this led to both intellectual and personal questions about how preferences develop and how people are often unaware of how they are socialized.

At that moment, however, I decided to use the colors in another way. I asked the students, already polarized, to choose the colors they felt most characterized their group and the other groups they perceived in the school. I didn't expect any profound results or resolutions. I did have to make sure there was no violence, and I had confidence that a shift of attention would be a relief to everyone. Beyond that, I wanted all of the students to leave the room feeling that they were free to express their most sensitive concerns at our school and that I was neither taking sides nor silencing anyone. I wanted them to feel that charged issues could be dealt with in a community of learners without causing the same violence that had brought Eve and Rhonda to Other Ways in the first place.

The test had the desired effect. It turned each student inward and gave each a moment to express preferences and time to listen to everyone else. Jena surprised us with her response, which, as usual, was brilliant and not exactly what had been asked for. She wrote this poem, which went to the heart of the matter:

> nude people dancing
> in a field of
> wild flowers
> beautiful colors
> striking gold
> majestic purple
> enchanting blue
> shocking orange
> spring green

        there are two of
        them, the male
        strong and masculine
        but very precise
        the womanly body
        graceful as the wind
        full of life
        and love.
        they love one another
        this is togetherness
        ones Ebony
        ones Pearl.

I asked Jena to read the poem to us, which she did, not once but three times. The students left the room quietly, looking at each other with eyes perhaps a bit more open and understanding.

By this time in my teaching career I had become pretty adept at improvisations that motivated people to learn and was willing to explore dangerous territory. So I designed an experiment for the next session: I asked the kids to divide up in clothes-preference groups.

That at least opened the door to crossing racial lines, but it had unexpected consequences. Eric and Roger, for example, who had middle-class backgrounds and one African American and one white parent, usually were part of the hippie group. They weren't sure they wanted to make such a choice. They represented the fault line between the groups and felt all of the pressures coming across the various boundaries that separated them. Their passionate commitment to not having to be classified was a driving force in our attempts to create a coherent student body, and they were often in the middle —in positive ways—of where the trouble was.

In class, two groups emerged: one African American, with the exception of Nonny and Julie; the other white and hippie-ish with the exception of five or six of the white students who never dressed out and looked more like college students than most Other Ways kids. Eric chose the hippie group and Roger chose the African American one. I met with each group privately and asked them to rehearse the style and behavior of students in the other group. The next day we would do a cross-dressing improvisation and students would have a chance to see themselves as other people saw them. I borrowed clothes from the high school costume room.

Eric chose to be the most exaggerated hippie possible, while Roger chose an equally exaggerated version of the smart clothes worn by twenty-five-year-old men on the street. We began with a grand entrance. I suggested everyone enter the room in slow motion, strike a pose they thought characterized the group they were imitating, and then freeze. After everyone was frozen in place I asked the students to look around at this portrait of what we thought of each other.

It was hilarious—African American students overdressed with beads and flowers painted on their faces, granny dresses, and torn jeans; hippie students with shiny leather shoes, wide-brimmed hats, tight skirts, heels, silk blouses . . . Some of the students, most of whom had been in the guerrilla theater troupe, cross-dressed by gender as well as social group. We had constructed our own bizarre wax museum, incorporating improvisation into the curriculum on tolerance.

I turned to the frozen figures and asked them to come alive slowly, in slow motion, and start introducing themselves to others in the room. The slow motion was my protection—I had to maintain enough control to prevent what might be a very funny and illuminating collective experience from becoming a mêlée.

Scenarios began evolving as the class time (classes at Other Ways were usually ninety minutes long) ran out. Before having the students change back into their usual clothes I raised the question whether, in changing back, they were just assuming another script, another scenario, another manufactured way to present themselves in everyday life.

This led to a discussion during the next few sessions of the sociologist Erving Goffman's *The Presentation of Self in Everyday Life,* which I'd planned to use in another context later in the year. After doing an improvisation like this, provoking a complex experience, event, or happening, I usually don't try to summarize or evaluate it with the students or force them to articulate what they have learned. It is usually more productive to introduce new intellectual material that deals with the issues, and come back to the event itself much later. Complex learning takes time to settle into a person; learning situations that are profoundly moving to some students might be simple fun or boring and silly to others. The intellectual follow-up and the discussion it provokes lead back to the experience but with a vocabulary and a perspective that allow for greater depth and analytic understanding.

Goffman's ideas worked beautifully after the cross-dressing event. I made a five-page selection from his sophisticated book as a text for us to read together next class. The selections focused on Goffman's vocabulary for describing how people use social masks to present themselves in various situations in order to manage issues of power, respect, and control. The central concept was from the title of the book: "the presentation of self."

For each concept I reproduced a scenario Goffman used to illustrate his ideas. Since there was a chance that some students couldn't actually handle the reading I decided to read the selections out loud myself, pausing to discuss questions the text raised and get at the issue of tolerance through a discussion of personal and group encounters. By building a language of ideas to discuss these experiences, the students gained a more thoughtful way to manage the conflicts they faced as they tried to define themselves in the world.

Every time I taught this class I used the following profile—actual results from one of the classes—to get students to begin to think about themselves and our group.

ELECTIVE AFFINITIES TEST

Instructions: On a scale of 1 to 10, place yourself according to that aspect of yourself you feel most affinity for. A "1" score is low; a "10" score is high.

Class responses:

	1–4	5–7	8–10
head	1	2	15
hands	2	3	13
body	2	11	4
feet	13	2	3
sexual	0	7	9
smell	12	6	1
sight	1	4	14
hearing	3	6	9
taste	8	6	6
touch	5	4	6
karma	—	17	1

We talked not only about the individual scores and what students learned about themselves but also about the possible significance of such a large number of highs on "head," "hands," and "sight," and such a large number of lows on "smell" and "feet." We considered a number of possible interpretations of the data and in particular talked about comfort in one's "head" and discomfort in one's "body." This led to discussions of how to integrate one's personality and become balanced and centered. Later on in the year we did the test again. There were dramatic shifts in some individual profiles. There was also a general shift to high scores all around, and since one of the underlying philosophies of the class was that a compassionate and holistic approach to life was healthy and desirable, I took this as a positive evaluation of our time together.

For as long as I remained at the school "The Unconscious and Decision Making" remained the center of my classwork with the students. We read and discussed texts in sociology, psychology, politics, and philosophy and considered how concepts like "double bind," "stigma," "conscience," and "self-awareness" helped people organize and manage their own experience. We read and wrote poetry as well as doing art projects together, and at the end of one semester we had an art show and poetry reading in a local art gallery. Sometimes students would bring in texts and we found time to include them in the curriculum.

I think the readings and discussions that students liked best came from a series of case histories of people under stress that I put together from sociological and psychological literature and fiction. We read Dostoyevsky and sections of Jules Henry's *Sanity, Madness, and the Family* as well as Oscar Lewis's *Five Families*. It was easy to discuss ideas and introduce concepts after we had considered a case history. The pedagogical power of starting with a moving story and then turning to intellectual analysis cannot be underestimated, whether the story is one of madness or the invention of a mathematical idea. The kids at Other Ways, and all of the other young people I taught, remembered what they learned with me through the tales the learning was pinned to. I learn in just the same way.

I planned the texts to have the classes move in synch with the political, social, cultural, and personal traumas the students were experiencing on an everyday basis. Between drugs, the Vietnam War, the murder of Martin Luther King, Jr., the occupation of Berkeley by

National Guard troops, the be-ins and sit-ins, I tried to put an intellectual face to the struggles we were all part of. I didn't want our students to run raging down the streets screaming slogans or attacking people who were different from them. I wanted to temper the loathing for whites that was, for many African American youths, the consequence of Dr. King's death. I wanted to help all of the students root their anger in their still-breathing dreams of living in a decent nonviolent world and use it to act, positively and with focus, to heal things. This meant, for me, drawing upon the literatures of the world, exploring culture and spirituality, and setting our time together in larger contexts.

I remember staff and students thinking I was crazy to teach ideas, read and discuss texts, and insist upon compassionate thought and critical analysis in the chaos of Berkeley. To some it made no sense to think about Sartre, Fanon, Plato, and Wittgenstein; to read Goffman, Jules Henry, and Paul Goodman; to analyze Richard Wright and Charles Dickens, or to explore the poetry of W. H. Auden, Amiri Baraka, and Sonia Sanchez at such urgent moments. Yet for me the role of a teacher is always to be on the side of growth, and that means contributing to the development of the mind and the nurturing of a spirit of inquiry under all and any circumstances.

Many of the students went along with my obsession with learning even though the school was under duress. One of the Johns made the following comments in a school evaluation of a class I taught at the Finnish Meeting Hall, where we had to clear out by four-thirty every day:

> Started out the year in a beautiful rented building called Finnish Hall. Herb's classes at Finnish Hall were unlike any other classes that I've ever taken. We dealt with some interesting new subject almost every day. We talked about things like prehistoric cave paintings, manifestoes, and family delineations. We visited a nursery school to observe sexism and racism in the kids. Sometimes we talked about things that came up that involved the school—the demand by the District that Other Ways be "evaluated," that the students be given "achievement tests." We talked about the racist aspects of these tests and possible alternatives to taking them. I remember one of the best classes was when Herb spent the entire period describing the birth of his son a few days earlier.

At one time or another I believe almost every student in Other Ways participated in the decision-making class, though the core of students who took the class each semester were mostly white or interracial. In fact, some of the kids described the class as a "white studies" class—which was the equivalent, for many of the European American students, of the Black and Latino studies programs we had at the school.

I have always been troubled by the apparent contradictions between choice and integration. At Other Ways we argued about whether males could attend women's studies classes, whether European Americans attend ethnic studies classes, and whether students of color should be forced into classes that were predominantly white. The sciences and math were excluded from this discussion, in theory, though in reality the various sections of these classes were often divided according to race. We tried a number of different approaches, such as having ethnic studies and history classes open to all students, with psychology classes and discussion groups separated by affinity. One year we had classes, open to all students, on African American history and on the media and its distortion of issues of race, class, and gender. These were very popular and well integrated. That same year we had classes on Black psychology and women's issues that were restricted on the grounds that they were designed to deal with sensitive issues that people would not discuss honestly in mixed company.

From an educational point of view, all these classes worked in bringing the students together. Everyone had an opportunity, in a group where they were comfortable, to speak about sensitive concerns and vent rage and anger. When run by skilled people, these classes allowed the students to develop the personal strength and confidence they needed to participate in all of the more academic programs we offered. They also created integrated leadership at the school. I was struck by how many of our student leaders had become more confident through learning to speak and think in small groups of their peers, where they felt comfortable.

The danger, which we encountered a few times, was when an adult consumed by the negative consequences of personal wounds used the groups to preach hate and instigate division in the school. On occasion I was able to pick up on that quickly and deal with it, but several of these divisive teachers remained after I left and weakened the school so that it became easy pickings for the district. One of the saddest educational experiences of my life was being sent an issue of the school's newspaper a year and a half after I left. The paper's name had been changed from *Other Ways* to *The Other Way*.

Other Ways was a four-year whirlwind for me. What began as a teacher-education program oriented toward the arts and writing turned into a full-blown alternative high school that managed to survive through some of Berkeley's most turbulent years. My role at the school was to do whatever needed to be done as a teacher, fund-raiser, administrator, and friend and advocate of the students. I tried to keep us steady and focused on education in the midst of a hurricane, and it was both exhilarating and exhausting. Rose, one of our student leaders, wrote this about me in her evaluation of the staff:

> Herbert Kohl, the problem man. Everyone had problems and Herb tried to solve them all and believe me if they could be solved Herb could solve them. In fact, sometimes I wonder if this was not his sole purpose in the school. When ever a problem arrived, someone always called Herb.

Several of the students collaborated on an evaluation of our educational adventure at the end of the third year. I believe it's worth quoting in full. Rereading it twenty-five years after it was written, I was moved by the sense the students conveyed of personal ownership of the school and the process of education, and by how powerful a community of learners can be in nurturing each individual learner.

> Other Ways is full of tests.
> Black/White, Between the Coke and carrot juice drinker, soul and rock and roll, white versus black poet, which has the heavier message.
> Fire Marshals—Not knowing from one day to the next if they'd take our building because something was not up to code. For awhile, the police were trying to bust our kids on the street. Mostly for burglaries that didn't exist. We had to print up school I.D. cards. A test of our mental strength as a community to see how long we could survive under these pressures.
> State Requirement—Herb turned us on to the fact that if you understand the psychology of the person who wrote the

test, you know what they want you to say, then you know the answers. We spent some time rewriting the S.A.T. and trying to psych the school board's mind by figuring out a good test for them.

Teachers—Teachers' roles are always changing. Last year there was a lot of emphasis put on students as teachers so we had some students teaching and some teachers sitting in on classes. It was status to be a student teacher, also, if you were good you got paid. This started a lot of kids looking at themselves, seeing what they could do.

Other Ways has got a lot of talented people. Especially musicians and poets. These have both been a very important source of communication at school. Reading poetry gives you a lot of confidence in yourself and if you are together in your art and mean what you're saying, it doesn't matter what your differences are, people will listen.

We've had some together jams. People show up with flutes, saxophones, guitars, drums, bass, piano (when available), trumpet, etc. Several bands came out of Other Ways.

If there is something you want to learn about and Other Ways doesn't have the facilities for it or teachers with that skill, first they'll look through all the students and see if they can teach you, then if they can't, they'll go find someone who can.

We can take classes at Cal, Merritt College, Laney, California College of Arts and Crafts, or any other public school in the Bay Area, and quite a few people do. In a few cases our students have turned papers in and the professors think they're Cal students and grade them. They do really well.

We don't take volunteers. We've had bad luck with them. They inevitably ask for money at some time and they usually take more than they give.

Other Ways will also fund you for projects, like one guy in our school is into electronics and they put out some money for him to build a computer and they'll buy material for sewing, etc.

Other Ways has weird classes. Some kids at school understand topology, have read through Yeats and Eliot, know how to build boats, survive in the woods or human behavior, but don't know basic algebra or how to spell.

This year there's a lot more emphasis on the basic stuff. Just a few things we need to know to survive in this society, even though a lot of people don't—reading, writing, and math. Once you've got those down, you're free to "do your own thing."

Other Ways just found ways to make learning more challenging and not so damn boring. Also, when it's not shoved in your face, you'd be surprised to find you might even like math; if you find the right book, you might dig reading, and writing poetry is a gas.

Most students and teachers have to go through a lot of changes before they can settle down and take in Other Ways.

The biggest one is the transition from a rigid environment where someone is always chasing you from one class to the next, one level to the next, etc. Other Ways is not a "Free School," we just put emphasis on where your head is at rather than what grade you're in or what your I.Q. is.

We think it's important to differentiate between Other Ways and a "Free School." Summerhillian or Free Schools were designed for kids with serious emotional problems. They assume that you are sick and full of aggressions and deal with you from there. On the contrary, you have to be very strong and together to survive the day to day changes and to get yourself to class. We assume that kids are sane and deal with them on that level.

Public schools don't even treat kids like they are sane and know what they're doing, and if you're treated crippled long enough you're going to walk funny.

When you treat people like they're together they get confidence in themselves and in that environment you start to develop skills. We don't let kids or teachers just talk about what they're going to do—we want to see it and if they're bullshitting, everyone gets down on them and if they continue to mess up, they're out.

School spirit is very important for survival. We have very basic rules. No dope or illegal highs, no ripping off, no fighting or illegal weapons, and with a few exceptions, people care enough and couldn't see the school close for some one's untogether actions.

Meetings are a hard thing. Everyone yells and it's hard to direct the energy to the immediate problem. Everyone's got their own personal problem they'd like to relay.

This year is very different. We have a building that we can call home. There are classrooms and schedules and not so many picnics.

Also, Other Ways is not Herb Kohl. Last year we were too dependent on Herb. When he'd take off for a day or two school would fall apart. During the last few months he's in his house writing and holds workshops for people serious in one field, a writers' workshop as opposed to a creative writing class.

That is the direction we're taking. When kids first come to Other Ways they usually don't know much about where they're headed, just that their tired of the schools the way they've been. Some kids we get aren't even dissatisfied with their schools. We've had straight "A" students come to us just out of boredom and we've had some kids that were on the verge of dropping out, some that had flunked out and some that were just going along with it all, that didn't care how messed up it was as long as they got a diploma. They've been told that with that piece of paper they could get a job and their parents will love them and maybe they'll even get a new car on graduation.

In the environment Other Ways provides we hope that everyone will find "their thing" and do it. Even though we have a lot of fantastic classes and push kids to get it together and make it to their classes, we also push that the heaviest most valuable teaching goes on outside the classroom and that what you learn in the classroom is useless unless you can apply it to your daily life.

One way Other Ways made money last year was going all over the country to conferences where teachers come, take their shoes off, sit cross-legged on the grass, and hear Herbert Kohl and other "radicals" into making change in schools tell them how to do it. We'd bring our Guerrilla Theater Troupe, poets, dancers, musicians, etc., turn the chairs upside-down and blow minds and they'd pay us. Then they'd go back after their refreshing retreat, pick up their yardsticks, sit in hard back chairs, read about the poor, starving Indians over cafeteria lunches and teach the same shit.

A brief description of our Guerrilla Theater Troupe. We did caricatures on society, rewrote Dick and Jane, a lot of emphasis on the masks that people wear in their roles from day to day, living out mental hospitals, draft board, public schools and other such oppressive institutions, etc.

Once you have found what you want to do, Fashion Design, Dance, Electronics, Photography, Science, Music, Poetry, etc., you have learned how to read, write and do math, Other Ways has done their job and will help you get work or into a school where you can continue your work.

GRADUATING TO KINDERGARTEN

I left Other Ways in the spring of 1971 and stayed at home during the 1971–72 academic year, writing and spending time with our three children, all of whom were under five. Judy went to weaving school and took time to learn something she cared about. I wrote *Reading, How To* and articles and reviews, got involved in Berkeley city politics, national educational politics, and—since our children were about to hit the public schools—parent politics. In a year Tonia, our oldest, would be in kindergarten. The year after that Erica would enter the system, followed in two years by Josh. Judy and I faced our children's education in the public schools with apprehension, even though we knew some good teachers in the Berkeley public school system and were willing to be aggressive in getting our children placed with them.

At that time I met Cynthia Brown, who had a doctorate in the history of education and had been active in the civil rights movement in her native Kentucky. She and I and a number of other parents, educators, and community activists in Berkeley, some of whom had taught with me at Other Ways, constantly met to discuss educational issues. Cynthia had seen Paulo Freire's work in Brazil at first hand. She introduced us to the specific educational techniques and strategies he and his students used.

Two themes that we kept coming back to were the need for teachers who were skilled in open and informal education and the need for more people of color to receive teaching credentials. These are abiding problems and ones I am still working on. We got to know a number of people who had B.A.'s but not teaching credentials and yet were working with children. A number of them worked with the Centro Infantil, a Latino child-care program that is now part of the Oakland school district. Two were teachers at the Samuel Napier Institute, the Black Panther Party school. Several others worked in Head Start, or at the Berkeley Parks and

Recreation Department. Some had only thought about working with children but didn't want to go to a traditional teacher-education institution.

I had seen many young people who had come into teaching because of the passion for service generated by the civil rights and antiwar movements. Many of these young teachers, equipped with credentials from traditional institutions, suffered from a lack of experience with the everyday practice of teaching in an informal environment that was also intellectually challenging. Their professors were hostile to the ways in which they wanted to teach, and most often the master teachers the students were supposed to learn from were the very models of the authoritarian teaching that young teachers rejected. However, their enthusiasm and desire to free children of the restraints of arbitrary authority and rigid learning were not enough to fill up a school day with learning experiences useful to children. Their training and their desires were at cross-purposes; many of them quit in frustration or moved into other fields where they could work with people and feel useful and be effective.

Teacher education commensurate with the demands of a caring, culturally sensitive, diverse, responsive, and content-rich classroom simply did not exist then, and does not exist now. When young people with a passion to teach and a commitment to the education of poor children come to me and ask where they should get their teacher education, there are few places to recommend. I suggest they go to school to get their degrees but do their real learning by finding schools and teachers they admire and by reading widely. I also suggest they find other ways to work with children before they teach—in volunteer programs, on the playgrounds, in arts programs. The main thing is to find a way to have positive and personal experiences with children who are similar to those you will teach. Too often teacher educators are out of touch with schools and remote from communities and children. One of the major problems of restructuring schools is that most institutions that credential new teachers are more concerned with self-preservation than with the lives of children and the support of bold and innovative teachers. This is true as much for institutions that embrace the rhetoric of school change without the soul of it as for those that simply act as if every attempt to change the schools will fade away and business as usual, failure as usual, is the nature of the job. If teacher-education institutions are premised on the idea that not every student can learn one can be confident that many children will not learn.

In 1972, Cynthia and I fantasized about creating a teacher-education institution from scratch, using our resources and experience and taking advantage of the many wonderful teachers in Bay Area public school systems who exemplified the kind of teaching and learning that we wanted for our own children and other people's. Cynthia discovered that a new, stricter teacher-education law was about to take effect in California; the old law would expire in three years. She had met a state administrator who was a closet progressive and who had told her that under the old law it was possible for a nonacademic institution, such as a tax-exempt nonprofit corporation, to be treated as an elementary education credentialing program if it met certain conditions. They were these: some college must provide credit for the classes the nonprofit gave; the instructors must hold the proper number of Ph.D.s and M.A.s; there must be a certain number of books on education available; the county must be willing to provide student-teaching certificates; and individual principals must be willing to make formal arrangements for student-teaching in their schools.

Between us, Cynthia and I were able to amass all the requisite credentials, books, permits, and requests. In the fall of 1973 we set up the Center for Open Learning and Teaching and declared ourselves a teacher-education institution. It took a full year to get the needed approvals so that we could submit records of all of our students as a group to the State Department of Education. The first twelve people who joined us understood that, for all our bravado, they might come away with nothing more than what they had learned in our classes and classrooms. The credential was, until the last moment that year, a gamble.

From a perspective of over twenty years I have to say that the fifty people Cynthia and I worked with over the three years during which the Center was able to function constituted one of the finest groups of educators I have ever had the privilege to work with. We found these people in the most unexpected ways. Some were friends of friends or had attended a talk I had given or had dropped into Other Ways. Some discovered us through the network of progressive private schools that existed in Berkeley at the time. A few came through political groups—such as Berkeley Citizens Action, which at the time controlled the Berkeley City Council. And a few simply walked in and said they had heard of us and had forgotten how but were passionate about teaching and would not teach against their conscience. They wanted to set up their own schools or change the existing schools—anything that would help children acquire skills without humiliating them or teaching them to forget their cultural backgrounds and social and community responsibilities.

The fifty ranged in age from about twenty-four to thirty-five. Many are still wonderful teachers or school administrators; some are artists or businesspeople. They all, in their hearts and in their lives, are fine, caring people who make it impossible ever to feel alone or abandoned in the struggle to make a sensible, peaceful world for our children.

During the first year of the program, I taught our credential students and pretty much stayed out of the schools. Cynthia organized and supervised the student teaching. My classes ranged from the theory and practice of teaching reading to curriculum making, the specifics of organizing open classrooms that didn't depend upon coercion, and the philosophy of progressive education. I also wrote and, when I could steal a weekend or a school vacation, met with teachers throughout the country in support of their alternative schools and attempts to create open education.

One of my major concerns was to organize opposition to conservative educators and politicians who were mobilizing what they called a basic-skills movement. I felt that people in the open education movement and other educational progressives were too passive in facing this assault on the idea that every child can learn. During the sixties and seventies much energy was focused on feelings, values, and social responsibility. All of these are essential—but so are skills: the ability to read, write, calculate, and compute. It seemed foolish to concede skills issues to conservative politics and to people who advocated obedience, overly structured learning, and mechanical performance, when skills have everything to do with the development of intelligence and sensibility, and, for young people, of an awareness that the life of the mind is an abiding source of power and joy.

Since the seventies and continuing to this day I have been engaged in confronting the basic-skills conservatives with another way of looking at basic skills. As I see it, there are at least six basic skills, which encompass all the trivial mechanical skills that people want obedient and passive children to acquire. This way of looking at skills respects the intelligence and moral sensibility of the young. These skills are:

- *The ability to use language well and thoughtfully.* This skill implies developing speech that is sensitive to the weight and meaning of words; acquiring the habit of reading intelligently and critically; learning to write coherently; knowing and saying what one means; and attending to the meaning of other people's words.
- *The ability to think through a problem and experiment with solutions.* This skill implies learning how to observe, question, listen, and experiment. It also implies that modes of thinking should be taught explicitly in school and not just implied through different school subjects.
- *The ability to understand scientific and technological ideas and to use tools.* This implies learning to use numbers, computers, and hammers, and having opportunities to apply language and thinking skills to scientific, technical, and mechanical problems.
- *The ability to use the imagination* and participate in and appreciate different forms of personal and group expression. This implies that serious attention be given to the arts from historical, performance, and technical perspectives.
- *The ability to understand how people function in groups* and to apply that knowledge to group problems in one's own life.
- *The ability to go about learning something yourself,* and the skills and confidence to be a learner all your life. This involves both learning how to deal with new situations, and developing new skills and interests throughout your life.

Most people who preach basic skills aren't serious about children becoming educated and sensitive citizens of a democracy. To be a citizen in a democracy means to be dangerous to anyone who wants to exert unquestioned authority and marginalize unpopular ideas or silence voices of protest. Teaching basic skills can be either liberating or pacifying, depending upon how you understand those skills. At the Center for Open Learning and Teaching in 1974, we saw basic skills as liberating.

During the first year of the Center's existence a student, Ray Nitta, invited me out to dinner and told me that he was troubled about my classes. They were too academic; he couldn't get a feel for how the kind of teaching I was talking about actually worked. And he said, in passing, that the students in our program would be better served if I were actually in the classroom as a master teacher, demonstrating what we could then discuss in classes at night.

I remembered my dream of teaching kindergarten while I was still teaching sixth grade at P.S. 103/79 ten years before; it took me three seconds to agree with Ray.

Fortunately, during my years at Other Ways I had made many friends within the Berkeley Unified School District. The day after my conversation with Ray, I approached Frank Fisher, the principal of our local elementary school. It was a five-block walk from our house; my oldest child, Tonia, was going to be in kindergarten there; and I had a number of friends on the staff. Frank had a reputation as a fighter for children; though he was a mild-mannered man he was ferocious in defense of his school and students. When I told him I'd like to teach a kindergarten class for two years he said he'd come up with something. Money would have been a problem, but I could afford to live off money from my books for two years; I was willing to invest that time in learning how to teach kindergarten and get our students at the Center credentialed.

Frank suggested that, with the agreement of the regular teacher, I informally take over one of his combined kindergarten–first grade classes. The teacher would be freed to do staff support and curriculum development work at the school, the staffing pattern wouldn't change, and I wouldn't be violating union rules or replacing a teacher. In fact, I wouldn't officially be hired at all; my formal status at the school would be that of a full-time volunteer, even though I would usually be alone with the children in the classroom. There were no legal or insurance problems, because I had a valid elementary school credential; still, the situation was obviously sensitive. However, during my two years at Hillside Elementary School I was treated like staff by all the other teachers and, to my knowledge, no one from the superintendent on down ever raised an objection to the arrangement. Maybe the school district's administrators were happy to get me out of their hair. During those years I wasn't about to cause trouble for anybody. Teaching kindergarten and first grade was the hardest teaching job I have ever had, and one of the most magical.

Frank insisted on several conditions. First, I would have to stay full-time for two years; second, I would have to come when other teachers came, leave when they left, share what I was doing with the rest of the staff, explain the arrangement to all of the parents and let them opt out if they cared to, and occasionally participate in staff meetings. I was not to travel around giving speeches or doing workshops, leaving the children and the class hanging. Otherwise, I could develop the curriculum as I chose, take Center students for their practice teaching, and structure the classroom any way I felt appropriate.

I agreed and began to plan for September. I would continue my Center for Open Learning and Teaching classes in the evenings, take student teachers from the Center into my classroom, and spend the day teaching five- and six-year-olds. Once in a while people asked me if such obsessive work on schools and schooling involved too much time and energy. My only reply was that my father and grandfather had worked at least fourteen hours a day and they didn't particularly like what they were doing. I was fortunate to use my time doing what I loved to do.

Hillside Elementary School, in the Berkeley hills, with views of the bay on two sides, had been built for the children of the wealthy and was spacious and gracious. The room I was assigned was ideal. It was large and light, with movable tables and chairs and a full set of enormous wooden blocks. There were bookcases and ample shelf space and a coat closet large enough for a workshop or a small science lab. Of the room's two doors, one led to the rest of the school and the other directly onto a small playground, which we shared with a wonderful preschool program. My daughter Erica was in the program; she loved it, and the teachers had become friends of ours. The whole environment would have been ideal for Other Ways; it was what young children deserved. I had more to work with as a teacher than ever before in my career.

Space, time, and content were three dimensions I could begin to plan. The fourth, personal dimension, which emerges from direct contact with the children and shapes the tone and quality of life in the classroom, is impossible to preplan. It differs from year to year and class to class. All the other planning is subject to modification, according to how life in the classroom unfolds. This is a powerful argument for overplanning and developing many options you may never use rather than for either functioning solely on intuition and sympathy or, at the other extreme, setting a rigid learning program to follow no matter who the children are or what the skills they bring to the class happen to be.

The first two planning dimensions I worried about were space and time. I wanted the children to have as much choice as possible, so I decided to create learning centers where they could participate in both independent and guided learning. I also wanted time for children to work independently and in small groups. And, crucially, I wanted time for us to be together as a class and to create a sense of community. I find completely individualized education counter to sensitive and sophisticated learning. It impoverishes the mind, depriving children of the opportunity to listen to each other and to adults, to plan large-scale projects together, or to learn to speak well in defense of their ideas and feelings. In order to put together individual, small-group, and community learning, and (given that I was teaching five- and six-year-olds) provide time for play, I drew up a tentative daily schedule.

The time structure was simple. I knew students came in at different times in the morning. This was during the desegregation of the Berkeley schools; half the students lived in the neighborhood and walked to school, while the other half came on buses from the valley in west Berkeley where the African American community is located. The children arrived over about half an hour; I wanted to use that time to get to know individual kids and to get the children started on their round of learning. Consequently we began the morning with children coming into the class, finding some learning center, and easing themselves into a project. Some children went to play with blocks, others to the science center, where they could play with magnets, pulleys, flashlights, bells and buzzers, and others to the math center–cum–pizza parlor, where they could play at running a business. There was also a dress-up corner, with costumes and puppets, where fantasy ruled. In the middle of the room was the reading-literacy-bookmaking-writing center. It had books, rubber stamps, stencils, simple equipment with which the children could make and bind their own books, two typewriters (this was before computers in the classroom), pens, pencils, and erasers. I chose to have my chair in this center, from where I could survey the whole room and also sit and read with children. During this first half-hour or so the children could come to me and read as well as play and explore on their own.

This was followed by a time together, which I kept open to use as things developed over the year but which every child was required to attend and participate in. At the beginning of the year I made it story time. Then would be time for individual and small-group reading, writing, and theater projects that I knew from experience would evolve over the year. After that time I wanted the children to come together again to work on a class project and then again form small learning groups. Fortunately, Judy reminded me that these were five- and six-year-olds and that in my zeal to teach them I had left out snack time, yard time, and in general time to be children. I abandoned that second learning period and shifted story time to the end of the morning, using our first time together for projects and discussion as well as for an occasional story.

The afternoon was different, and easier. Only the first graders would stay all day, so there would be no more than fifteen children. I wanted to concentrate on reading and math and on fun projects in theater and dance, as well as to experiment with filmmaking. I'd never made films before, but Fred Perry, a former Other Ways student and by now a friend, had gotten me interested. Figuring that the afternoon didn't need as much structure as the morning, I planned to spend time with individual children and small groups; we'd follow up, on more complex levels, some of the things we'd begun with the whole class in the morning. Apart from that, I'd let the afternoon develop and concentrate on the substance and content of the morning.

Then there was content: I wanted the children to be learning *about* something, not just acquiring skills. I divided the school year into six-week learning units, the length of a practice teaching experience for our student teachers at the Center. That way the student teachers would experience a full curriculum cycle, and my little ones would be able to cover at least six different areas over the course of a year. I planned, among other things, science units on light, water, and sound, and a unit on African culture that illustrated the complexity of life on that vast continent, with excursions into traditional Ashanti culture, Muslim culture in northern Africa, and modern Tanzania.

As school approached I found myself ready in all ways but one for the arrival of the children. I had decorated the classroom, leaving plenty of room to display students' work; had gathered books and material for the unit on Africa I wanted to open with; had even chosen an Anansi the Spider story as the introduction. I set up the learning centers and discussed my plans with the student teachers I would work with. I held a few parent meetings, at which I explained my plans, the structure of the classroom, and my ideas about how children learned.

I had dealt wth everything—except for my fear of the children. What would happen if all of them started laughing the moment I opened my mouth? What would happen if they started running around? Never, in my whole teaching career, had I felt that I was facing such potential for chaos. I couldn't sleep for nights before the first day of school. Tonia was six and Erica was five; they had friends over all the time, so I knew what some five- and six-year-olds did at home. But twenty-nine of them, and just me, in a room together?

The teacher who had loaned me her class was going to be around for a few weeks, but the teaching was mine. She and Frank had given me the freedom to plan the room and set the curriculum in exchange for my taking the responsibility to work directly with the children. They stood aside to see if I could indeed do it.

Day one was easier than I'd feared, but not so easy. The children came into the room, wandered around for a while, and then sat down on the rug in the center and looked to me to tell them what was going to happen. I began to talk about behavior and structure—to lecture, despite myself, about discipline and order, revealing my own insecurity. Some of the children started fidgeting. Others got up and began walking away from the circle or started chatting with each other. A few of the boys began to edge toward the blocks, while two others took toy cars out of their pockets and began racing them across the room.

I was clearly too abstract, too worried, and too remote from the children. My instincts told me that the best thing to do at that moment was to read a story, and I had ready my copy of *Anansi the Spider,* an illustrated book about the West African and West Indian trickster figure who uses his mind to outwit stronger animals. I had planned to get to the book in exactly four days, providing prior background material about West African traditional culture and how these tales worked as sources of strength and cultural survival in the West Indies throughout the slave era.

However, my overplanned curriculum had to yield to the immediate need for a compelling story. I grabbed *Anansi* and read it as dramatically as I could. It worked; everyone was drawn back into the circle of learning through the story. In fact, Tamara asked me to read the story a second time, and I did. Then Carl wanted a third reading. Instead, I asked whether anyone remembered enough of the tale to tell it in her or his own words. Paul tried and did a delightful rendering of Anansi's wickedness, throwing in some new adventures made up on the spot.

I then asked the children to draw pictures of Anansi. The result of my first few weeks of work was instantly reorganized and the children jumped in, drawing and painting; some of the first-graders made their own little Anansi books.

In about half an hour the children were fully absorbed in what they were doing; my role was to wander from group to group and child to child, answering questions and helping with spelling or erasures. I ended up teaching the two kids who were bored by the whole thing how to play checkers.

It was a delightful surprise. I found myself plunged into a complex learning environment with none of the preliminaries. That was the virtue of overplanning and carefully setting the environment. I knew where things were, had resources to fall back on, and didn't have to resort to discipline or mechanisms of control as long as there were interesting things for my students to do.

The challenge of the second day was what to do with the events of the first day, how to use what I'd learned from the children to tease complex learning out of the group. Anansi had been a hit, and everything else had gone smoothly, so I decided to move from Anansi to the Ashanti the next day and also, first thing in the morning, introduce the centers and have a walk about the room. However, as soon as Leon and Kwame, the two boys I had begun to teach checkers, arrived the next morning they set up a game and gathered an instant crowd. Some of the children already knew how to play and wanted to be champions. Others wanted to learn how to play. About half the class, those uninterested in checkers, went straight to places in the room that had obviously intrigued them and began to play or read. It was clear that the children had thought about the environment overnight and had made decisions of their own about where they wanted to be within it. The first hour of the day passed quickly and I let the children work unsupervised. It was a great relief to me to witness their voluntary engagement with the learning opportunities presented by the space. It seemed that all my planning had paid off.

Of course, there were a few disagreements, but I found them easy to manage. At least eight children wanted to play checkers and there were only two boards. However, we had an art center and a small workshop where I stored wood and plastic scraps, so it was easy to direct the children to make their own boards and pieces. Before the end of the hour we had at least six new—and, I thought, beautiful—checkers sets.

Then came story time. I put up a map of Africa and was about to give a short talk on the Ashanti, illustrated with gold weights and pictures I had gathered. But the kids wanted to hear the Spider story again. Martin raised his hand and asked for it and I hesitated, at which point Leo and Malcolm began chanting, "Anansi, Anansi," and soon most of the children joined in. I noticed some of the shyer children mouthing the words while looking down, giving covert support to the mini-revolt. It was a delight to hear the call for a story, so I read *Anansi* again and again. The third time I rebelled and asked the class if anyone remembered the story. Sage and Cheri volunteered that they did, and we got two new versions of the story, which I wish I'd transcribed. I do remember thinking that these elaborated tales had an energy and magic missing from the book, and that I had forgotten, in my rush to teach content, how much young children love (and need) to hear a favorite story repeated and to let it sink in and become part of their knowledge of the world.

As they retold the Anansi story, the children filled in and invented details. Cheri added a conversation between the Spider and his mother about being sure to clean up his room before going out to do tricks; Sage described Anansi's argument with his brother. The ease with which invention and memory mixed became characteristic of our storytelling time throughout the two years I spent at Hillside; now I try to recreate that ease and flow of the imagination in my work with college students and prospective teachers.

Over the next few weeks I did get to Ashanti culture; the children made fabric with Ashanti symbols, listened to a friend from Ghana describe contemporary Ashanti life, and put on a play of one of the Anansi stories. With the help of Elombe Wagner, my first student teacher, we made an animated movie of the same story. Elombe, who knew a lot about traditional and contemporary African cultures and society, took over the class a few times and Elombe and I moved the subject from Ghana in West Africa to Swahili-speaking East Africa. He gave the children some language lessons, and each day we both traced the route from Berkeley to Accra and from Berkeley to Dar es Salaam on a world map.

Beginning this way was part of keeping a promise I had made to myself in Harlem. Children there told me that they'd learned in school that Africa was a country where black people lived in jungles. It shamed me to be part of the perpetuation of that racist myth. I tried to counter it in my classroom, and I also resolved that when I did work with younger children, I would start them out with a sophisticated, appropriate sense of the complexity of cultures and their transformations through history, beginning with a look at some of the many faces of Africa. I wanted all of the children to begin free of the stereotyping that most early social-studies curricula plant in their consciousness.

After getting to know the children a bit, I introduced one more daily feature: a letter. A few of the children had come to school knowing how to read. Most of the first-graders knew the alphabet and had a modest informal reading vocabulary. Some of the kindergartners and two of the first-graders had what could be called *Sesame Street* confusion. They knew jingles, letters, and rhymes, but had no coherent sense of how all the pieces they had seen on TV went together to make reading a book possible.

I decided we needed a daily dose of reading that the whole class could participate in. My aim was to design a learning experience that would catch up those students who had not learned to read at home or in preschool and would still challenge the most advanced readers in the class. So I bought dozens of sheets of large poster board, wrote down each child's first name on a three-by-five index card, and during one class meeting explained that for the next few months we would choose one special letter a day—the first letter of the first name of someone in the class—and then see how many words we could come up with that began with that letter. I put all the cards in a hat from the dress-up room and asked Carolyn to draw one. She came up with "Malcolm," so our first day's letter was M.

I wrote "M" in the middle of a piece of poster board and sounded it out in as many ways as I could. I play-acted "Mmmmm," as if it were delicious, growled it like a monster, hummmmmed it. Then I asked for contributions; the children came up with "mother," "man," "maybe," "me," "monster." I wrote them down and asked for volunteers to draw pictures under them. I told the children that anytime they thought of an M word or came upon one in their reading, they should tell me and I would add it to the poster, even if it meant filling the whole room up with "M"s. James, who read beautifully, ran to the reading center, picked up a dictionary, and asked me to add all the M words in that. He had a way of showing off his intelligence that often defeated my educational intent, so throughout the year I had to maneuver in ways that both recognized his accomplishments and protected the other children from his arrogance. On this occasion, I suggested he make an "M" dictionary: pick the most difficult "M" words and write them in an illustrated book, which I would copy for all the children. I turned him into a teacher, honoring his knowledge and helping him see how to use it to help everyone.

I didn't care whether all the letters in the alphabet were covered by this exercise and if a letter came up more than once we could push ourselves to find or make up new words. What I wanted and did manage to achieve was to have everyone engage actively in reading-writing-thinking-playing as a unified, ordinary, daily activity. This was a way of equalizing the knowledge and skills the children brought to school with them while raising the standards for all. And besides, children simply do not learn how to read in linear ways, no matter how they are taught. They take what adults present to them, look at the written page themselves, and more often than not, figure it out themselves, as long as adults are around to answer their particular questions.

The afternoons went well. I spent my time learning about the first-graders' skills in one-to-one reading and arithmetic sessions. I used my informal diagnoses to build a program for these children. I also encouraged the children I wasn't working with directly to pursue group projects, taught a few of them chess to take my game program a bit further, and tried to set up an informal situation that could be structured by the projects my student teachers would plan and teach. The goal of the afternoon was to develop community, make children feel comfortable with me as their reading and math teacher, and prepare them to become active senior contributors to some of the morning learning programs that involved the whole class.

The romance ended after a few weeks. I trusted the children to work with simple tools, but kept an eye on the workshop at all times —fortunately, because one day a boy named Matt tried to hit Sam on the head with a hammer. Matt was a year older than the other children; his family had just moved to Berkeley. He'd been placed in my class as a special favor by the principal, and I was told that he'd had problems in his previous schools. That turned out to be an understatement.

Matt was tall, lean, and pale. He had blue eyes and blond hair and, when he wanted to, could look disarmingly innocent. I learned quickly that those innocent looks were storm warnings. I caught him just before the hammer descended on Sam's head. The next day's incident involved a saw with which he seemed ready to part Tamara from several of her fingers. When I temporarily closed the shop Matt turned to the block corner and just missed Martin with a block the size of a small two-by-four.

Sam, the smallest child in the class and one of the shyest, was Matt's main target. One day it was a stick carved into a dagger. Another day it was a rock or a pair of scissors. Yet Matt never actually injured anybody; indeed, I noticed that he made sure I was around and watching when he was about to strike. I was patient with him and had private conversations with him and his parents. I ended up suggesting he hang around me and tell me, before he picked something up, what he was inclined to do. He agreed; his parents begged me to hang on with him; and my inclination to work as hard as I could to get kids out of knotted self-destructive and dangerous inclinations rather than expel or punish them countered my constant anxiety over what he might do. It was a matter of my teaching intuition, which led me to feel that this was a solvable problem. But, I have to admit, Matt pushed me to the limit of my skills and patience.

One day he went after Sam with a small pocketknife. I grabbed him and was about to sit him down roughly and tell him that the price of continuing his attacks was simply to be thrown out of the class, but he cracked and started screaming and attacking me.

The other children stopped everything they were doing and turned to watch us. Times like this create major moral and social dilemmas. I had to control him and protect the other children while keeping him in the process and helping him maintain some dignity and face, so that he could be with the other children the next day and not have to feel that they had made him their enemy or seen him humiliated. I also had to show him that I would not let him go berserk in the room, for his own sake as well as mine and the other children's.

I picked him up. He was screaming and kicking; I turned to the class and, calling on my theatrical skills, said in a calm and confident way that we would be back and that they had to show how strong they could be by running the class without a teacher for a few minutes.

In the hall, I sat Matt down in a chair and held him there. By now he wasn't screaming or kicking but struggling not to break down and cry. I still held him tightly but told him it was fine to cry. On the chance that he was ready to talk, I asked him why he hated Sam so much. He did break down then, and sobbed that Sam hated him, that all he was trying to do was make Sam his friend, but Sam kept running away from him so he had to hurt him.

I nearly laughed: here was a normal desire turned pathological because Matt just didn't know how to be someone's friend. Developing acceptance and love through violence: he just didn't know that it never works.

I also noticed, while he was crying, that there was not one healthy tooth in his mouth. I rarely pried into my students' home arrangements, but when health is an issue I'm adamant and tenacious about their getting care. Matt needed a total remake of his mouth; he must have been in constant pain for years. He couldn't make friends; he never stopped hurting: that was enough to encourage me to try harder.

So I spoke to Matt's parents and they took him to a dentist who fixed his teeth and alleviated the pain that drove him to be so volatile in class. Matt and I set up afternoon getting-to-make-friends lessons. For a few weeks, during what would have been our one-on-one reading time, he and I playacted making friends. I was Matt and he was Sam. He needed that role reversal—which in spirit and intent was not so different from the schoolwide cross-dressing we had done at Other Ways. And it worked better: little by little he became Sam's friend. This was great for both of them, but for a while it meant trouble for me, since one of Matt's first impulses in the friendship was to show Sam some of the techniques he had developed to hurt children and get away with it.

Both boys stayed with me for two years and by the end of that time were close, compassionate friends who also lived in reasonable and ordinary peace and tension with the other children. I still hear from Matt and his parents. He is a delightful person and a well-integrated, successful computer scientist. I could never have guessed that he would turn out that way. In this case, at least, I can say with certainty that I did make a difference: he, as an adult, has told me I did.

Robert was a different challenge. Dan Peletz, a wonderful pre-school teacher whose early learning center was across the playground from our classroom, asked me to take Robert and promised to help me with him. Robert had severe kidney problems and was not given long to live. He had to wear diapers, which he had learned to change for himself. He was a charming, mischievous boy who asked nothing but to be treated the same as the other children. He loved to run with the wildest and most active children. Though he was always a step or two behind, he was so persistent and feisty that all the children slowed down a bit so he could keep up.

I was nervous about accepting him in the class. My parents wanted me to be a doctor, but I throw up at the sight of blood and can't dissect a frog without feeling like a murderer. Dan sat me down and said that I had to learn to see Robert as a child, not as a patient, and give him what I would give any other child. I trusted Dan so Robert joined the class. But at first I was nervous. Would he be all right? How would the other children treat him? Would his supply of diapers run out? Would he get sick in class? Should I teach him to read, given that he had so little time to live, or were there more important things he needed to know?

As it turned out, I did not have to explain much about Robert to the other children; most of them had gone to preschool with him. And Robert taught me what he needed, which was simply to be a child, to run with the other boys, to cause mischief, to learn to read and pretend I was making him work too hard. He jumped into everything, and his enthusiasm was infectious. One day at story time he asked a provocative question and I realized he was trying to trick me, so I crafted an answer that I hoped would surprise him as well. Later that day I noticed that I had stopped worrying about Robert without even thinking about it. Somehow that direct engagement with him beyond his problem defused my anxiety. Thus I learned to be useful to Robert by forgetting about him. This may sound paradoxical, but I didn't worry about every child in the classroom at every moment. If I had, there would be no time to teach and have fun with the children.

For the rest of the year, Robert was his delightful self. He had planned to continue with us the next year; however, he became too ill for school and, though he fought to stay alive for several more years, this courageous child did not live to see ten.

Robert was a member of the Pee Wees, along with Martin, Paul, Hal, and three or four other boys. Here was a thoroughly male, thoroughly integrated band of troublemakers. The boys all wore sweatshirts, which they pulled down over their knees. During recess and snack time they wandered around the classroom and the playground hunched down so that they looked as if they had no feet. They chased girls and boys who weren't Pee Wees and played at scaring them. The song of the Pee Wees was "I'm a Pee Wee, / You're a Boo Boo, / Get the heck out of here." Occasionally they would make someone cry or end up in a minor skirmish. Once I tried to bring the Pee Wees up before the class and talk about whether they should be prohibited or not. It was one of our first experiments in student governance and part of my plan to turn over to the children as much as possible of the maintenance of civil order in the classroom. Everyone agreed that fundamentally the Pee Wees were harmless and fun. Carolyn even argued that if we got rid of the Pee Wees then the girls who played in the dress-up corner and had a secret club would have to stop, too. The other children agreed that so long as no one was hurt mischief wasn't too bad a thing and could be fun.

I remember some other mischief, created by my daughter Erica and several of her friends during my second year at Hillside. Near the reading center was a rug which we used for class gatherings and stories. A chair and a large movable chalkboard stood at one end of the rug. I sat in the chair when reading stories, and often the children took turns sitting in the chair and making a presentation to the whole group themselves. It wasn't *my* chair but "the storytelling chair," a place from which anyone who wanted to address the whole class could speak and command a respectful audience.

I used the chalkboard to draw stick-figure illustrations when introducing new concepts or vocabulary. During one of my geography lessons I decided to draw a diagram of the school and add directions to show which was north, south, east, and west, based on where the school was with respect to the San Francisco Bay, the Berkeley Hills, and so on. Erica knew that I easily become hopelessly confused about directions; I navigate on the basis of familiar landmarks, not a rational understanding of the points of the compass. Over the week, while I used my diagram as a way of introducing map-reading skills, Erica and her friend shifted the chalkboard or changed the drawing so that it never faced where I claimed it was facing. By the end of the week I was facing a giggling class as I pointed in the direction of the Bay on my map and the students pointed out to me that someone who followed the lines on the board would end up northwest instead of north, or south instead of east. Hopelessly confused, I ended up letting my student teacher plan a series of more sensible corrective lessons for the next week. By this time in my teaching career I found it delightful that the children had thought things through well enough to play a trick on me. It certainly doesn't hurt children to have an occasional experience of outwitting adults, or be appreciated for that cleverness.

Another time I passed out metal mirrors to all the children. This was the beginning of a month-long unit on light, during which I wanted to teach about topics from reflections and symmetry to color theory. I gave the children the mirrors in order to have them notice the reversal of left and right in mirror images. Matt immediately took his mirror, captured the light of the sun shining through the window, and reflected it directly into my eyes, temporarily blinding me. I suppressed my impulse to take the mirrors away and instead asked all the children to do what Matt did and try to blind me. The children turned from looking at Matt and me to looking at their mirrors and the sun, and then to thinking about how to capture the rays and reflect them toward my face. Once they caught on, I asked them to make light patterns on the wall and then, as a challenge before we broke up, to draw what they thought was happening when they got control of the sun.

I had intended to begin our study with symmetry and handedness, but instead shifted to reflection. On this occasion, as on others I've encountered over the years, I saw how mischief can be turned into learning if you're prepared to respond with teaching instead of discipline.

Not all of the mischief in the class was creative, however. Lewis was the biggest child in the class and was the kind of African American boy who, too often, is singled out as a troublemaker and then made into one by teachers and administrators who seem to see him at the age of six, seven, or eight as a six-foot, 200-pound eighteen-year-old. At times during the beginning of the school year Lewis arrived sullen and angry. He would push other children out of his way, or knock over their games and scribble on their work. But on most days he was the gentlest, most charming, most considerate person. He was articulate—he called me Herbie the Grouch every time I got angry at him—and a master of both praise and insult. It was impossible to tell from one day's behavior how he would be the next morning. In other words, Lewis was the kind of child who can be a great challenge and joy to a teacher. If you engage his intelligence and win his respect, you can change his identification as a trouble-maker into an expectation of future excellence.

Lewis was usually the first student I called to read, or at least the one I looked at first. I watched the way he walked into the room, noting the set of his brow, how he held his hands and fists, how his eyes scanned the room. At the first sign that it was going to be a bad day I jumped in with:

"Lewis, today you'll take care of yourself. . . ."

"Lewis, you read first today. . . ."

"Lewis, keep your hands to yourself. . . ."

"Lewis, do something . . . sit down . . . enjoy yourself . . ."

"Lewis, don't . . ."

I knew how he'd respond. Grouch, Grouch, Grouch—that's what he called me, and the other students picked up on it. I didn't like being called Grouch and tried to joke off the name. On the other hand, I couldn't let Lewis continue to harass other students, destroy their work, and hurt himself with the internal warfare between his intelligent, creative self and his aggressive, defiant self. Whatever the causes of that conflict, my job was to intervene in it and help him grow more confident of his mind and more compassionate toward the rest of us. I simply had to accept a minimally Grouchy role until I figured out a better way to work through the situation.

It became easier, after a while, to set limits on Lewis's behavior by sitting on him at the beginning of the day. However, the tone this set for everyone began to be uncomfortable, and I found myself showing a tough face even when it was no longer useful. Lewis and other students would look at me occasionally and tell me to turn the Grouch off, pointing out that they hadn't done anything wrong. They pointed out that on some days I let Lewis play around or make noise, and that on other days I didn't. This was caused by the Grouch factor, they claimed. Lewis said one day during a class meeting that the factor was located somewhere in the back of my brain.

I immediately saw that he had given me a way out. Admitting that there *was* a Grouch factor, I went to the blackboard and drew a head and a brain. At the back of the brain I labeled a section "The Grouch's House," and we began to discuss what brought out the Grouch in me—and in the others as well. For the idea of a Grouch in the brain allowed many of the students to acknowledge that they, too, had days with their Grouches out.

We decided that there were inside reasons and outside reasons that set the Grouch off. I admitted that sometimes I Grouched because I'd come to school in a bad mood. At other times I Grouched because some of the students were fighting or bothering others and I had to set limits. Lewis acknowledged that he woke up some mornings with his Grouch out. On those mornings his Grouch got my Grouch going. The discussion was more sophisticated than I had expected five- and six-year-olds to be capable of. We were able to use the Grouch image to think about and analyze complex behavior.

The notion of a Grouch factor even changed behavior in the class. One day we speculated on what kept the Grouch happy, and the students suggested jokes, snacks, praise, and isolation. We talked about ways we had of bringing angry feelings under control. I suggested that the students remind me when my Grouch was showing, and told them I would do the same for them. It was no longer necessary for me to look at Lewis for signs of aggression. I could look at his Grouch, and I could appeal to him to control it when he came in angry.

Since the problem was his Grouch and not *him,* Lewis began to assume responsibility for its behavior. He learned to leave other students alone, to scribble on his own work, to go outside and break a stick instead of a game or a sculpture. After a month, the Grouch became boring. The powerful metaphor became a stale cliché and we no longer referred to it. But it had helped cement community, keep Lewis part of the group rather than alienated from it, and taught me about indirect ways of dealing with so-called discipline problems.

Over the years I have discovered that there are times when indirect ways of discussing feelings are the most helpful in neutralizing a situation. It is possible to use superheroes, animals, imaginary friends, TV characters, athletes and other real-life heroes, and astrological symbols as tokens of thought to create discussions, dramas, and writing that deal with pain and conflict. Such substitution is one powerful way of turning problems of self-discipline and control over to the children; by letting them speculate on how they do behave and how they might behave, you can help young people assume responsibility for their own behavior.

During my first year, Lewis wasn't the only one with the potential to disrupt our learning community. There were times when what could have been a bit of fun and creative mischief turned into group disorder, especially in the middle of the rainy season, when the children had been cooped up in the room all day or when there was a violent incident on the bus or playground. I discovered something that settled the class down one day when things were so out of control that I was ready, despite my best intentions and strongest will, to grab and shake a particularly troublesome student. Some of the children began fighting; others made a circle around the fighters; and a few moved into the corners and tried to hide. With the most menacing look I could muster, I moved toward the child I thought had instigated the fight and swept him off his feet. The class turned silent, waiting for the hammer to fall. I gritted my teeth, turned the student over my lap, and raised my hand as if to spank him. Then, lowering my hand as slowly as possible, I proceeded to mime spanking the child, whispering to him that his role was to pretend to cry. He let out the most drawn-out and mournful moans. The other students, catching on immediately, wanted their turns at being play-spanked. I obliged a few of them, then asked everyone to sit down and told them we would try something new. There would have been no use going back to what I had originally intended for that day.

The class sat quietly and expectantly, which surprised me. I asked two of the most restless students to stand up and get ready to fight each other. Then I told them that they could move only in slow motion and must not touch each other. They had to mime a battle. They also had to control their bodies so that they never broke out of the slow rhythm of the mime. I asked one of the two students to practice, and she quickly realized that it wasn't such an easy thing to slow up her body and take conscious control over her movements. After this practice, the students fought their mock battle. Then I asked them to pretend to embrace. Next I asked the whole class to stand up as slowly as they could and raise their hands as high as they could, and when they couldn't go any higher to get up on their tiptoes and pretend that they could take off and fly.

After the exercise was over, the students fell on the rug and giggled and rolled around. After a while everyone quieted down and asked for more improvisations. I drew on my experience with the high school students at Other Ways and used exactly the same improvisations we had done. I suggested that the children all lie down on their backs and close their eyes. Then I asked them to imagine that they were asleep; I would become a dream master for the moment and suggest they live in a dream for a while. I filled their dream world with water and said we were all underwater and could only move the way fish moved. I suggested they begin to test themselves in the water and swim around, thinking of the kind of fish they were, whether they were sharks or minnows, beautiful tropical fish or fearsome blowfish with poison spines. The spell was broken by a fire drill, but I remained amazed at the self-discipline some of the most defiant and undisciplined children in the class had shown.

From that time on I did warm-up improvisations almost every day and found them a good way to lead children into larger theater projects and acted-out storytelling. These improvs became a way of bonding the children to one another, helping them master long narrative structures, and teaching them to discharge the hostility and anger that occasionally invaded the classroom from home or the streets. Once again, theater had become a way to overcome difference, anger, and fear.

I have always prided myself—perhaps even more than I do in the skills my students acquire and the intelligence of their conversation— on the fact that all my classes have come to feel at home with and care about each other. Sometimes this passage is difficult and takes up almost half a school year. At Other Ways, to develop that kind of bonding was a constant struggle, which succeeded only with constant, strenuous effort to overcome the racial tensions at the school. Other times, as at Hillside, things click right away. A visitor can tell if we've reached the stage of conviviality by watching how students greet them and introduce them to the classroom. My students express joy in ownership, delight in learning, and a wicked sense of knowing all of our secrets, having that special knowledge that makes one an honored member of a group and not merely a visitor.

Throughout the two years I spent at Hillside I was amazed by the open and democratic sentiments the children expressed and by the logic and sensitivity of their arguments over questions about maintaining order in the class. We had fights; a new student was caught stealing other children's things; cliques were formed and some children felt rejected. Everything happened that usually happens with young children, but we talked about it—and the children raised issues of fairness and caring about each other that delighted me. They gave me occasion to introduce ideas and stories and poems that clearly spoke to their concerns about happiness, safety, and order.

My first year at Hillside was the year of divorce. One day in November I noticed Sage crying at the door. She refused to come into the room and wouldn't talk to me. I thought someone had hit her, or that she had lost something or had been teased. My daughter Tonia, who by this time had transferred into the class, ran over to her, along with Susan, Carolyn, and Ann. They stayed in the hall talking through the first hour and refused to come to the circle for story time. Now, these were my story freaks, the children who would grab any book read aloud and take it home and memorize it. I told them, very sternly, that they knew attendance in the morning circle was required, and I insisted that they knew how important that was to what we learned in class. Tonia turned to me and said that what they were doing was more important. The other girls agreed. Something in their tone made me back off, and I said it would be okay— just once.

During lunchtime the girls, including Sage, came up to me as a group and explained that Sage had just found out that her parents were going to divorce. She didn't want to stay home with them that day, as they'd suggested, but just couldn't come into the room. Carolyn and Susan then explained that Sage needed them: their parents had already been divorced and they could help her.

For the next several weeks they and Tonia became Sage's counselors and supporters. They told her how to develop a world of her own, helped her deal with her anger at both her parents, and in very small ways nurtured her through this hard time.

Sage's experience was the norm in our class. Except for Tonia and a few of the African American children, every child in the class came from a one-parent family, a family that was on the verge of collapse, or a (usually successful) second marriage. During my first year, about a third of the children in the class experienced the dissolution of their families. The majority of the parents were European American, middle-class, and well educated. Given the way in which the stereotyping and stigmatizing of the poor has become fashionable, it is essential to underline that many children in great need are those whose parents have succeeded on the terms of the society but have caved in under the pressures of that success.

My way of trying to be useful to the children was to keep them focused on the future. This was more a matter of creating hope than of healing old or current wounds. My role as a teacher was not to deal with the children's coming to terms with their past so much as to make them feel strong and enthusiastic about the future. That meant helping them through the current pain but not dwelling on it; instead, I gave special attention to their personal skills and inner dreams. This meant discovering what they liked to learn, what they cared about, and how they could use these things to have safe, pleasant time with themselves apart from their grief.

For example, Carolyn, who also experienced the disintegration of her family, always gravitated toward books on mechanical inventions. When I remarked on this to her, she said she loved to create things. The next day I presented her with a construction set with gears and a motor and other components that allowed her to make moving machines. Then I set aside a small place in the classroom where she could work with the set when she was done with her other work. It was a learning center for one.

I frequently give my students learning gifts, and by the time Carolyn got her invention kit the other students knew it was another one of Herb's "presents for learning." I borrowed this term from the nineteenth-century German educator Friedrich Froebel, who first created kindergartens and who built his curriculum around giving children specific gifts that would contribute to their learning. What I was doing was just a reconceptualization of what some progressive educators had been doing since the mid-1830s but without the rigid system that developed around the gifts.

It was a delight to see Carolyn work on her wonderful inventions. It was a time-out from grief, a passage into accepting a new way of living, and a chance to refocus on herself and discover how to develop her own path in what would probably be a difficult few years ahead.

I also did a lot of work in the class on families throughout the world. I dealt with culture and family, with the understanding of what it meant to be a member of an emotionally caring community, and with mutual assistance. This might sound abstract, but when such ideas become integrated into everyday life in kindergarten and first grade they become specific and immediate. For example, we spent a few weeks looking at how towns are built and on building our own ideal town. We designed a community square and talked about the kinds of things kids wanted to do and the kinds of spaces they needed to do them in. We talked about how children and adults might relate to each other in an ideal town and wrote stories and drew pictures on the theme "Life as It Might Be: Our New Town." Then we built a cardboard model of our town and made up some plays in which kids had to deal with adult problems, set up a town government, and play adults trying to figure out how to make new lives for themselves when their old lives weren't working. The children's work was delightful, often hilarious, sometimes scathingly critical of grown-up ways. We discussed the issues raised by the plays and skits and stories; however, I deliberately refused to tie things up with a neat summary after a discussion or event, or to draw a moralistic conclusion about what was a good or bad way to be. It was up to the individual children to figure out for themselves how they felt and how what we did could help make sense of the problems in their worlds.

Of course, many things besides divorce happened that first year, one of which led to the theme that played throughout my second year at Hillside. That theme was the politics of food.

Ray and Sharon Nitta, a brother and sister of Japanese and Hawaiian descent, were part of the first group of students at the Center for Open Learning and Teaching. They brought incredible skills, sensitivity, and experience to our group. Ray is a traditional Japanese carpenter (meaning, among other things, that he does not join wood with nails but uses wooden pegs) and a healer; he has extraordinary insight into the structure and nature of games and puzzles. Sharon had a degree in nutrition before she came to us, and her holistic view encompassed classroom learning, food, health, and the making of a convivial, multicultural school community. Though neither she nor Ray had ever taught children before joining the Center for Open Learning and Teaching, both understood how people learn, had neither fear of nor respect for dysfunctional institutions, and were willing to follow their instincts and the children's lead to completely rebuild schools if necessary.

During the time Ray was a student teacher in my classroom, the children constantly complained about the school lunches. Both the food and its packaging bothered them. Some of the children took one look at their lunch and dumped it whole into the garbage. Those who did eat, dumped aluminum foil, plastic, paper, and other leavings into garbage cans, which were carted away at the end of the school day.

Ray's curriculum theme was environmental sanity. We had talked in class about recycling, about the problems waste creates, and about how it is possible to live simpler and more satisfying lives by taking care of our environment and taking collective responsibility for keeping it beautiful and whole. One of Ray's exercises was particularly effective. He suggested that the children in our class collect all the aluminum foil thrown away every day and see how large and heavy a ball of aluminum we could come up with after a month.

Garbage became part of our curriculum, as it had at Other Ways. During one of the evening seminars at my house that focused on curriculum development, Sharon offered a suggestion that reminded me of my resolution, made years before when I was teaching at P.S. 103/79, to do something about school lunchrooms. Her idea took us beyond critique to a schoolwide experiment in conviviality that directly addressed the issues of multiculturalism, nutrition, waste, and community involvement, and that helped children become part of an organic community of learning. The class came up with a radical, sensible educational idea that provided a small but powerful model of school restructuring, and we decided that with the help of the principal, Frank Fisher, we would make Sharon's dreams a reality at Hillside.

Here is the simple, radical idea: Make the school kitchen into a nutrition-education and curriculum-development center involving parents and students as well as food-service workers, and turn the lunchroom into a restaurant, meeting place, multicultural art gallery, and recycling center. In other words, turn eating into a communal and congenial time and make the lunchroom gracious, educational, and environmentally responsible. From Ray and Sharon's perspective, one which I readily adopted, we could develop schoolwide learning centers and expand to the rest of the school what we were trying to do in our classroom. Ray even wanted to extend the idea further; he suggested that we could develop a solar greenhouse, and a year-round rooftop garden. We could use the food we grew for school lunches, and the gardens as natural-sciences learning centers.

Over the next year we did all that and more. With Frank Fisher as our central supporter, and with the enthusiastic cooperation and participation of most of the staff and many of the parents, the school's lunchroom and roof underwent major transformations. This didn't happen easily; we got approval for our program only after we turned out about a third of the parents and children at a Berkeley school board meeting where we requested and got local control of our lunchroom.

We took out the long tables and benches in the lunchroom and replaced them with tables Ray had built to seat three, four, five, or six people. We obtained nice chairs for the children to sit on. With the assistance of some of the school's older children, Ray built partitions and put in a hi-fi sound system. Frank was ingenious about finding sources of money for these changes.

One Monday I arrived at school to find an enormous fish tank, tropical fish swimming around in it placidly, right in the middle of the lunchroom space. The fish seemed to have a calming influence on the children. When everything was up and working the children took turns selecting appropriate lunch music, helped with cleanup, and ate in a civil, intelligent, and gracious way. For my class, at least, the new lunchroom made all the difference in the world. The children came back from lunch ready for an afternoon of learning, and I no longer had to spend the first half hour calming them down or worrying that some of them were hungry.

The menu completely changed as well. Sharon helped the food-service workers, as well as community volunteers, cook foods from all over the world. She emphasized food from the cultures our children represented. Each week she put out a printed menu, which was also a multicultural curriculum bulletin for everyone in the school. On one side she had the daily menu (with vegetarian options) and several recipes for the foods that would be featured during the week. On the other side she had a world map indicating where the food had originated, along with puzzles or folk tales or statistics. The menu was prized by the teachers, who used it in their classes, as well as by the children, who could share it with parents and siblings.

Sharon planned a chicken meal once a week. Each week the chicken would be prepared in a different way: we had chicken curry from India; fried chicken and collards; *arroz con pollo;* boiled chicken with latkes; chicken shish kebabs with Thai sauce. The meals were carefully balanced and there were always vegetables and salad. Sharon tried to balance nutrition and cultural habit in a way that would provide the children with the best meals possible. She also went around to classes and had tasting sessions, preparing the children for meals that had new and interesting flavors.

In a very quiet and warm way, Sharon and her nutrition program became an integral part of the school's learning program. The new program actually cost less than the old lunchroom and had practically no waste. We replaced the plastics with dishes, silverware, and glasses and hired some dishwashers, expanding the food-service staff with money that otherwise would have been spent on disposable packaging.

Ray's roof garden was taken over by several of the third-grade teachers and began producing lettuce, carrots, herbs, potatoes, and other vegetables for school lunches. The flowers they grew were used to decorate classrooms, the lunchroom, and the school office. In a way we had not planned at all, Ray and Sharon, with Cynthia's and my help, managed to infuse the school with gracious and civil living habits at no extra cost to the public.

In the classroom, I connected all this to the United Farm Workers' grape boycott. One of the children asked me privately whether we would allow grapes in the lunchroom; her parents didn't buy grapes because of the farmers. I suggested she bring the issue up when the class gathered, and we had an intense conversation about the table-grape boycott. Some children felt that the boycott existed because Safeway was a bad company. Others thought it had to do with farmworkers but no one seemed sure of what a farmworker was. So, along with my student teacher, I developed a grape curriculum in which we spent a few weeks looking at the path grapes took from the vine to the table. We didn't just look at the grapes themselves, as all the elementary school textbooks I perused did. We looked at the human context in which grapes were grown, picked, distributed, and consumed. Then we met some members of the United Farm Workers, who were delighted to provide an illustrated and animated discussion and playlet about their struggle for better wages and working conditions. I even invited someone from Safeway, who turned out to be quite sympathetic to the boycott and explained to the children that Safeway did not grow grapes and was indeed taking the works and actions of the UFW and the boycott very seriously.

Some of the children, including my own, eventually joined their parents on the picket lines in front of supermarkets. Some didn't, and one or two had parents opposed to the boycott. I had explained to all the parents my intention of discussing the farmworkers' situation in class, and I had told them my position on the issue. However, I assured them—and they knew from the rest of my practice in class —that my major concern was that the children understand what the issues were and what was happening. Having spoken with our children about such political and social matters I knew that five- and six-year-olds were perfectly capable of understanding social struggle and could develop informed opinions. I'm not so romantic as to believe that these opinions would be based on complex logical reasoning backed by careful historical and factual analysis, but I do know they would be more carefully weighed, more thoughtful, and more sensitive than most of the political and social opinions held by many adults in our society. Education for democratic citizenship should begin as soon as children first gather to learn from adults and with each other.

In 1975, the new California state teacher-credentialing law went into effect and we no longer qualified as a credentialing program. So after three years, during the last two of which I taught at Hillside, we had to end our teacher education program and close the Center for Open Learning and Teaching.

Looking back at those three years, I believe we accomplished several major things. We managed to get credentials for forty-five people, most of whom, twenty years later, are still doing wonderful, caring things with or for children. Two-thirds of our graduates are people of color, so we made a major contribution to the diversification of the teaching profession in the Bay Area. I have visited many of our former students' classrooms and they are welcoming places for children. Finally, I have been blessed with lifelong friendships that emerged from the program. I would do it again tomorrow, perhaps this time on a middle school level, if the possibility presented itself.

At Hillside I was able to show that it was possible to move from desegregation to respectful diversity, and to deliver skills to the children while creating a working classroom environment that crossed boundaries of class and culture through respect and inclusion. The curriculum was pervasively multicultural, as were the adults the children came in contact with, from guests to student teachers. The children felt good, spoke well and thoughtfully, and learned skills. This is not the contradiction some critics of open and multicultural education make it out to be. In fact, for me, the essence of good education is rooting skills in the more important and sophisticated understanding that develops in a convivial learning community.

However, there were some failures. Over my two years at Hillside three or four of the white parents pulled their children out of the class because I wasn't permissive enough. I refused to allow their children to do whatever they wanted, whenever they wanted and instead insisted on group participation, or at least respectful attentiveness during group time. I also refused to allow these children to follow their impulses and whims if it meant monopolizing the resources in the class. I believed they had to learn to share, but their parents felt that this was an unwarranted intrusion on their children's freedom. The only way we could deal with this major difference in educational orientation was to suggest that these children find a more congenial place, which they did at one or another of the private Free Schools in Berkeley.

My failure with Peter, one of the African American students, bothered me much more, since we were together for a year. Over that time he was in my class, he and I totally failed to connect and he acted as if he despised me. I couldn't find a way to break through his hostility; several times I asked him if he wanted to be in another class. He said no, they were all terrible. I did not teach him to read, did not succeed in making him feel better about himself, nor discover anything that interested him or might motivate him to learn or just to smile. To this day, I cannot figure out what happened to create such a relationship or what else I could have done to change it. It bothers and saddens me, and is a reminder of how difficult it is sometimes to teach.

As wonderful as our work at Hillside was, its effects did not last long. This was not because of the principal or the other teachers we worked with, but because of the disastrous spiral of the Berkeley Unified School District from busing and desegregation into resegregation through absence. The district had been about 50 percent European American and 50 percent people of color; after major white flight, 80 percent of the students in the district are children of color, while the European American children are in private schools or in the suburbs, as are many middle-class African American, Asian American, and Latino children. There has been a major exodus from the public school system in Berkeley, enrollment in which, over the past fifteen years, is down by about half.

With the withdrawal of the middle class came the withdrawal of political support and financial assistance for the schools. As funding and enrollment decreased, there was a retreat to "the basics," meaning the idea that such aspects of education as decent cafeterias and gardens were just frills, no longer affordable. And with that, our Hillside programs were dismantled.

This retreat from public education brought with it a deterioration in the quality of education—not an intensification of learning, as some of its adherents claim. When schooling is spare, minimal, and obsessed with skills without content you get the impoverished thought and marginalized imagination that show up, as children enter adolescence, in terrible test scores and scorn for school and everything it represents. Without conviviality, school comes to resemble a minimum-security prison, a depressing holding pen for people who want to get out and get on with their lives. Learning becomes a secondary matter; control becomes central.

It is disheartening to see people abandon the public schools, not merely in Berkeley but throughout the country. For me it is a dangerous way of quitting on democracy and is bound to increase the tensions and violence our children will have to live with in the future. These days, when so much negative is said about public education, my experiences at Hillside remind me of what is possible and provide me inspiration and energy I need to keep working at nurturing public education. Young children, five- and six-year-olds, bring the fullness of their being to school, and all children, no matter how damaged they might be by everyday pressures or horrors or how privileged they are, should be welcomed and shown the same high regard that the wealthiest people can afford for their children.

Chapter 5

FRESH WATERS ARE EVER FLOWING

You cannot step twice into the same river; for fresh waters are ever flowing in on you.

—Heraclitus

ALDER CREEK

Alder Creek, where the North American continental tectonic plate rubs against the Pacific plate, and the San Andreas fault runs out to the Pacific Ocean, is about five miles north of my home in Point Arena, California. I love to take daily walks along the creek and out to the sea with my golden retriever, Mazi; together we have seen three years of the creek's transformations. Walking along the fault feels dangerous, as if we are daring the earth to split again. At the same time stepping on ground where tectonic plates meet infuses a simple daily experience with a sense of the planet as a whole. Though the creek is not spectacular and there are many more dramatic beaches in our area, a daily visit to Alder Creek has become part of my life, much as writing and teaching have.

Taking daily walks, stealing an hour from work to stretch and simply breathe without an agenda or purpose, is a recent phenomenon in my life. For the first fifteen years I lived in Point Arena I probably walked by the ocean or went to a beach less than once a month, and then only when Judy or my children dragged me or when some guests just had to be taken to see the ocean. I realize now that I had imposed certain limits on my own freedom because of my obsession with getting work done, being "relevant," and "making a difference." It took an encounter with potentially life-threatening high blood pressure to make me realize that everyday speed was a threat to lifelong effectiveness, and that the energy and intensity I wanted to bring to every moment would be better gathered up and parceled out sensitively over time. Walking every day, listening to the ocean, watching the changes the creek lived through in its yearly cycles were not a waste of time that could be better spent writing, teaching, or agitating for change. Rather, this was proportioning time, time to meditate—to ruminate, as one of my high school philosophical heroes, Spinoza, put it, *sub specie aeternitatis*, "under the aspect of eternity," as if one could step out of time and observe all of history, fixed and ended once and for all. From this metaphysical distance everything one does or dreams of doing is final: important on a moral scale and insignificant on the level of ego.

What I love most about Alder Creek is the way it changes *and* remains the same, much the way writing and teaching for me over thirty-five years are always different and the same. As I became a regular at the creek, the words of Heraclitus, another philosopher whose ideas have fascinated me for years, took on an inner life and at times echoed in my head like a trite melody or phrase that's impossible to get out of the mind:

> You cannot step twice into the same river; for fresh waters are ever flowing in on you.
> We step and do not step into the same river; we are and are not.

During the course of a year the mouth of Alder Creek changes from a small, almost stagnant lake that reaches toward but never spills into the Pacific Ocean to a roaring stream that sweeps silt and uprooted trees, sometimes even second-growth redwoods, into the sea, which in turn tosses driftwood and logs back onto the shore or shoots them—and occasionally the bodies of dead birds, seals, or even a dolphin—up the creek during high tide. In the midst of summer there are lovely warm swimming holes nestled in caves created by cracks in the rocks along the north bank of a gently flowing stream. During a winter storm descending from Alaska there is no discernible creek; the ocean rushes over the beach, obliterating it and tossing all the driftwood onto what used to be its far bank. So I walk and do not walk along the same creek over the course of a year.

I first visited Alder Creek about nineteen years ago, during summer. About half a mile upstream, some of the local high school students had made a delightful short film about summer love and one of the actors took me to visit their shooting locale. At that spot the stream flowed gently through some alders and around a gravel bar with a touch of grass growing over it. For years that was my fixed image of the creek. Compared to my present dynamic sense of the creek as the total of all of its cycles, moods, and variations over the course of time, this image is merely a snapshot, one momentary step into an ever-changing environment. And I know that even my daily experiences with the creek are inadequate to grasp the fullness of its being. The tectonic plates move apart three inches a year; the earthquake fault responds to underground pressure; the frequency and intensity of storms hitting the shore vary from year to year; and the silt coming down the creek, which affects its banks and the life it supports, changes according to various conditions upstream ranging from logging and land development to annual rainfall and gravel mining.

The reason I have been so drawn to Alder Creek and obsessed with its changes these days is that now, at sixty, I've been thinking a lot about the paradoxes of identity and change in my own life and work. Like the creek, I've experienced small and easily understood changes, more subtle long-range changes in patterns and strategies, and wild storms that produced major diversions or disruptions. Beyond my own personal changes I've been thinking about the changing faces of the students I work with and the continual shifts in their environment. Most recently I've also been thinking about the dangerous ways in which schooling seeks to suppress organic change and force growth into artificial channels that not only control learning but actually shrivel the imagination and impoverish life.

For many educators, planning for a school year consists of setting a time schedule, fixing on the course sequence, deciding beforehand what to evaluate, and determining the norms of acceptable performance. If you took a cross section of any day of the school year you would find the same structure and the same kinds of activities, especially on a secondary school level. The content might differ according to some preset sequence of learning, but the rhythms of the day and the life surrounding learning would be the same. It would be as if the U.S. Army Corps of Engineers, coming in to normalize Alder Creek, enclosed it in a large tunnel, turned its bed into a concrete chute, and set up computer-controlled water flow. The result would be the spiritual and physical death of the creek. A similar dissolution of imagination and spirit takes place in the channeled and constricted learning environments characteristic of most schools.

In the spring of 1986, when my son Josh was a junior in high school, he and a number of his friends certainly felt that way about their own schooling, and they let the staff know it. As troublemakers, they were peculiar. They had no problem with the formal demands of schooling; with a minimum effort—in some cases, *no* visible effort—they did as well as they cared to do in the boring and undemanding environment of Point Arena High School. This gave them the freedom to think about what was wrong with schools without having to agonize over whether they were stupid. They reminded me of the original Other Ways students—of Fred Perry, Jena, Jennie, Katy, the Johns.

Josh and his friends Abel, Oona, and Sean first focused their critique of the school on "Senior Slave Day." One day toward the end of each school year, the seniors would hold a mock slave auction to raise money for their class trip. Each senior was auctioned off to an underclass person and made to do silly things. Most students and the entire faculty thought it was a harmless, fun event.

"Senior Slave Day" was not unique to Point Arena High. The writer Alice Walker lives in a neighboring school district whose high school did the same thing; she wrote a powerful and angry letter to the local newspaper saying that the event was an insult to African American people and an example of the subtle ways in which school rituals make light of racism and therefore reinforce it. The local school board and principal defended the students, and the event continued for several years, creating rancor and divisiveness in the community.

Josh and his friends took Alice Walker's letter to their principal and student council. The issue created serious debate among the students, a rare and refreshing event. During the event about a dozen students held a protest with the explicit support of Judy, me, and a small number of other parents. Two friends of Josh's who were seniors refused to participate in the auction. For that, the principal told them they had to pay extra to go on the class trip—they hadn't raised their share of slave money. Reuben and Bryce decided to stay home instead of pay up and to this day feel that they did the right thing.

The next year the name but not the structure of the event was changed. It became Senior Service Day and the "services" of the seniors were auctioned off. Josh and his friends became even angrier at the school.

Josh, Abel, Oona, and a friend of theirs, Ian, who had graduated from Point Arena several years before, had a reggae band, which practiced several nights a week in our living room. Both Judy and I loved their music and the energy they put into creating a wonderful sound, so for the most part having the practice in our house was a privilege. During one band break, Oona jokingly complained to me about having to take civics, sociology, and economics during senior year. She said that economics was nothing more than learning how to borrow money, use credit cards, and write checks. Josh added that sociology at Point Arena meant safe-sex and drug and alcohol education. Either Ian or Abel added that civics was all about obeying the law and conforming. Oona, who was a brilliant straight-A student, added that she would love to have a challenging and interesting course for a change, and Abel suggested that I teach sociology, civics, and economics the next year.

It was an intriguing idea. My plan for that year was to write in the mornings and figure out a way to work with young people in the afternoons. I knew I was not welcome at the high school, having been part of a group of parents and educators who had tried and failed to reform it, and I did not feel like teaching in a hostile environment. If I could teach at home, have a class of reasonable size, control the curriculum, and structure the time so that my mornings were free to write, maybe it would work out.

Several things made it possible for the class to go ahead. Judy and I live on eleven acres, which we share with a small education and development center we created, the Coastal Ridge Research and Education Center. In addition to our house and Judy's studio, we have three cottages. One is a residence for visiting educators, a second my office and study. The third and biggest building is a library and seminar room, ideal for a class of about a dozen people.

Consequently I had fully insured, comfortable facilities in which to hold the class. I had the appropriate teaching credentials, so there was no problem with state and local education codes. In addition, it was possible to schedule the classes for a double period at the end of the afternoon so the students wouldn't have to run back and forth from school to our place, about three miles outside of town. Civics was a year-long class, and economics and sociology each lasted a semester so the double period in the afternoon would suffice.

The major problems were the curriculum and the approval of the principal. To my surprise, he was open to the idea of my taking eight students for special sections of sociology, civics, and economics. I'm not sure why, though I believe a number of factors played a role. An advantage of a small-town school (there were only 128 students, with about thirty-two in Josh's whole senior class) is that there's no school bureaucracy to worry about. The principal and I could talk things through, and as long as he had the approval of the school board he was free to make decisions about adding classes. That left the curriculum. There were course descriptions for all three classes, and I had to find a way to cover the material they outlined. The principal and I agreed to give the class an advanced-studies designation; I agreed to cover the course descriptions—and add more complex material as well, if he would let me do it my way. In addition, we agreed that I would write out class descriptions showing how my sections would cover the required material, as well as an additional description of how my sections would differ from the usual classes.

I had no problem with these requirements. My goal for the class was not to reform the high school so much as to experiment with different ways of teaching mandated curriculum. I looked at the official class outlines and at the list of educational materials usually used to teach them. Each class had a commercial textbook. The class outline was no more than a summary of the text's chapter outline. It was not clear what came first, the text or the outline of the class. In fact, according to students who had taken the course before, anyone who'd read the text and the teacher's manual and passed the classes with a B or better could probably have taught the classes. It was strictly by-the-book teaching, with an occasional optional research paper for people who wanted to get extra credit or make up for missed homework or failed exams.

I didn't want to use a textbook. Instead, I wanted to use original sources, to put the students in touch with the thinking and writing of people who had shaped sociology, made and interpreted the Constitution, and reflected upon economics. In addition I wanted to set the three classes in the context of the world, not just the United States.

Many critics of educational reform worry about the erosion of standards that they claim accompanies progressive curriculum reform in general and integrated, theme-based teaching in particular. But doing things differently does not mean doing them less well or making fewer demands upon the students. High standards don't trouble me. What does is how the adoption of specific standards becomes an excuse to regulate the form and structure of education as well. However, there are many routes to the same goal; some are linear and fit into a textbook, step-by-step curriculum. Others take meandering paths, pausing for conversation and the exploration of topics and themes that are not in the curriculum per se but that illuminate the ideas being taught. Creative teaching and learning need the freedom to find a route to the standards that suits the students' and teachers' knowledge, experience, and interests. I knew I wasn't going to use the textbooks but rather find a way to actively engage my students in a project that could lead to a working internalized understanding of civics, sociology, and economics.

In Point Arena, with Josh and his friends, I took the "Aims and Objectives" straight from the standard curriculum and worked them into a creative curriculum that, to return to my Alder Creek metaphor, became part of teaching within a moving stream.

The final approval for the classes came in June, so I had the summer to finalize my list of students and plan the class. Josh, Oona, and Abel decided to join; since he was interested in teaching, I hired Ian to be my teaching assistant–apprentice teacher. Thus we involved the whole reggae band in the class.

Ilana, the school valedictorian, who was a good friend of Josh and Oona, also signed up, as did our next-door neighbor Amanda and her friend Sage. Another friend of theirs, Melissa, indicated interest and joined us for a while but dropped out. There was Dominique, an exchange student from Belgium who insisted on coming to class despite considerable opposition from her host family, which was extremely conservative and had been overtly hostile to my educational work in the past. Also with us was Sean, a friend of Josh's who had the reputation of being extremely smart and relentlessly resistant to authority. From third grade through sixth, Oona, Ilana, Josh, Amanda, and Sean had all come to a summer camp Judy and I ran and been in plays I directed. Sage and Dominique were new to me as students, though I knew Sage's mom from the days when Sage and Josh were on the T-ball team I coached.

Some friends in New York didn't believe me when I said I'd volunteered to teach a public high school class for nothing and even paid for a teaching assistant out of my own pocket. In addition, they worried about what this implied for the union. That wasn't a problem: as when I'd taught at Hillside Elementary, I didn't take any teacher's job or prevent any new teacher's hiring, and the regular classes were still offered. Basically, I absented eight students from the high school for two periods five days a week for one school year in order to set up a laboratory of learning. My goal was to explore, in a somewhat ideal setting, how learning could take place; later I'd try to apply what I'd learned to more usual public school settings.

In addition to being small and off campus, this class differed in another way from most urban public high school classes, even those in small, experimental high schools. If you have children of your own in a small town like Point Arena, it is almost impossible not to know everybody else's children too. Teaching Josh and his friends was very different from teaching in other circumstances, because with the exceptions of Dominique and Sage, I had watched all the children grow up and had worked with them in one way or another for about ten years. I could talk to them over the summer and find out about their current concerns and interests. And I could inform them, as my own process of planning the class developed, of what to expect from me.

What came across in my summer discussions with the kids was that they were bored in school and looking for an intellectual challenge. The problem was not to keep them from playing around but to fulfill their expectations of being exposed to new and exciting ideas. One of the main demands on educators' ingenuity is how to be serious and challenging with adolescents without boring them or creating discipline problems that interfere with learning.

I didn't want to waste my students' time with textbooks that they could easily read themselves if they chose to. On the contrary, I wanted to create a class during which they would be drawn into an understanding of citizenship and get a feel for how money and work were intertwined and how resources were shared or hoarded throughout the world. I also wanted to help them understand culture and class and to work toward some useful definition of the health of society that could be used to weigh the quality of one's life. Most of all, I wanted them to feel that the class was a voyage, an exploration of fundamental human issues that connected them with the intellectual traditions and academic knowledge involved in building a democratic society. I wanted them to become engagé—that is, passionately concerned with understanding and shaping the world they lived in.

In structuring the class, I had to overcome the separation of content and process. What we studied and how we were to study it were not two separate or separable aspects of learning. By 1986 I had developed an integrated planning process; for once, I would be able to implement and test it in a learning environment I was free to modify however I wanted.

Such ideal settings, which cannot easily be reproduced within a public school, are important if we are to expand our notion of what young people can and will do. We have to extend our knowledge of how learning takes place beyond what happens within the confines of a classroom and the social and academic constraints of a school. This extended sense of the possible can lead to a rethinking of the relationship between context and content in education. Institutionalized expectations and imposed limits on what is offered to students trivialize the process of learning and inhibit intellectual and personal growth. Having a place of my own to teach, and the freedom to plan within the incredibly wide parameters set by agreeing that the focus of the class would be civics, sociology, and economics, led me to spend the summer of 1986 obsessed with the unity of process, content, and place, and with the creation of an environment for *these* students, at *this* time in history, in *our* community, using the resources we could scare up.

I started by clearing the planning wall in my study. That wall, which is about five feet long by nine feet high, starts out as a blank slate and over the course of my thinking through the structure of a book or an educational project gradually fills up with notes, ideas, and suggestions. At the beginning of a project the wall is very loosely organized. Anything relevant that occurs to me is noted on the wall. I don't try to impose a premature structure on the material I'm gathering. The idea is to achieve a sufficient density of possibilities before beginning to group the material under categories, which emerge from the material itself rather than from some preconceived structure.

As an example of how these categories develop, one of the first things I began thinking about and making notes on was the strengths the students brought to the class. First, there was the reggae band, whose members were beginning to realize that it had to be run as a small business as well as an artistic group. Clearly they had a personal interest in understanding the economics of small business. A note to this effect went up on the wall: "Bands as small businesses." And another raised the question: "How could the band develop a spread-sheet?"

Sean, who was a surfer and a skater, could make and repair surfboards and skateboards; he was skilled with epoxy and wood. That led to several notes on making things out of wood, on epoxy modeling, and on the public order and safety issues relating to surfing and skating.

Oona was an excellent writer; her interests led me to think about desktop publishing and, once again, home businesses and small businesses.

Before the band became his passion, Josh had been a model builder; he had spent several years obsessed with making a perpetual-motion machine. Again I noted model building, and began to think about the kinds of models students could build for a class on sociology, civics, and economics. The analogy of physical models with economic models was obvious, so a note stating that went up on the wall. Then it occurred to me that architectural models, and perhaps a model of a society, could also play some role.

My thoughts about models and building something with the students were reinforced by the fact that Amanda, whose mother made and sold beautiful one-of-a-kind dolls, was a skilled artist and craftsperson; she had worked on her mother's dolls and her own line of crafts since she was about ten. Amanda could take an idea and create a marvelous physical representation of it. "Dolls" went up on the wall. Through free association, so did notes about masks, social roles, pretense, stigma, and, by extension, role models, socialization, peer pressure, fashion, and popular culture.

I also considered major events that had taken place during 1985 and 1986 and reflected on how they might be used to illuminate the subjects we were studying in class. I noted events like the Tower Commission report, the protests and strikes in South Africa, the coming Bork confirmation hearings, and Surgeon General Everett Koop's congressional testimony supporting condom distribution and warning about the danger of AIDS. These events could spark discussion of important sociological, civic, and economic ideas.

In addition I started stacking up resource materials and pasting up notes on how I might use them for our reading and discussion. Among the dozens of things I posted and gathered were the following:

Plato's dialogues, in particular the following Socratic dialogues, which everyone concerned with democracy and issues of conscience ought to have an opportunity to read and discuss: *Phaedo, Crito,* and the *Apology.* I also included the "Allegory of the Cave" section of *The Republic* as a possible reading assignment.

Jefferson's drafts of the Declaration of Independence (from historian Carl Becker's book *The Declaration of Independence*) along with the document as adopted; we'd use these to study the process Jefferson and others went through as they tried to articulate their notion of a democratic society and government.

The Constitution and the drafts of the Bill of Rights. The U.S. Government Printing Office was a prime source for these. For example, they provided a document called "The Making of the Bill of Rights," which reprinted the original drafts, containing fifteen proposed amendments, as well as the final Bill of Rights.

A collection of national constitutions from Namibia, the Soviet Union, and France as well as selected parliamentary papers from England. My idea was to contrast parliamentary democracy with our system of the balance of powers and to illustrate how a country without a written constitution (Great Britain) could develop democratic forms of government.

An assortment of human rights documents, including the United

Nations International Declaration of Human Rights, the Emancipation Proclamation, the French Declaration of Human Rights,
and the "Declaration of Sentiments" of the 1848 Seneca Falls
Convention on Women's Rights.

A similar collection of essays and excerpts from works on sociology
and economics, as well as a stack of cartoons, quotes, charts,
and graphs and reproductions of posters, paintings, and photos
related to the various topics we might consider. I included many
essays that examined culture and community from a multicultural
perspective.

Poems and short stories, by a variety of writers representative of the
many peoples of the United States, that illuminated the subjects
we were studying.

Documents from the civil rights and women's movements and from
struggles over freedom of speech and other Bill of Rights issues.

U.S. Department of State Post Reports, one for the Bahamas dated
August 1985, and the other for Saudi Arabia dated May 1986,
which I discovered at the GPO on a visit to Washington, D.C.
These documents, produced by the State Department, are given
to diplomats and their families being posted to different parts of
the world. They provide practical information on how to dress,
behave, shop, get settled, treat local people, and understand local
government and politics. What made them particularly interesting for my purposes was that they were specifically intended to
inform U.S. government officials how to behave in various cultural and political contexts.

I organized all this material into what I call a casebook, by analogy with a legal casebook. Each student was to produce an individual
casebook that would include her or his own work, copies of some of
the work of their classmates, and the readings we actually used.
Instead of having a fixed textbook, we would have an evolving one,
specific to what we studied that year.

After a month of accumulating ideas and materials my wall and
floor were a mess. Nevertheless, clusters of ideas had begun to develop, and some overriding themes and broad concepts began to
emerge. They promised to unify the class while giving it the unpre-
dictable and creative nature of a flowing stream that keeps its identity
within difference. My overriding concern for the class was to make
sure that my goal of having the students learn about citizenship,
society, and economics would not crowd out the students' creative

input or take on a didactic character that would prevent them from thinking through important issues and developing their own well-reasoned and sincerely held beliefs. The themes of model building, small systems, autonomous institutions, local power, and conflict resolution recurred over and over in the material I selected. The problems the students faced—AIDS, drugs and alcohol, feelings of alienation and powerlessness, sexual identity, economic security, trust —all occurred in the context of defining a world for oneself, of making a meaningful place in a hostile environment.

This wasn't surprising. Point Arena is a complex community, many of whose people have retreated from urban living to try to create small, convivial communities. The parents of more than half the students (Amanda, Sean, Oona, Ilana, and Abel) had moved to the country to find some succor and freedom that they couldn't find in the city. At some point in their lives, they had been dreamers, flirting with alternative lifestyles and learning, during their years in the country, how to be self-sufficient. Their children had grown up around Point Arena and were comfortable with country living but also encountered local conservatism in their school and in their social lives. In addition, they didn't accept all of their parents' ideas and values. Some of them, as I found out in the course of the class, quite thoroughly disagreed with their parents and had much greater faith in the larger society and the opportunities it provides than their parents did.

Sage and Melissa were what might be called crossovers; they came from a more conservative part of the community but were open to all kinds of ideas and people. The bridge between them and the other students was Amanda who, though she came from a "craft" and somewhat bohemian environment, was also very comfortable with people whose lifestyles were more mainstream.

Judy and I do not fit comfortably in any of the usual categories that Point Arena people use to describe themselves, and we are about ten years older than most of the other youngsters' parents; we're closer to the civil rights movement and the beat generation than to the Haight-Ashbury generation many of them belong to. And, having worked in poor urban communities most of my adult life, I am still a city dweller, a Bronx New Yorker, learning to live in the country and get on with my work. Josh reflected this history; he'd lived in Berkeley until he was six, and he was comfortable in both the city and the country. He got along with many different types of kids and, through the band, had a bridge to almost all of them. In keeping with the social and political struggles for justice Judy and I were involved in outside the community as well as within it, Josh had a keen sense of partisanship. During 1984, when we lived in London, he had been a member of the Youth Campaign for Nuclear Disarmament and participated in many antinuclear and antiracist demonstrations. Issues relating to decency and justice were very much on his mind as was the pacifism he adopted when he was twelve (and still, at twenty-six, conscientiously maintains).

Ian brought a number of other concerns to the table. He lived with his grandfather, who'd been one of the Tuskegee Airmen, and he was very interested in issues of culture and dignity. Abel, equally concerned with these issues, was beginning to explore his Cajun roots at that time.

I decided to integrate sociology, civics, and economics through the following scenario:

> There has been a major earthquake and people are unsettled throughout the state of California. The class has been designated as one of many Resettlement Authorities throughout the state. A population of 8,500 people must be resettled on land assigned to the class. The land is located in the same geographic zone as Point Arena but is not on the coast. It measures twenty miles by fifteen miles and has a river running through it and some hardwood forests. Animal life and plant growth are what they were before communities were settled by European Americans. The land was to be considered uninhabited.

Here I made a mistake, which I would correct for the next time I taught the class. I should have recognized that the land would not have been uninhabited. Later in the year I included discussions of how to work with the Native American population on any resettlement program. This slip of mine shows how easy it is to fall into racist ways of thinking and by neglecting the reality of other people's lives, set up a learning situation that misrepresents and denigrates them. I wanted reality in my students' imaginings, but neglected a significant part of it myself.

The goal for the class was to design this community as realistically and exactly as possible, and to set up a scenario for the resettlement of the people. I knew that this was impossible to achieve in the time we had, but I was also confident that all the aspects of civics, sociology, and economics covered in the high school curriculum would be dealt with in challenging ways. Our last day should, if the class succeeded, find us in the midst of the project, raising new questions and figuring out new directions for our explorations in the design of a decent community. This was to be a flowing stream in one season of its existence, the same and different, substantial and yet fluid, always subject to the creative input of the participants.

However, I didn't want to step into the water the first day of class and let everyone be swept away by their first impressions and wildest ideas. I believed the students ought to have certain tools before they embarked on the planning, and some conversations about the issues we'd be considering. I wanted, in other words, some more formal learning to precede focusing primarily on the project.

Many child-centered and progressive educators would disagree with me on this issue, believing that all the skills of thinking and researching should emerge from project learning and the students' experiences. I find it easier, more systematic, and more effective to do direct teaching once in a while or to set a topic for conversation that none of the students could possibly decide on.

The first text I chose for group reading during the first class was *Crito*. None of my students had ever encountered Plato or would have suggested we study these texts. But the death of Socrates seemed like a wonderful way to introduce dialogue, argument, and logic while at the same time going directly to issues of democracy, conscience, and responsibility.

The students needed a number of skills if they were to develop a sophisticated understanding of the subjects. These skills all centered on the ability to analyze a text and to discuss ideas and write about them. The challenge was to provide my students with a vocabulary of ideas and to acquaint them with question-raising skills and the art of serious intellectual conversation. In addition, their writing skills had to be honed. This meant taking advantage of what I'd learned when I taught in Harlem in the 1960s and at Other Ways; I would provide, almost daily, short writing exercises to develop fluency in writing about the ideas that I hoped would develop through classroom conversation. During the summer I created a list of central concepts in economics, sociology, and civics, which I derived from college texts, academic journals, current discussions of issues, and my working knowledge of the fields.

In fact, I believe that all classes for all age levels could profitably begin by providing students with a core conceptual vocabulary that would help them navigate the subject matter and learn how to speak intelligently within the field. I don't mean we should provide students with jargon to use mechanically. Rather, the goal is to be specific about concepts that will allow students to be more thoughtful in their engagement with a subject.

Here's a sampler from my list of the core vocabulary of Civics, Sociology, and Economics. I clustered some of the words in order to introduce students to continuums and clusters of ideas:

> right / obligation / entitlement / duty / privilege / radical / liberal / conservative / moderate / reactionary / progressive
> free market / socialist / communist / communitarian / capitalist
> thesis / antithesis / synthesis / dialectic
> alienation / anxiety / angst
> necessary / sufficient
> rage / anger
> proof / justification / excuse / reason
> caste / class / race
> commodity / profit / ownership / value / labor / means of production / capital / inflation / recession / wages / stocks / bonds
> matrilinear / patrilinear / matrilocal / patrilocal

I didn't begin with all the concepts on the list at once. I did, however, give the students the complete list and tell them we would cover the ideas. And, I urged them, if I or another student used the words and someone didn't understand the nuance of meaning or particular weight we were giving the concept, he or she should speak up.

One of the most frustrating habits students learn from test-obsessed and textbook-oriented schooling is to acquiesce in their own lack of understanding. Students become conditioned to get through a chapter rather than think it through. They are always swept off to the next quiz or test, and when they don't understand something they learn to fudge it. This is partly because they are afraid to display their ignorance to the teacher. If they read the text and don't understand a concept, that's their problem. Instead of being a challenge, "not knowing" is internalized as a sign of some inner deficiency that should, at best, be hidden from public view. What I try to do is encourage my students to feel comfortable enough with me and with the rest of the class to let their lack of knowledge show. When this freedom to struggle toward understanding becomes part of the class mentality, a vibrant and challenging intellectual life begins to thrive.

In conjunction with an understanding of concepts and a respect for the weight and power of words, students need to develop a tight, thoughtful way of writing about ideas. Again, old habits of learning interfere with the development of complex skills. Students are accustomed to writing for a grade, not to writing as an exploration of ideas. They cut the subject small, try to be certain about issues that are elusive, and attempt to tie everything up at the price of simplification and overgeneralization. My short writing exercises were designed to lead to discussion, not to be graded and then forgotten.

Finally, I combined a heavy dose of propaganda analysis and critical reading of texts with the vocabulary and writing exercises. These were all tools for understanding the core issues of living and working in coherent and convivial groups—that is, sociology, civics, and economics.

I had never before tried to teach such a multilayered class and was lucky to do it in such a modest and congenial setting. Here are the main components I tried to weave together into a coherent educational whole:

a large-scale community-planning project;
a series of skills-building lessons;
class readings and research relating to issues of community building;
lectures and briefings from me and guests on civics, sociology, and economics, and also about problems relating to community planning; and
student-initiated and student-developed group and individual work relating to community planning

To understand how I went about organizing these different strands of learning, the Alder Creek metaphor becomes useful. I was fully prepared for a school year that would be an adventure without a clear, determined shape or content. However, I did have goals, the central ones being these:

> to have my students engage the pressing social, economic, and civic problems in our society in an intelligent and personal way;
>
> to help them understand something of the historical and international contexts of these problems;
>
> to get them to dream up solutions and then think through ways to turn parts of these dreams into concrete action; and
>
> to give them a working appreciation of the privileges and obligations of being part of a society struggling to become a working democracy that serves all of its people well

BUILDING A WORLD

I began with Plato, returning for the first time since 6-1 to Greek culture—but this time in the context of a curriculum that was multicultural and honored the insights and wisdom of the Greeks as some among the many contributors to our knowledge and development.

We began with the trial and death of Socrates. I knew the material was new to all the students, so none of them would have an academic leg up. In addition, the dialogic nature of the pieces was a model for the class. Serious discussion about issues of life and death, in which living and dying were intertwined with principle, conscience, the rule of one's inner voice, and the decisions of the majority would sound all the major themes for our year together. I could think of no better way to open up dialogue than through an encounter with the pleadings of Socrates' friends and his stubborn insistence on dying.

During the first few classes I gave a short lecture on Socrates, the Greek polis, and Athenian democracy with its small voting citizenship, its slaves, and its disenfranchisement of women. I refused to romanticize Athenian democracy and provided a short selection from I. F. Stone questioning Socrates' belief in democracy and pointing out Socrates' derision of the masses. The contradictions of life in classical Athens would illuminate our study of similar antidemocratic elements in the U.S. Constitution.

Then we read the *Crito* out loud, going around the table taking turns reading a few paragraphs at a time and discussing them. Reading a text out loud, word by word, and then examining what has been read both slows people down and begins to develop the habit of comprehension, which is the internalized refusal to read something through without understanding it. It means querying the claims of the author, looking up strange words, and slowing down when the text gets tough. This out-loud close reading and conversation, with its emphasis on comprehension and elaboration of the text, has been at the center of all of my teaching throughout my career.

The two Socratic dialogues were perfect. *Crito* begins with a bribe (the jailer is tipped and lets Crito into Socrates' cell in the middle of the night). The setting is dramatic and the conversation personal, philosophical, and moral at the same time. We went through the dialogue, taking our time, talking not merely about what Socrates and Crito meant, but about the issues themselves. The discussion was a model of the class as a whole. I didn't have a set number of questions that the students had to respond to, nor did I have intended outcomes or specific issues. I teased questions out at times, but mostly followed what interested the students. Occasionally, when someone went off on a tangent (a personal discussion of someone who was stubborn like Socrates, for example), I brought attention back to the text.

At first things were a bit awkward. Ilana and Oona tried to anticipate what "Herb" wanted, and had a hard time listening to or thinking about the text. Sean became really engaged, but then went off on a tangent meant not to illuminate the text but to anger Amanda by some personal reference I didn't get. Sage jumped in to defend Amanda, and I had to jump in on Socrates' behalf.

While this was going on I gave the students a specific commentary on the class, a meta-commentary meant to help them understand this new, nonjudgmental yet highly critical way of functioning as a group. We spent several classes on the *Crito* and then Ian, my assistant, conducted a class on the *Phaedo* while I stepped back and observed. The discussion of Socrates' death was quite emotional and its rhythm and tone made me more confident that we were moving in a sensible direction.

Here are some informal notes on that class and the assignment I created to follow up on the discussion of Socrates:

9/18/87: We went over *Phaedo* today. We brought up the points of spirit leaving the body at death; who is responsible for political murder, the person giving the orders or the person carrying them out; and Socrates' satisfaction with death because he could finally be well and through with his life on earth.

Assignment: Write a Platonic dialogue. It should contain the following:

1. more than one character, and conversation between them
2. a setting in which the topic they discuss has significance
3. personal as well as intellectual drama
4. a questioner with seemingly greater knowledge
5. a learner
6. a question with no simple clear answer
7. doubt at the end of the dialogue

We discussed the nature of the assignment and I linked it to the special character of the Socratic dialogue as a form of education we would use in the class. I managed to save Josh's dialogue:

Josh
Nathan Crito is a young man of 24, who lives in a small town in Georgia. He is white, and was recently arrested in a large fight, that was inspired by racial tension. Socrates, the legend, appeared to him one evening while he was brushing his teeth, about to go to bed. He was out on bail and trial pending.
CRITO: Hey who are you? what are you doing in my house?
SOCRATES: Oh I thought I'd stop by, we have something to discuss.
CRITO: Who are you, what do you want?
SOCRATES: My name is Socrates, I don't believe we've met.
CRITO: What am I to say? A great cloaked and quite ancient seeming man with flowing white beard and all appears before me! A ghost I would assume! If you are a ghost tell me and leave! I've done nothing! Don't stand and haunt me.
SOCRATES: I am no ghost, and to haunt is not my intention. But you say you have done nothing. Have not we all done something or another at some point in our live surely you've done something sometime?
CRITO: Well yes . . . this questioning interest me what are you saying?

SOCRATES: you are in legal trouble are you not my son?

CRITO: Yes I am that is correct. Something tells me to proceed cautiously.

SOCRATES: I have been in legal trouble myself you know. What is your crime?

CRITO: Well, it isn't really a crime, but it is illegal.

SOCRATES: We will get in to that latter. What was your action?

CRITO: Just me and a few friends beat some sense into a couple niggers who were drunk and needed a bit of learning.

SOCRATES: These men you spoke of as "niggers" where did you find this name?

CRITO: Niggers? why that's what they are!

SOCRATES: A name. Isn't a name given by oneself or parent, or a community as a whole, naming itself?

CRITO: Yes, I guess, whatever.

SOCRATES: Would it be new to you to learn that this "nigger" you use is not only not a self given name, but an insulting name. Like if I was to call you an asshole and not only you. your "nigger" mothers, parents, children, fathers, unborn children. Your own child would be insulted every time that chilling word was heard if you were black. Did that occur to you?

CRITO: No. It did not.

SOCRATES: These men you beat sense into what happened? What was the circumstance?

CRITO: Well, A couple nig. . . . uh guys were going home after a late night at the bar, and so were we (me and my friends that is) and we see them walking, a bit tipsy and we ask them which way they were headed "home word" they tell us. A couple of wise guys, so me and the others (there were 5 of us) jump them. Beat em up good. It would have been good and safe hadn't that old rich nigger been watching. Makes me sick they let the rich ones take a white man to court.

SOCRATES: you were yourself a bit tipsy at the time I assume?

CRITO: Well a bit.

SOCRATES: and that is no crime, correct?

CRITO: course not!

SOCRATES: Than may I assume that you did not beat the men because they were tipsy?

CRITO: Well; . . . no I suppose not.

SOCRATES: And I presume they held no threat against you.

CRITO: No threat.

SOCRATES: than more than anything else, you beat them for their blackness.

CRITO: Rightfully so.

SOCRATES: You then support there being wrong in blackness, and every black person is bad

CRITO: Certainly.

SOCRATES: If a black child was brought up in a white family, would they be bad?

CRITO: No of course not.

SOCRATES: If a white child was raised by black parents, would the child be bad?

CRITO: Most definitely.

SOCRATES: Then may we assume upbringing and not color influence a character?

CRITO: Well, I suppose.

SOCRATES: Black and whites alike are raised to hate each other, yes?

CRITO: Uh . . . I guess.

SOCRATES: Then what makes them different?

CRITO: Uh . . . Nothing I suppose. Not in those circumstances.

SOCRATES: Nor in any other, correct.

CRITO: I have nothing further to say Mr. uh . . .

SOCRATES: Socrates!

CRITO: Oh yes. . . . Socrates.

There were about two weeks of class before we turned to the resettlement project. During that time we read several case histories from *Sanity, Madness and the Family* by Jules Henry. Each had to do with a person who was driven mad by others—that is, whose every act or word was negated, undermined, misrepresented, or contradicted by every member of her or his social circle. I chose these cases because they led to detailed discussion of how people affect each other in social situations, and to an understanding of the influence of context and situation on behavior. In addition, Judy ran several classes on gift giving, sharing, and communication, and their relationship to social organization among the !Kung people of the Kalahari desert.

All these class sessions were designed to help the students distinguish sociology, economics, and civics, and at the same time understand that they overlapped. For me, these subjects are ways of parsing experience, which has many dimensions and, in itself, is unified in the everyday lives of people. I wanted the class to see that the academic organization of experience and of the world is a consequence of human choice and interest. My goal was to set a critical tone for the class, which would question the nature of the concepts we used as well as using those skills to examine particular cases. For example, I wanted the students to be able to understand the cultural dimensions of racism while at the same time understanding that many racist attitudes have economic origins. This means acknowledging that while racism might be part of the cultural life of poor whites in the South, that cultural hatred might have economic roots and be inseparable from the dynamics of poverty in the United States.

These first few weeks were fairly formal. They were run like graduate seminars I had participated in and taught myself. There were no grades, no critical evaluation of the participants. The center of energy and concern was the subject matter itself. All of the students participated and began to feel comfortable being part of an intellectual community, one in which learning became the focus. For some students, fear of being judged dissipated. Others forgot their internalized opposition to formal schooling. The seduction of the subject began to take over. People being driven mad, a man who died for his ideals, a culture whose values were fundamentally different and in some ways more humane than ours were all intriguing things to learn and speculate about. The power of learning about a world larger and more problematic than usually presented in school was my best ally in creating a community of learners.

At the end of September I opened the class up a bit by introducing the project. The students' response, however, turned a gently flowing creek into a rushing stream. I handed out a small map of the land we were to resettle, as well as a description of our task. Then I suggested that we translate the map into a plaster of paris model of eighteen inches by three feet. That way we could have a visual image of the terrain as we planned the density of settlements, the placement of houses and public facilities, the development of commercial places and farms, and so on. Sean said the idea was dumb and that the model was too small to have fun with. Ian, Josh, Amanda, Abel, and Sage agreed with him. Oona, Dominique, and Ilana thought my idea of a small model was better.

Sean said if we made a model it should be large enough to put in details. Abel followed with the suggestion that we should make small houses and docks and boats to put on the model, as if we had already built it and had planned for them. Ian suggested that Sean's idea was feasible, that we could build an epoxy model on top of a four-foot-by-eight-foot sheet of roofing insulation. Amanda suggested we paint it and maybe even add channels so water could actually flow through it. Sage added that we could build a table for it outside the classroom and even make a shelter to cover it during the rain. Even Ilana, Dominique, and Oona caught the fever. They added that we could experiment with the placing of settlements and land divisions and have many models of what was possible instead of just one.

It was Friday and I was nervous. I had no idea how to work with epoxy, wasn't sure about taking up so much space and time with a model, and wondered if what could be learned from doing this would be worth it. Instead of making a decision, I told the class that I would think through the issue over the weekend.

I spent Saturday and Sunday in an internal struggle, the teacher in me wrestling with the educator.

The teacher had been conditioned from the time I entered kindergarten: School was for learning. Time must be filled up with measurably meaningful activity. Work must be demanding and have an edge that proves it's serious. The goals of learning must be set out clearly and measurably. Part of me has not been able to escape the feeling that if I can't control learning and know what my students are doing, then learning isn't taking place and I'm not doing my job.

The educator in me knows that the teacher is often misguided when it comes to understanding how learning takes place. Trusting students, letting things move toward goals in diverse and frequently digressive ways, following enthusiasms, and responding to events and experiences are not diversions or wastes of time. Rather, they are the essence of substantive learning. From the perspective of the teacher, the four-by-eight model was a digression, a potential waste of time. For the educator, it was an opportunity—indeed, not one opportunity but many. It meant learning about epoxy and model building from the experienced surfers, skaters, and craftspeople in the class. It meant giving the students real ownership of the community-shaping project. And it provided time to speak casually of where we might go with the project as hills, mountains, valleys, rivers, creeks and streams were shaped.

Leaning toward the educator in me, as I usually do, I prepared for the adventure. However, I could not completely silence the teacher in me, so I tried to think of how the students could do much of the construction outside class time. That old demon efficiency was still bugging me—but obviously not the class. Josh told me that Sean and Abel had gotten the epoxy and tools, Amanda had come up with the paints and brushes, and everyone had agreed that we would start on the model Monday. Josh just wanted to know if he could take our truck to the lumberyard and charge the insulation board, plywood, and other materials needed to build a table for the model. Abel, Oona, and Ilana would be coming over in the afternoon and they planned to have the table finished by Monday's class.

So much for my decision making. I confessed my hesitancy, and Josh told me not to worry, reminding me that the students had initiated the class because they wanted a learning adventure. My resistance crumbled and on Monday we began to build the model—or, more accurately, the students began to build the model and collaborate on designing the physical world that would frame our planning. My map had indicated only a river with an island in the middle, some flat land, and some forested hills. The model developed to include a watershed, a logical unit for the development of a sustainable environment. This meant studying how a river might actually flow through the land, where its source and its mouth might be. It meant getting specific about the climate and the flora and fauna. And it also meant, for each of us, becoming familiar with the characteristics of the land in a way that I had not anticipated. As the model developed over a week we had a chance to talk about swimming holes, good places to camp, places we wanted to preserve from people's compulsion to develop and overplan. The themes of the rest of the class were sounded informally, without any pushing from me or attempt to organize them.

The next Monday I took advantage of the discussions we were having and the common focus model building had created. I suggested we have a brainstorming session, putting down everything we could think of that might have to be considered when planning a community. We generated a list of variables that represented about a hundred different aspects of planning and then grouped them together into tasks. The next step was to set up planning committees. We formed a Commission of the Whole divided into five planning groups: Surveying, Land Development, and Finding Resources; Laws and Government; Transportation and Housing; Water Usage and Waste Disposal; and Communication, Economic Development, and Entertainment. Each committee generated questions they had to answer, taking account of scientific knowledge and social theory. Then they did the research, reaching out to experts in the field and using library and computer-based resources for suggestions for the development of the community. The committee work took up about half of the class time. During the other half we read resource materials, tackled some shared questions, and read and discussed materials I had selected to enrich our discussions. There also were weeks off to investigate some issues in depth as a group. One of these investigations was on the role of the arts in society. We also took time to read constitutions and bills of rights and to draw up our own governing documents.

Here is a sampler of the questions and issues the committees decided to work on:

Surveying, Land Development, and Finding Resources. (Much of the committee's work lay in determining specific aspects of the land, based on the geography and geology of actual land in a similar zone.) What kind of vegetation grows here? What kind of soil conditions are we working with? Where is the tree line? What is the annual weather cycle? What kind of power might be developed? What part of the land should be developed for human habitation? Should it be clustered or spread out? What kinds of land allocations should be made? What would ownership be? What about land for agriculture? Should farming be done communally or individually, and how much land should be allocated to it? How deep is the river? What are its resources? What natural gas, metals, minerals, and so on, are available in what quantities, and how are they to be preserved or exploited? How has the earthquake that necessitated the resettlement affected this land?

Laws and Government. How should we enforce laws? Who votes, and who is voted for? What basic freedoms or rights do we have? What basic rights pertain to the following areas: marriage, children, gays and lesbians, minorities; questions of education, leadership, the

First Amendment, food, health care, housing, transportation, animals, entertainment?

Transportation and Housing. Housing codes? Planned communities or just live where you want? Bikes; kinds of fuel; roads, paths, and trails; water vessels, tolls or free transportation; public or private transportation; parking; commercial vehicles; provision for transportation to and from the outside world and for trade.

Water Usage, Waste Disposal, and Environmental Protection. Common water systems, wells, sharing of water resources, environmental protection of watershed, rules to govern use of resources, common or private ownership of natural resources, import/export regulations, recycling, composting, human waste recycling, intelligent usage of resources and sustained development, prohibition of pesticides or other forms of pollution, balance of development versus preservation. Questions: How much land and water does it take to feed one person? What does this depend upon?

Communication, Economic Development, and Entertainment. Community TV and radio, community-owned presses, computers, and copy machines, newspapers, what kind of press and publishing businesses to develop, a poster brigade, telephones and other communications with outside world. Art studios, concert halls, availability of instruments, art supplies, and so on, free or for pay entertainment. What kinds of public and private businesses should we have? What happens with profits? Taxes? Do we allow outside development and large corporations, or is self-sufficiency a major goal?

After the committees met and sketched out these various themes for investigation we all met together. The students read out their lists and I wrote down their suggestions on butcher paper. Soon every wall in our seminar room was covered with the makings of a small community, mirroring the planning process I'd used during the summer for the class itself. The bewildering options displayed by this brainstorming provided us with a vision of the miracle of everyday life, in which the simplest and most ordinary activity presupposes that many complicated structures are in place and functioning. It was a dramatic illustration of how we are surrounded by culture, by social institutions, and by norms of organized behavior, and yet are not explicitly aware of how much we are part of this nexus of structured interactions. The vocabulary word that described these semivisible underpinnings of everyday life was "infrastructure."

Recently I asked Josh what, if anything, in the class influenced the way he looks at the world these days and he said it had to do with infrastructure. From the time we stripped off the covers of everyday life and exposed the infrastructure, he has taught himself to look beneath the surface into the hidden structures of things. Of course, he may be atypical, given that he's a contemporary classical composer and builds complex structures in his music all the time, but it's nice as both a father and a teacher to think that our class enriched his perception of the world.

As the class reflected on the infrastructures of social life it became clear that we could not adequately deal with everything in the space of one year. We had to develop priorities. I pointed out that this need to make sense out of bewildering complexity is what leads to theory making. Here was a marvelous and unexpected opportunity to dig in intellectually and study some aspects of the relation between theory and practice.

I had had no intention of studying the process of planning and the nature of theory when the class began, so I had to rethink where we were going just when I thought we would get down to working on specific aspects of community development. However, since I think of my teaching as participatory research I felt free to range far in my search for intellectual tools for community planning. With so many factors determining the shape and character of a community, we needed a sensible way to sort them out.

Instead of beginning with a lecture on theory versus practice I asked everyone to read through the lists and look for common themes. I believe it was Josh or Oona who pointed out that some things were contradictory. For example, if we wanted all the houses clustered in one place, people wouldn't be free to choose to live where they wanted. If we wanted to develop agriculture, we would have to destroy some of the natural habitat. If we wanted radios, TVs, computers, and so on, we would have to sacrifice economic self-sufficiency, and also find a way to establish economic relationships with the outside.

During our discussion of these dilemmas the following general points emerged: One, we needed some agreement on overall principles about what kind of life we wanted to have within the community before we could go ahead with the plans. Second, we had to let facts —that is, what is possible according to current science and knowledge—also determine what we included in the final draft.

This latter came out in the vegetarian wars. Josh had managed to include in one of the lists a stipulation that the community would be vegetarian. He was a philosophical vegan and, at that stage in his life, was also a proselytizer for that cause. Sage pointed out that she didn't want to live in any community where she couldn't have a hamburger. Others felt that with a well-stocked river it was foolish not to eat fish, and that with so much land it was equally foolish not to raise chickens. Sean felt that hunting should be permitted as well, and that deer and wild pig should be consumed. The tension over this issue diverted attention from all other planning issues. I decided to let it play itself out as a way to introduce some theory and order.

First, everyone agreed that maximum self-sufficiency should be an overall principle guiding community planning. From there came the problem of hamburgers. Philosophical arguments about keeping cows, slaughtering animals for human purposes, beef and health, a good diet and the right to eat yourself into the grave went on for a few classes. Then Dominique raised a simple question: Could we afford cows? What would raising beef to feed the population cost by way of resources and the environment? I remember the students turning to me for an answer and I replied that we hadn't raised cows in the Bronx. Research was in order; we needed facts to inform our moral and philosophical musings.

A temporary working committee on cows was set up. I love to use temporary structures as in organizing my teaching. A small group for welcoming guests, a committee to solve a problem, a standing team ready to be the research branch for someone writing a paper, a temporary construction or model-building crew, a music or art brigade—all these temporary and usually invisible structures add to the whole group's learning resources. They also make it possible for everyone to have a chance to be the boss, the leader of a team, the expert in a particular task, or the director of a certain activity.

Josh and Ilana were assigned to call the California Department of Agriculture and find someone who could tell them about raising beef cows. Abel, Sage, and Dominique were to visit local dairy farms and find out how much land they used per cow and why they were in the milk business rather than the meat business. Sean was to call the Meat Council or the Cattlemen's Association or whatever professional organization he could find, explain our class project, and ask them what was needed for a cattle ranch.

I reminded the students that, if self-sufficiency was one of the main values in our community building, then they had to find out about fattening the cows, slaughtering them, distributing the meat, and so on. At that point I turned to the concept of wayfinding. This is a planning strategy that takes into account both the space in which an activity occurs and the time and processes it involves. When planning a football or baseball stadium, you have to plan for more than the playing field. Among other things, you have to consider how people will find their way from home to their particular seats in the stadium. The path from the parking lot to the seat, if not taken account of in the planning, can lead to frustration and chaos. The same is true in planning airports, transportation systems, and recreation and shopping facilities. One must be specific about such things such as what facilities are needed and how paths should be designed. Wayfinding also means paying careful attention to seemingly simple aspects of design such as where signs should be and how they should be designed.

I suggested that the concept of wayfinding should be applied to the production and consumption of beef and that we should draw a diagram of the path from a cow's birth to its consumption, noting all the facilities, resources, and processes needed along the way.

Pursuing the vegetarian wars was much more than a diversion. It gave the students content to wrestle with at the same time that they were struggling to define themselves through diet and philosophy. Food wars are not minor matters; people have killed each other over eating habits. Here was a concrete opportunity to integrate scientific information with struggles over health, style, and culture. The subject involved hard knowledge and research but was shaped by philosophy and tinged with passion.

Josh was set against killing cows, no matter what. This drove Sean, Amanda, and Sage to hard positions in support of beef. The food wars drifted over into culture and environmental wars—reggae versus country music, clearcutting versus sustainable-yield agriculture. We had some intense disagreements over these issues; I let them play themselves out, choosing an explicitly Socratic role for myself. I tried to question everyone equally and lead them to produce reasoned defenses of their positions rather than fall back on their emotions. I wondered whether there is a place in the strong vegan position for the possibility that plants have emotions and that therefore neither animals nor plants should be consumed, a consequence that would lead to lethargy and slow death for human society. To the beef eaters, on the other hand, in the wicked spirit of Socrates I raised the question of cannibalism. If people can't eat each other, what about eating pets? Or cute domestic animals they knew? Say, Wilbur the pig in *Charlotte's Web*?

The research proceeded as the arguments raged. However, we did finally come to an agreement, one which was very important for how the rest of the class proceeded. It was that we would honor the most current reliable factual information on a subject of our deliberations. We accepted the principle that scientific evidence had an important regulatory role in the development of ideas.

This decision, as obvious as it might seem, had important implications for our deliberations. First, it implied that we needed to do some research and find out what was known about an issue before we began arguing about it. Our food wars would have been much clearer, and perhaps resolvable, if we had known more about beef before the shouting began.

Second, it implied that we had to think about the reliability of information that claimed the authority of science. Are polls reliable? Does a medical or psychological test done on three people justify concluding something about how all people function? Does science extend to the judgment of quality in art, music, and literature?

The food wars led us to a short and profitable digression on the role of evidence in argument and the scientific grounds for making claims. We agreed that there were many arguments that could not be resolved by science or decided through observation, but that it was easy to get lost in vague argumentation or end up in shouting matches if evidence was ignored and research not pursued.

Awareness of the need to prepare for reasoned argument rather than simply fall back on emotion was one of the aspects of critical thinking I had hoped would emerge in class. I had prepared some wonderful curricula to illustrate this point later on in the school year, but our discussions over beef made them redundant. Once it's clear to me that students understand something, I try to move on to more complicated content rather than stick with plans or use prepared lessons, no matter how clever they are or how much time I've invested in them.

When the results of the beef research came in, everyone, myself included, was astonished by the quantities of land and resources needed to raise cattle for meat. It was clear that wooded areas would have to be cleared for pasture and for places to grow feed. The waste-management problem meant we had to plan for the protection of the streams. The squeeze on space meant that we had to cluster people, give up a diversified crop base, and devote a disproportionate amount of resources to beef processing and storage facilities.

On the basis of these facts, the argument over food changed. We would not have beef. But that didn't solve the vegetarian wars so much as shift the grounds of the argument. Sean, Amanda, and Sage, now with the agreement of Ilana, Oona, and Dominique, advocated for raising poultry and fishing as well as farming vegetables. Josh and Abel held out for pure vegetarianism in the community, though they agreed that research shows that well-managed fisheries and free-range chickens could contribute to the community's food self-sufficiency.

At this point Ian took over the Socratic role: So, what was the problem? Were Abel and Josh holding out as a matter of health? Or of some other moral stance? Abel held out for health. He was countered by many arguments about the nutritional value of fish and poultry. Josh had more metaphysical and spiritual arguments. The discussion was finally resolved by a question Oona directed to Josh and Abel. She asked them if they believed in democracy and went on to suggest that they were trying to turn the community into a dictatorship of the righteous. She specifically asked whether Josh felt he had a right to tell other people how to eat and whether he believed he could decide other things about people's lives against their will.

Josh backed down and the group agreed on a mixed food economy, referring the matter back to the economic and land-development subcommittees. However, I insisted we keep open the question of how far the community could go to restrict the rights of individuals. This issue became a central concern as we developed a bill of rights.

Before beginning work on our bill of rights and constitution, we read the U.S. Constitution and all its amendments, the French Declaration of Human Rights, and the United Nations Declaration of Human Rights, as well as several articles on the lack of a bill of rights in Great Britain. We also looked at Amnesty International material on human rights violations and studied the work of Amnesty. Some of the Amnesty national briefing books and case histories made very moving reading about the consequences of violating human rights.

In addition, we had the hearings on Robert Bork's nomination to the Supreme Court, which were broadcast live on radio, to dramatize the notion that political and judicial struggles over the meaning and scope of personal rights were living issues that affected the students' own freedoms. Actually the students didn't "have" the Bork hearings, except for Josh, who was part of our family conversations on the hearings. None of the others even knew there were hearings going on until I brought them up and had the class listen to testimony I'd taped from the radio. I was shocked at the indifference of the high school teachers and the larger community to such important matters; it took quite a bit of prodding and selective taping of the proceedings to convince the class that the Supreme Court was a living institution. Something at home, in their schooling, and in the media made government, in all its aspects, seem remote, hostile, and not worth knowing about.

The Bork hearings provided an occasion to help students develop and articulate their own views on rights, responsibilities, and the role of government. Bork has very strong and controversial views on the right of the government to regulate private acts and on the relationship between morality and government. I felt a strong need to inject the larger national reality into my students' lives. The Bork hearings were an ideal opportunity. I introduced a tape of a long session concerning sexual privacy, in which the question of the government's right to bar certain kinds of sexual activity was raised. Soon we were swept up into debates on abortion rights, gay and lesbian rights, and the role of government in guaranteeing health care. We even considered questions of whose obligation it was to financially support the rights granted to people.

It was interesting how, as the students discussed questions of specific rights, read human rights documents, and made up their own bill of rights, almost every subject in the regular school's civics curriculum description was covered, only in greater detail and with thorough and often passionate class involvement. The sixteen articles of the bill of rights the students developed provided a vision of a democratic society with participation open to all who cared to be part of the political process, and where the basics of a simple though decent life were guaranteed. This bill of rights interminged personal, political, and economic rights, with the economic component being much more prominent than it is in the U.S. Bill of Rights.

Our Bill of Rights

Article 1. Freedom of religion, press, speech, assembly, and petition.

Article 2. Freedom from unwarranted search or seizure of person or property.

Article 3. The right to a trial by a jury of peers who are registered voters.

Article 4. The right to breathe clean air.

Article 5. The right to be considered innocent until proven guilty.

Article 6. All persons of the age of seventeen and older may vote, and those younger who have successfully participated in a course in political awareness may also vote. Those however, who are extremely emotionally or mentally disturbed whose disturbance prevents them from having the ability to be politically aware cannot vote. However at any time they can take a course on the political and voting system and show they can understand the material they are eligible to vote.

Article 7. All people are equal and are to be treated in the same way by the community consistent with the rights and responsibilities spelled out in the Bill of Rights and the Constitution.

Article 8. The right to as much education in the field of choice as desired at public expense.

Article 9. The right to free birth control, abortion, and adoption with the infant's future secured.

Article 10. Freedom from slavery or involuntary servitude unless the service is the sentence by a jury for a criminal act.

Article 11. The right to free medical, dental, and orthodontic care, except for frivolous and unnecessary cosmetic surgery.

Article 12. The right to a private residence which adequately satisfies the needs of the household, at public expense.

Article 13. The right to unpolluted water and to food that meets nutritional needs at public expense.

Article 14. The right to free and safe day care for working parents.
Article 15. The right to care and a decent life for those unable to
   work for physical, psychiatric, or mental reasons.
Article 16. The right to freedom of movement within the community and to and from the community.

The making of this bill of rights coincided with the students'
discovery of themselves as citizens. Every article was cause for discussion, research, and reflection. It was fascinating to see the class raise
questions about county politics, examine the issues before the Point
Arena City Council, and talk about how they would vote and even
how they might more actively participate in government as they got
older. This curiosity led to discussions about national political issues,
about current happenings in the world. The class could go anywhere.
It was like Alder Creek during a winter storm.

Toward the end of the school year we held a constitutional convention. We had divided up the land and set up areas for agriculture;
for government and community affairs, including a center for the
arts and entertainment; and for dwellings. We had determined some
general principles of a mixed economy with a strong safety net and a
place for small businesses. The group responsible for public utilities
(roads, electricity, water, waste) decided to work with the housing
group and not put in a utilities grid until people decided where and
how they wanted to live. One of the main principles of community
design that the students came up with was that human issues, wherever possible, would determine design and the use of technology.
Thus, instead of putting in a sewer, electricity, and water grid first,
the students determined that housing choices would take precedence
and determine how utilities were organized. This is the opposite of
large-scale development principles, but is consonant with many of
the principles of appropriate technology, which we were studying.

In the course of the year, we did not try to plan a utopia but to
resettle real people, with all of their history of decent and imperfect
behavior. Therefore we had to deal with issues of taking in people
with criminal records; of dealing with people with AIDS; of whether
we wanted prisons, what substances to legalize, whether to develop a
police force, and how to deal with public safety.

The right to vote was one of the most difficult and contentious
issues we faced. The question of qualification for voting, which I

think was never fully resolved, had to do with whether people who didn't understand the political system and espouse the community's goals should have the right to vote. Some of the students held that would-be voters should have to pass a citizenship course; others objected that the class could be controlled by special interests. A few of the students wanted universal suffrage from the age of twelve, while others felt that there should be a cutoff age. The arguments over voting rights were the most charged we had all year. I think the reason was that the class consisted of people whose opinions, such as advocating pacifism and opposing U.S. support of the Nicaraguan Contras, caused them a lot of trouble from the many students at the high school who were less well informed and who took an unthinkingly militaristic and chauvinistic attitude toward anything Reagan's administration advocated.

The school year ended with a partially finished constitution. Here's what the students came up with:

Constitution

Preamble: Dear Reader,
It is not the intent of this constitution to tell you what to do or to suggest you live like the founding members of this community.

Act on your own consideration of each situation and change the rules when they become obsolete.

Always remember that everyone and everything deserves to be closely evaluated before being judged.

Most importantly, don't let anyone mess with you!

Section 1: The Structure of the Government
1a. There will be a local council consisting of 5 people for each 100 registered voters, to be elected by those voters. The local council will be determined on the basis of geographic proximity of the voters, and new zones will be created if the number of registered voters increases.

1b. Each 1,000 registered voters (10 councils) will constitute a borough. The borough will be governed by a legislative body consisting of one elected representative chosen from each council by the 5 elected representatives who serve in that council. The borough will consequently be governed by a body of

10 representatives each of whom is accountable to their own council.

1c. There will be a body entitled the FUNKADELIC which will make the laws and rules for the community as a whole consistent with the BILL OF RIGHTS and the powers reserved to the boroughs and other local political units. This body will consist of a congress of all of the borough representatives.

Section 2: Constitutional Conventions

There will be a constitutional convention every 5 years. Three representatives will be chosen from each borough and a two-thirds vote of the representatives is needed to pass a change to the original Constitution or to the Bill of Rights.

Section 3: Citizen Initiatives

Petition by 50 percent of the voters can put an amendment to the constitution or the bill of rights on the ballot. Two-thirds of the registered voters are required to pass the amendment.

Section 4: Any Violation of a Person's Constitutional Rights Is a Crime.

Section 5: A Vote of 2/3 of the Funkadelic Makes a Bill a Law.

Section 6: The Funkadelic Has the Right to Set Up Trade and Commerce with the Outside World.

Section 7: The Government Will Provide Protection for the People on a Community and Borough Level.

Public safety people will be accountable to the boroughs and the community at large. Police officers will be full-time employees that will be trained. Firefighters will also be trained but would work on a rotating basis.

Section 8: Everyone Accused of a Crime Will Be Entitled to a Trial by a Jury of Peers.

There will be a group of people called *mediators* who will preside over the trials and give a voice to all parties concerned. The jury will judge guilt and determine penalties.

This is one class that I have been able to evaluate, since I am still in touch with the students ten years after teaching it. Only one of the students lives in Point Arena at present. All say they are registered voters and have voted in local as well as national elections since they qualified to vote. They attribute their engagement, in large part, to many of the things we did and discussed in the class. All of them also claim that it played an important part in their intellectual development and connected them with learning and intellectual discussion in a positive way. It played a role in negating their alienation from education, and opened a number of them to continuing their education. Josh is a contemporary classical composer and conductor who lives in Seattle. Sean is a carpenter in Seattle. Abel does computerized comic-book coloring and his work has appeared in comics published by all the major comic book publishers. Oona is in graduate school. Ian is the drummer of a successful reggae band, and Ilana is a real estate agent. Dominique is a lawyer in Belgium; Amanda runs a nursery school. Sage is married and living in a small city about fifty miles from Point Arena.

I have described the work of this class to many teachers and administrators. One common response is hostility to the idea that what could be done with eight students in a rural setting, off campus and with no administrative constraints, is irrelevant to public education and particularly to the problems of urban schooling. Another response is a grudging acknowledgment that many of the ideas and exercises of our class are useful and that in minor ways they can be applied to enrich the regular curriculum.

However, over the years I've concluded that you take the teaching as the opportunity presents itself, that all young people have the same hunger to learn, and that good teachers can take a sensible idea and make it useful wherever they teach. One of my former students from Hamline University in St. Paul confirmed this about a year ago when he sent me a document from his Minneapolis junior high class. It was entitled "An Anti-racist Constitution: An Interdisciplinary Exercise on the Nature of Political Thought for Urban Middle School Students." I had shared my casebook with him and conceived of using the creation of a constitution and bill of rights to help students deal with issues of racism and political power. Here is a brief excerpt from one of the constitutions his students created. It illustrates that we do not know the limits of what young people can do and that it is up to us as teachers to push the envelope. Wherever you work, do something different when what is mandated does not work for the children.

The Preamble of Spenlin

We the people of Spenlin promise to serve and protect the citizens of our country. Our purpose of government is to make sure everyone is pleased with the job that the government is doing. We are a government that cares and listens to what the people say and want. In our government our power is split up, no person has the right to govern the whole government. The people in our society have civic virtue and will pay taxes. They will be good citizens. All of us here on Spenlin will protect each other.

Our collective view on what society should be like is:

1. People who are in gangs that hurt people will be put in a reform school.
2. For everyone to have equal rights and to be treated the same.
3. We will not have any pollution. All of our air, lakes, and rivers, etc. will be free of pollution.
4. Everyone will have a home, they will have a bed to sleep in, and a table to eat on. Everyone will have an education, at least they will have a high school education. No one will steal from one another. If someone wants something, instead of stealing it they should ask the person if they can borrow it. There should be no child abuse, or family abuse. Families will argue, but there will be no hitting. There will be no drugs, even if there is, people wouldn't take. It because they know it will kill them. No one will be an alcoholic. People can drink a few beers but no one will be addicted to it.
5. There will be no racism. Everyone will be treated equal and they won't be judged on what their race is. There will also be no sexism. It won't matter if you are a boy or a girl.
6. Our taxes will be lower than In America. People will have enough money to pay their taxes
7. We will lower prices on food so everyone has food to eat, will also lower prices on transportation and other things.

8. You must have a permit to own a gun. You must also have gone to hunting safety or to know how to use a gun, before you can actually own a gun.
9. The people in our country will be loyal, hardworking, they will pay taxes, and most of them will have civic virtue. Overall they will be good citizens.
10. Every one will have a Job so they can have money. If they have money then they can have a home and food.

CULTURE SKIRMISHES

It is easier for creative teaching to flourish in kindergarten than in college, though teaching five-year-olds is no less challenging than teaching twenty-year-olds. When I taught kindergarten in the 1970s and again in the mid-1980s, class time was mine to shape; the content of learning could be almost anything that engaged the children in reading, math, science, and the arts. There was no pressure for tests, and time was available for discussion and play for its own sake.

The transition to first grade, however, meant a major change in structure and the demands on teachers and children alike. Test results and specific increments of achievement became overriding concerns. Each subject had to be given its proper amount of time. The first and last day of the school year had to be equally crammed full of doing. And compared to the flexibility still left in teaching elementary school, where you have your own classroom and can close the door and shape things more flexibly than the lesson plans suggest, college teaching is an enormous challenge to the creativity of any teacher.

In college you don't have your own classroom and have no walls to decorate or space to leave things behind. In the humanities there are no lab centers where experimentation and play can take place. The bells ring and classes change even more relentlessly than in high school; students learn to expect little of their teachers. With the notable exception of some self-motivated lovers of learning, students tend to feel on trial all the time. Self-esteem is tied up in every little response, and for some students the fear of failure is so great that it paralyzes all creative activity.

Yet these days, college teaching—that is, working with young people in their late teens and early twenties—has become a delight to me. I feel drawn to it as I did to teaching fifth and sixth grade in the early 1960s. It may be a matter of age. My own children are all out of college, but I spend time with them and their friends and am intrigued and impressed by how they are trying to make sense of the cynical times in which they are growing to adulthood. Their company is a challenge and a source of renewal for me. And I recently realized that my sixth-grade students were closer in age to me in 1962 than my current college students are. Consequently I teach college with the same energy, curiosity, and commitment, though with more craft, than I remember having when I taught at P.S. 103/79.

In the spring trimester of 1995 I taught a class on multicultural education at Carleton College in Northfield, Minnesota. There were fifty students in the class, mostly juniors and seniors, and about a third of them were young people of color. The students all brought to the table their own vision of what culture meant and their own strongly held views about the value of multiculturalism.

When Judy and I arrived on campus in late March, we walked into a university-wide event that transformed my expectations for how the class would be structured. The experience was the equivalent of meeting Larry and reading Fred's Leibowitz essay at P.S. 103. Charles Murray had been invited to the college to talk about his book *The Bell Curve* (coauthored with the late Robert Herrnstein) and discuss it in a public forum with the African American psychiatrist Alvin Poussaint. There was a campus uproar. A number of faculty members objected that Murray's scholarship was questionable and the conclusions he drew about the intellectual inferiority of African Americans as a group were racist. They said that the university should not dignify his work with a public debate. A group of students were even more forceful in their objections to Murray's appearance on campus and had formed a group to plan a response to it.

Many of the college's students of color were furious and felt pushed out of the college community. The anger was not limited to African American students but was felt just as keenly by Latino, East Asian American, and Asian American students. They claimed that by paying Murray (whose lecture fee was rumored to be $20,000) to appear at a campuswide event, the administration was calling into question their status as legitimate members of the college's intellectual community. The pain felt by many of the students, who said they were deprecated as affirmative-action babies no matter how well they performed in class, was intensified by the event.

Certainly I could not avoid dealing with that issue in my class. At the same time, I did not want to make Murray the topic of my class. So, in the few days before the class began, I looked at my reading list, restructured the order of the readings, and planned a responsive class that would deal with complex issues of multiculturalism and not get lost in the general tension created over Murray's visit. Murray's visit did have one bonus: the issue of racism was on the surface when I arrived at Carleton, and no preliminaries were needed to tap into my students' fears, rage, confusion, and despair.

I began by assigning a paper designed to evoke a personal rather than an academic response. I wanted my students to understand that, from whatever background, ethnicity, or class they came, they were all products of respective cultures in which they were raised. I wanted to establish at the beginning of the class, in a way that students would internalize, the idea that multiculturalism was not the study of "them," the minorities, by "us," the majority. For the majority students, the idea was to level the field, so that every student would think about herself or himself as culturally shaped and realize that the culture she or he belonged to was no more permanent or special than other cultures. As for the other students, I wanted them to see themselves as parts of a whole, not separate from it or marginal to it. And for all the students, more than any other thing I wanted to hear their voices—not in academic prose, but with the inflections and images of their childhoods. I hoped that the responses would have the power and conviction of the P.S. 103 "My Block" essays.

The assignment was to respond to the following:

> Remember yourself as a young child before you ever went to school. Think and write about: how you learned to ask questions, what kind of questions you asked, and how the people around you answered the questions you raised and asked you questions in return.

I explained that the responses could be written, taped, painted, sung, danced, or collaged. I also made it clear that I would react personally to the students' work, and not with a grade. Given that Carleton is a school where there is a great deal of competitive academic pressure, it was clear that the students would suspect my motives. Their entire college experience had taught them to feel that I had some ulterior intent and was testing them in some subtle way. I wasn't. The educational studies department had agreed to let me deal with student evaluation in nontraditional ways; I had decided that every student would begin with an A and would have to do some pretty irresponsible things, such as fail to turn in papers or to make any effort to write well or to attend classes, to unearn that grade. My preference would have been to eliminate grades altogether and enter into an agreement with the students that they had to attend classes, do the reading, and submit work in order to get credit—period. The rest would be dialogue and response. However, the A was a concession to Carleton's system; as it happened, several students did work their way out of that grade.

My major goal was that the students grapple with issues of multiculturalism and racism on both a personal and an intellectual level, and that they come away from the class with informed opinions on cultural differences and the problems of social cohesion in our society.

Several of the students were bold. I got one taped response to the question, one collage, and several illustrated essays. The rest of the fifty-two students wrote papers, which took hours to read and respond to. I had underestimated the time commitment it would take to teach this class well and respond to the voices of all my students. However, reading these first papers was like being let into the lives of fifty-two interesting and complex people whose ideas and opinions had to be taken seriously.

I shared the papers with Judy just as I had shared the papers of my thirty-six students in Harlem; our conversation enabled me to think through how to respond both to the voices of my students and to the issue of racism, which informs all attempts to discuss multiculturalism but is not identical to it. Here is one of the responses that provoked thought and conversation throughout the duration of the class:

A Childhood story to treasure

Ge Vue

Growing up in a refuge camp along the border of Thailand and Laos, I remembered sneaking out onto the porch at night to sit on rice sacks with other children from the village and listened to folktales that men young and old were telling. Some of them were great orators and told elaborate tales about ghosts, love, wars, and broken promises. Other story tellers tend to be more cunning and told series of funny tales about a goofy but extremely intelligent court jester who constantly made a fool out of the emperor by playing tricks on him. Yet, others would recall tales about the innocent sufferings of orphans. In a rigid clan system where one's worth was measured by the size of one's clan and the parent (more specifically the father) was one's intrinsic link to the community, an orphan child with no parent was disconnected from the community and dangled at the bottom of the social status. However, because of the orphan boy's kind heart, Shoua, the all powerful being who overlooked all living creatures on earth rewarded him with a beautiful wife and riches. Although the orphan boy tales always have a happy ending, such tales would grab me and drown me in my own sopping nonetheless. I was about four or five years old then, but I already could locate myself in the stories because many of my village friends whom I played with every day lost their father in the war. Although my family was "safe" in the refugee camp, every day my dad still attended meetings with the Nationalists who were determined to regain the home country back. As a child with a wild imagination, it frightened me to see my dad leave every day; for I feared he may not return.

I don't remember the exact circumstances surrounding this story I am about to tell. May be my brothers and I got into a fight so Dad set us all down to tell us this tale so we would understand the power of kinship. May be Dad noticed my weeping eyes one morning as I watched him leave and told me this tale to comfort me. May be he thought that as a quintessential five year old, I was old enough to internalize something consequential or as the feeble child who was deprived of his mother's milk, I must learn to be astute. Whatever the reasons, this is the tale Dad impart with me when I was a little child.

There once was a huge elephant. He was the biggest, "baddest," most feared creature in the jungle. Where ever he went, animals, trees, and rocks would move out of his path. Because the elephant was so powerful, he became very arrogant and all the creatures of the jungle despised him. Every day, the elephant would marched tall and proud through the jungle recklessly knocking trees down and ripping branches from here and there to eat. One day as the arrogant elephant was about to tear a branch off with his powerful trunk, he heard a mother bird cried out from behind the leaves.

"Mr. kind elephant! Please don't eat the branches from this tree. My little baby birds have just hatched and they are too young to fly to safety. If you eat this branch, my nest will be knocked down and my fragile babies will surely die. There are many trees in the jungle and around you that are just as good or better than this one. Please spare my babies and don't eat this tree. If you must, at least wait a few days until they are strong enough to fly away."

The mother bird pleaded and pleaded with the elephant, however, being such a pompous elephant, her persistent pleading only infuriated him more. He was the king of this jungle, yet this frail, tiny bird was trying to tell him what he should and should not do. Furious, the elephant torn the whole tree down and stumped on the mother bird's nest killing all her babies. Horrified but helpless, all the mother bird could do was weep and weep.

When the father bird came home and saw the mother bird weeping, he knew what had happened and tried to console her, "Please stop crying. Your tears cannot bring them back nor will it solve anything. I have a friend who might be able to help us. Why don't we go find him instead."

So the mother gathered herself together and they both flew out to find their friend, a large bird with broad, powerful wings and could see far and sore high—a falcon. When they told the falcon their story, the falcon was appalled but she was not surprised because she had heard of this elephant and the atrocity that he has committed before. The falcon was very eager to help them and told them that she has another friend who would willingly help them too once they told him their story. With that the falcon brought them to another bird.

This bird was very colorful and had a very sharp, sturdy beak which can peck holes in the toughest tree in the forest—a woodpecker. After the mother and father bird told the woodpecker about the elephant and what had happened, the wood-pecker also acknowledged that he knew that contemptuous elephant and would be more than willing to aid them.

The woodpecker also had a friend who shared their griev-ance and he was confident his friend would help them too. Thus the woodpecker led the mother and father bird to the edge of a pond to meet his friend—a big, fat, and ugly frog. After hearing their tale, the frog agreed to help them and also introduced them to yet another friend, a fly this time.

So between the five of them, they devised a plan. The falcon with her keen eyes and powerful wings soared high and far to search for the elephant. Once she located the elephant, she flew quickly back and tell the group. The woodpecker then sneaked upon the elephant and with his sharp and fierce beak, pecked furiously at both the elephant's eye blinding him. Next, the fly flew over and laid hundreds of tiny eggs on the elephant's bleed-ing eyes infecting both immediately. Blind, terrified, and in pain, the elephant rampaged aimlessly throughout the jungle. After the elephant was worn out from his reckless running, the frog hopped to a steep cliff and began croaking loudly. Upon hearing the croaking sound, the elephant was misled to believe that there was water nearby. Remembering how thirsty he was, the elephant rushed toward the croaking noise. Instead of finding water to quench his thirst however, the elephant plunged to his death instead.

At different stages in my life I find myself reflecting back on this tale. And each time, the story takes on new meaning. The true power of stories does not lie solely in its context. Stories are powerful because they are personal. When someone imparts with you parts of his life experience, when he shares with you something from his heart, it touches your heart. Words especially when spoken eloquently as story tellers often can do, paint images in your mind that are difficult to forget, and therefore you will always remember a tale once it touches you.

The papers made it clear that, across culture and class, all of my students had raised questions when they were children. This seems like an obvious fact, but the ability to question can be honed and encouraged or manipulated and diminished. In some children it can even atrophy or become latent, only to explode later in life when the whole world can seem meaningless and the question of the value of life itself becomes urgent.

Childhood questions are often attempts to understand patterns in the world. As those questions were answered (even silence is a kind of response), a view of the world begins to take shape, not merely in the answers adults provide, but in the way they provide them. In addition, the students not only asked questions and got answers but themselves contributed to shaping and interpreting the responses. However, self-questioning skills rarely become central to the process of formal or informal education. Culture, with all of its strengths and biases, as well as its bonding and alienating characteristics, is most often antagonistic to questioning itself. And yet understanding the role of culture in one's life and the subtle ways in which every person, above and beyond her or his individuality, also filters the world through unquestioned cultural modes of perception is central to cross-cultural understanding and communication. The study of multiculturalism—to say nothing of the forging of ties across cultures—has to originate with the continual and profound questioning of culture, one's own as well as other people's. And this requires specific attention to the skills of questioning and to the development of an awareness of others as questioning beings who are trying to understand the problems of your culture while you question theirs. I wanted to complicate my students' understanding in order to open the door for them to communicate across cultures. To do so required that each student feel that her or his voice would be heard in the class.

Culture is not a matter of something some people have and others don't. We are all accculturated. Developing an understanding of this was a central goal of my class, and meeting it was more difficult than I imagined.

In the days before my class began I asked several white Carleton students not in the class what they thought multiculturalism was. The responses ranged from "the study of minorities" to "how we [the white majority] relate to people who are different" and "how to get rid of prejudice toward them." These responses were given by intelligent, sensitive, academically sophisticated college students. Despite their success at a very fine college they had a blind spot toward their own cultural identity and its place among other cultural identities. Because of this, they framed the dialogue about multiculturalism in us-them terms, with the "us" an unquestioned given, under assault by a "them" that had to be studied, understood, or placated. This was very different from the situation in the sixties, when many of the white youngsters I taught felt they were on the side of "minorities" and in struggle alongside them. Now the situation has shifted to a subtle yet nevertheless distinct sense on the part of most of the white students I worked with, including liberal ones, that there is an opposition and antagonism between them and minorities and that they are the ones under siege.

One student in my class at Carleton failed to show up for discussions or hand in assignments but tried to get credit by writing a long paper at the end of the semester. In the first paragraph, the student defined multiculturalism as the study of minorities. To avoid misconceptions like that one, my idea for the class was to explicitly introduce the proposition that everyone has culture, and that people make and transform culture over history. That meant being able to question culture and understand its development and modifications. Events like the Murray presentation were cultural and had to be examined in their cultural and historical context. Certainly it made sense to respond to Murray on a personal level. However, to refine that response with a cultural analysis of how Murray's presence at Carleton fit into current cultural, political, and economic skirmishes made more sense for a class whose goal was to understand multiculturalism and the nuances of racism. Murray's presence was an epiphenomenon, an event on the surface of deeper cultural disturbances that we had to understand. Setting up for the students a context in which Murray could be understood without letting the class be dominated by that event meant introducing students to the idea of multiple narratives—that is, to the concept that cultural actions and historical events are often viewed through the dominant culture, in what the scholar Nathan Irvin Huggins has called "the distorting mirrors of truth."

Huggins's work tried to correct those distortions with a call for an African American narrative view of American history to inform and correct the distortions of a European narrative. My goal was to have my Carleton students understand and articulate their own narratives and begin to find a way to do what could be called narrative shifting: looking at the same events as if they, the viewers, were culturally other than who they are. This might mean, for European

American students, attempting to understand Latino or African American narratives, and for African American and Latino students, trying to understand the many faces of white narratives (labor, women, poor whites, the wealthy, Italian or Jewish Americans as well as Scandinavian Americans, and so on).

The goal was to understand that there is not one way to look at events in the world, not one single history, but rather a multitude of possible narratives within which history is created and judgments of events and people are made. I wanted my students, for example, to think of statements such as "The 1950s were the best times in U.S. history," "American children have too many possessions," and "In the past, the schools taught all children to read and write" from within different narratives. Was a given statement as true for African Americans in the South or poor whites in Appalachia as for white middle-class Americans? What could it mean to Latinos or Japanese Americans on the West Coast? How did it privilege one narrative and neglect others? And how does a consideration of multiple narratives modify the kinds of statements one makes about events?

This was not to say that all narratives are equally valid, or even that within one cultural group there is a single narrative. Rather, my goal was to help people see that within our society, composed as it is of many peoples from many different cultural traditions, understanding cannot come from within a single narrative perspective, and therefore complex thinking and shifts of perspective are essential tools of intelligent living.

My first assignment achieved two things. First, it got me engaged in the lives of my students. They were all interesting, and that made it impossible for me to fall into the mistake of saying "The white students think this" or "The Latino students think that." It also gave me a sense of the diversity within the class, a diversity I wanted to emphasize rather than minimize so that the students would feel how strong the pull of their own culture is despite how neutral they may think themselves.

Second, the assignment got students to write in their own personal voices rather than the academic voices they used for their other classes. Carleton teaches its students academic prose quite effectively, but there is a danger of loss of voice when all the writing one does is confined to a nonvoiced genre. The papers provided a way for my students to learn to write about ideas in intelligent, sophisticated, and at the same time personal ways.

I responded to the papers as a whole in class, trying to portray the range and variety of responses. Some students' papers indicated that their parents encouraged them to ask any question whatever; others were told that they should keep their questions to themselves. There were cultural clusters among the personal responses, but these did not diminish the power of the individual responses so much as add an illuminating cultural dimension to our analysis of the work.

Since this was a class in multicultural education and many of the students intended to become teachers, I tried to connect everything we did in class to similar things they might do at work. With respect to this assignment, I also suggested that when they became teachers they think of how groups of papers as well as individual student assignments can be pedagogically interesting, and I pointed out that a powerful teaching technique is to give a general response to a set of papers as well as individual responses to each student.

I intended to write extended personal comments for each student and suggested we reproduce and share all of the papers. Two unexpected events intervened. My mother died after a long and difficult illness, and I had to go to New York for the funeral. I simply could not concentrate on the students' writing enough to make fifty-two individual comments, though I was able to do that later in the semester. Also, we had an unanticipated blowup in class after the Murray lecture. A student group opposed to his visit held an alternative event at which staff and students spoke out about issues of racism and provided a critique of Murray's scholarship. In my class, several of the white students who had participated in the alternative event mentioned that it felt wonderful for them to be able to express their concerns about racism in public. Several others said that they believed Murray's presence on campus was healthy because it forced many students who avoided the issue to think about racism. At this, several students of color exploded, expressing rage at the idea that it was acceptable for an academic forum to consider whether people of color were inferior. They accused the white students of expressing liberal racist ideas, of believing that the university existed for the pleasure and intellectual delectation of whites at the price of the dignity and self-respect of people of color. One of the students suggested that the white students wouldn't need to confess their own racism or proclaim their antiracist sentiments if they had the guts to directly confront the racists on campus.

Just before the end of the class I jumped in to say that the most important thing about what was happening at that moment was that the wounds of racism on campus were open and bleeding: since racism was a poison in the system, we had to let the bleeding continue, keep the issue open, throughout the year. The pain everyone in the room felt had to become the generative source of learning for that class. I stuck to my private resolve that despite evidence to the contrary prejudice is a disease curable by good teaching.

I was both troubled and relieved by what had happened in class —troubled because of the pain expressed by the students of color and misunderstood by most of the white students, and relieved because having a problem on the table is always better than having it hidden and unspoken. As a class we had a common experience, one to reflect upon from multiple perspectives but nevertheless to come back to as a group. It was a bond that I had to figure out how to use positively.

A few days after the blowup in class, two white students—the students who had said they felt that Murray's visit was a good thing for the school—came to see me during office hours. They told me that they felt silenced, not only in my class but in many of the classes they took. And they wanted me to know that they weren't racist, but that they did feel that all views should get an airing. We discussed the difference between all views being expressed and examined and one view being given institutional sanction. However, these students' problem was much larger than Murray's visit.

Like many other white students, they felt, and then allowed themselves to become, silenced. The silence led to resentment and suspicion, and my intuition was that these in turn would plant the seeds of racism.

Not all of the white students shared this experience. A few had fought explicitly against racism in student groups and had consequently developed friendships across ethnic boundaries as well as confidence in dealing with issues of racism.

On the other hand, the students of color who had reacted with such vehemence also felt silenced and discriminated against; they spoke their minds only when they were pushed or felt safe. A number of students of color expressed exasperation at having to live with the presence of race and ethnicity as an issue. They wanted to be *students,* to learn chemistry, biology, and literature, but found themselves de-personalized, picked out in class to speak as representatives of their group or asked to listen to white students' confessions of confusion over issues of race. They sensed the uneasiness of many of the white students, and some faculty as well, who acted as if students of color were not members of the college community. Thus they felt a con-stant strain on their ability to function well academically (though a number of the students in my class managed to graduate Phi Beta Kappa and with high honors).

The issue of race and ethnicity affected everyone, yet there were few explicit discussions of racism at the college. As a visiting profes-sor, most of whose teaching time is spent with younger people in urban public schools where integration is not an issue and never was, I was surprised and troubled by this sad tension between white students and students of color. I have since discovered that the situa-tion I found at Carleton is common at colleges and universities across the country: interesting and lively young people act stereotypically because they have no precedents for dealing with the issues of race, and no older people around who had such experience either. Most of the professors were as inexperienced and frustrated as their stu-dents; they simply wished the problem would go away, perhaps even wished that students of color would simply disappear from their classes.

It was not a situation of the guilty and the innocent, the right and the wrong. I saw the situation as a trap that inhibited learning and led to unspoken hostility and unarticulated self-doubt for just about everyone. By taking the position of being explicitly and unambigu-ously opposed to racism in all its manifestations, I adopted a goal that was perhaps impossible to achieve.

I knew how to provide an environment in which students who felt stigmatized by racist attitudes would feel safe to learn and free to express what they thought and felt. I also knew how to pick up signals and gestures and read faces, a skill that enabled me to mini-mize hurts and to tease responses out of shy and reluctant speakers. While I knew how to create dialogue over sensitive issues, I did not yet understand the specifics of why the white students acted so threatened or why they allowed themselves to be passive in the class and yet walk away still feeling in control as soon as they left the classroom and could avoid students of color.

In the case of my class at Carleton, I first had to overcome my ignorance of what the students, and especially the white students, were thinking. The chat I had with the two young women who had welcomed the Murray visit affected me profoundly. One of them believed she understood the effects of racism and was not in any way a racist herself. She felt attacked and intimidated by the students of color and those white students who supported the alternative event, even though no one had said anything directly to her. The other young woman was angry, as a woman and as a scholar, at being silenced by anyone. And yet both of them admitted that they had learned to stay quiet whenever such issues arose in "mixed company"; they informed me that what happened in my class, even though I went out of my way to ask people to express their feelings and opinions, was no different. Yet they did come to me, and I listened, not knowing what to do but understanding a need to rethink once again the nature and structure of that class with those particular students at that moment in the history of their educational careers and personal development.

Understanding the need to make such adjustments and to shape the content of a class to fit the pedagogical needs of the moment as well as the demands of the subject is what I have come to call situational teaching. Situational teaching requires a teacher not only to plan the reading and the organization of content, but also to raise and find tentative answers to the following questions: Who are my students? What is happening in the world, the nation, the community, and the cultural and social lives of the students that can be brought to bear upon their mastery of the subject? How can the class help develop the students' minds, their imaginations, and their ability to deal with complex issues as well as hone their skills?

In referring to how works of art develop, the painter Ben Shahn said, "I would not ordinarily undertake a discussion of form in art, nor would I undertake a discussion of content. Form is formulation —the turning of content into a material entity, rendering a content accessible to others. . . . Form is the very shape of content." *

* *The Shape of Content* (the 1956 Norton Lectures at Harvard), Harvard University Press, 1956, p. 53.

I remember sitting in the Hayes Bickford Cafeteria with Shahn and others very late at night, sometime during Shahn's residence at Harvard that year, and discussing the meaning of that last line: "Form is the very shape of content." We dealt specifically with the applicability of that idea outside the arts. I was curious about whether form, in that sense, was essential to the expression of a philosophical position or the development of a mathematical idea. Ludwig Wittgenstein's *Philosophical Investigations* had just been published in English, and many of us in philosophy were trying to get through the puzzle its form provided. The book consists of loosely connected paragraphs clustered around themes or ideas, punctuated with aphorisms, enigmatic statements, asides, and anecdotes. The whole was an attack on the very enterprise of philosophical system building, and its form embodied that intention. In mathematics, we were studying Gödel's incompleteness theorem; its form, too, could be interpreted as the shape of its content.

Shahn was intrigued by this notion and suggested it could be taken even further into the realm of process. Could the form of a society be meaningfully interpreted as the shape of its cultural content, or the form of history and economics be meaningfully studied as the shape of material content? No conclusions were drawn, but the phrase "Form is the very shape of content" has stayed with me over the years and helped me conceptualize some of the educational work I do.

Situational teaching involves the shaping of content. It means taking the particular subject one is teaching, or the theme or problem one is addressing, including all the texts, information, and resources available, and creating an educational form in which that content is embedded in the lives and concerns of the students and in the social, cultural, and historical situation in which one is teaching. The goal is to shape the class so that life and learning are convergent and students' voices and responses contribute to the specific way in which the subject is examined.

In the case of my multicultural-education class at Carleton College, situational teaching meant finding a form that would allow students to express their own understanding of multiculturalism, feel free to articulate their views on race and culture, and begin to communicate across culture. Consequently I decided, for the first half of the course, to deemphasize the question of teaching multiculturalism and concentrate on the nature of culture and the ways in which racism functions in our society. Murray was the negative experience that framed the class, and I wanted a positive one to balance that. Fortunately, during the spring of 1995 there was an exhibit at the Walker Art Museum in Minneapolis entitled "Asia/America: Identities in Contemporary Asian American Art." Judy and I had visited the show and were moved by the range and variety of expressions about being Asian in the United States that the artists conveyed. There were sculptures, constructions, environments, paintings, illustrations, and multimedia installations. The artists' families had originated in Southeast Asia, India, Pakistan, China, Japan, Korea, and the Philippines. It was impossible to stereotype the art or the artists. The diversity of response to the American experience was compelling and complex, full of bitterness and hope, disappointed expectations, experiences of racism, material success, and cultural devastation—as well as cultural affirmation.

What was perhaps most lacking in the experience of almost all my Carleton students—a lack that contributed to their difficulty in communicating with each other across cultures— was lifelong friendships with people who were culturally and ethnically different. The great majority of white students had come from homogeneous communities where neither they nor their parents had friends of color. Some of the students of color had lifelong white friends, but most of them had grown up in barrios or ghettos with few white residents or none. As a group, the students in the class were victims of residential segregation. The opportunity to communicate with peers whose experiences were different first arose in college.

My white students in particular—and perhaps the majority of white teachers in the United States—were likely to continue the patterns of segregation in their residential and social life after college, even if they ended up teaching in schools where the students were predominantly children of color. As I saw it, developing peer relations across ethnicity was the major educational challenge in my class, not learning techniques for teaching what the African American scholar Lisa Delpit called "other people's children."

Judy suggested that the exhibit at the Walker might help all the students approach cross-cultural understanding. Many of the artists in the show belonged to the same generation as my students, and all of them spoke about part of the experience of being American in the

1990s. I arranged for the class to visit the show. The assignment was to go through the exhibit three times, first looking at all of the works without looking at titles or reading any accompanying material; second, reading all the annotations and the artists' biographies; and third, looking for one piece that spoke to you particularly intimately. After choosing a piece, the students were to sketch it, not with a view to the artistic quality of their own work, but to become more familiar with what the artist was doing and saying.

To judge by my students' responses, the experience created the opening I wanted. We discussed some of what people saw and felt, and I tried to get the class focused on the effort it takes to listen when you feel attacked. Specifically, I wanted to develop the idea that what people hear, they filter through their experience. There are times when people who come from a dominant culture and people whose lives have been characterized by oppression or inequality have different perspectives on the same conversation or lecture. What are cool intellectual discussions for some people are matters of respect and dignity—even life and death—for others.

The museum experience was a beginning. However, I still had to do more to understand my students and help them learn how to listen and learn across cultures if they were to become good teachers. Consequently I decided to have an hour's talk, individually, with all fifty-two of my students.

These conferences paid off in ways I had never anticipated. A theme common to many of the white students was their anger at being held accountable by many of the students of color and some of the "radical" white students for the racism of the past. They did not feel guilty about what had happened before they were born and did not believe they themselves were racist. They hated being called "white students," which is just what I'm doing here. In a society in which race is so intertwined with identity and every aspect and detail of life, it's impossible to deal with some issues without categorizing people, and yet to be put in small boxes is infuriating to the people so categorized.

Many things that white students did or said were perceived as racist by students of color, sometimes creating impossible binds for both. For example, if white students claimed that they understood the experience of African American or Latino students, they would be considered racist for assuming the ability to fully comprehend the nuances of the injuries of race. If, on the other hand, they said they didn't understand, they would be accused of indifference to and complicity with racism.

Often the students of color complained that they were constantly being asked about race and told how welcome they were at Carleton, with the underlying assumption that they were guests at a white institution. Either neglected or overindulged, they felt that they were always on display.

Two of the most poignant conferences occurred on the same morning. One young African American woman, Roberta, told me that she had grown up in Scandinavia and attended international schools with the children of diplomats from all over the world. She had not experienced racism, having grown up with diversity and equality among people with power. Her first U.S. experience was at college, and there she learned what race meant in America. For the first six months she was shell-shocked. She had not been a participant in racial politics before; at home she had been looked upon not as a minority but as an American among Europeans. It was hard for her to learn that she wasn't considered the full equal of white Americans. Roberta had come to college to be a *student,* but found herself forced to be a *student of color.*

After that conversation I wasn't prepared for what Michelle, a European American student, brought to the table. She had grown up in a welfare family that struggled to get her to a good college. At Carleton she became painfully aware of what it meant to be poor among youngsters of privilege. The other students made simple assumptions about being able to afford to hang out in restaurants, go to the theater, or buy new clothes or CDs. That Michelle could not afford these things separated her from the majority of Carleton's students, a very affluent group. She resented some students of color —who, she felt, trivialized the things she had to go through to make it at college and acted as if they were the only ones with difficult lives. At the same time, she expressed personal abhorrence of racism and complained about how frustrating it was to be unable to be understood and to focus her opposition to racism on some common struggle. She had discovered, through the responses of the students of color, that she was "white," and was annoyed by the label.

Michelle wasn't alone in being angry at discovering that she was "white." Many of the students had come from upper-middle-class white communities. Before they reached college they had never been identified ethnically or racially. They were simply "normal" and were always treated as individuals rather than as members of a group. Initially, they welcomed the diversity at college as a way of broadening their experience. However, in considering themselves as "normal" and students of color as "different," they fell into the trap of treating students of color as less than individuals, as exotics to be encountered as a learning experience. I heard white students refer to other students as "African American," "Asian," "Asian American," or "Latino" with no self-consciousness and yet take umbrage at being called "white." They didn't understand that placing themselves outside so-called multiculturalism and creating a fictive zone of normality is a form of racism.

During the many hours of conversation I had with my students it became clear that all of them were pained not only by issues of racism but by issues of categorization in general. For many of them, college was the first time they found themselves forced to deal directly with some of the contradictions of class and culture inherent in American society.

One of the hardest things for the white students to deal with was that they were beneficiaries of white privilege, which manifested itself most notably in their being considered as individuals and allowed the freedom of casual association and easy access to community resources. Many had a hard time understanding that not being treated in a special way was a privilege.

One particularly sensitive young man confided to me that he was feeling intimidated because of his conservative Christian beliefs. He was opposed to racism on strictly Christian grounds. I found his argument compelling and his efforts to speak out admirable. There was a general attitude at the school that Christianity did not have a place in discussions of serious intellectual issues. I hoped, in a small way, to provide an opening for his voice. We had a number of conversations about the relationship between religion and politics, and I came to respect the sincerity of his views despite my fundamental disagreement with the substance of much of what he believed.

Perhaps the most difficult meeting I had was with an African American student who was not a member of the class but came because he had heard from other students that it was okay to talk with me. All he wanted was for me to listen to what was happening to him in an advanced physics class. Until the Murray lecture he had been doing fine, struggling along through the problem sets like everyone else. Since the focus on *The Bell Curve,* he'd found that despite the strongest resistance he could muster, when faced with a difficult problem he began doubting his own intelligence, and found himself giving up rather than diving in as had been his habit before. The debate itself had eroded his confidence and invaded his consciousness. He wanted to be reassured that he wasn't going mad with rage and self-doubt. I listened and tried to reassure him, though with what effect over the long run I can't predict. But the horror of it is still with me.

None of my students was explicitly racist, and I believe that every one of them believed in the possibility of a multicultural society at peace with itself. However, they had no way out of the social and cultural traps of a racialized society. We, as a group, had to work our way out of racism to multiculturalism, and that is what I tried to help students do, both in the private conversations and in class.

Learning how to say what you actually feel and mean is difficult when so much of speech is judged and monitored in school. A high regard for the content of what you say is one route to effective communication. As the class progressed, I could see students both slowing down to think about what they contributed and becoming bolder and more willing to take a stand they felt comfortable defending. I encouraged the students to open themselves up to criticism and opposition. My feeling was that if they couldn't feel safe disagreeing in the classroom, where else would they feel safe making public statements that might oppose popular thinking?

The goal was to deal with fear and rage, to allow fear to be expressed and rage channeled into intelligent argument. I wanted the class to become a forum for airing the most sensitive issues of race and culture, which are so dominant in education these days. And, indeed, I felt that the silence of some of the students was slowly being broken, while the rage of others was beginning to be understood as well as expressed in ways that opened rather than closed dialogue.

Then came the bombing of the Murrah Federal Building in Oklahoma City, and the ugly face of racism became public once again. One of the students, Irum, who was a Pakistani American Muslim, came to the class distraught. I feel terrible classifying her in such a cold way, but it was precisely because of those classifications that she was so enraged. The first response to the bombing was that it was done by "Middle Eastern Muslim terrorists"—and Muslim Americans, no matter how long their families had lived in the country or what part of the globe they had come from, were the enemy, strangers, not "real Americans." So it wasn't only me who turned her into a "Pakistani American Muslim," but also the media and the other students.

Irum picked up on other students' responses, listened to the newscasts, and then had to endure the incredulity of the same people when they found out that the act was done by a "real American." Whether or not the terrorist was a Muslim, she *still* wasn't a "real American." When we discussed this she screamed at the class, "I'm sick and tired of people asking me where I'm from. I'm from Des Moines, goddamm it!"

The other students could not ignore this outburst. We all had distinct and explicit proof of how the representatives of white culture manufacture and perpetuate racism. The challenge to everyone was to feel the world as Irum felt it at that moment, to understand what it was like to be a Muslim in the United States, to be of Pakistani origin in the United States and immediately become defined as the other, one of "them" rather than one of "us." There is no way of soothing these wounds.

I was lucky enough to have many conversations with Irum during my time at Carleton and to work with her on issues of racism within the sciences. She graduated Phi Beta Kappa and summa cum laude, so obviously she was not crippled academically. It was her heart and soul that were assaulted, and my concern was to offer her support and work with her against racism. My hope was that many of the other students in the class would analyze their responses and stand with her. I also hoped that in the future, no matter what their careers or vocations, they would choose to fight against racism and embrace multiculturalism. Ultimately, of course, this was their choice and nothing I could—or would even want to—compel.

Throughout the changes that happened during the trimester, the class still covered the reading list I had planned at the beginning (and I added a few essays that seemed particularly relevant). I kept on coming back to the central concepts that I had intended to teach. We explored the meaning of culture, the complexities of communication across cultures, the complex of culture, class, and ethnicity, and the interplay between individual voices and cultural conventions. Toward the end of the class we considered how to use the process the class had been going through in an elementary or secondary classroom, and how to design a school.

The class ended as an unfinished conversation. We didn't solve the problem of racism or figure out the best possible way to teach multiculturalism. But I felt, at least, that we had achieved the goal of opening up serious educational discussions on the nuances of multiculturalism and the problems of class and race. It's up to the students to evaluate the effectiveness of the experience. I came away with great respect for how all of these young people wanted to face and overcome the most intractable problems within our society.

"To the Foot from Its Child": Teaching as the Discipline of Hope

·The child's foot is not yet aware it's a foot,
and would like to be a butterfly or an apple.

—Pablo Neruda, "To the Foot from Its Child"

Six years ago I walked into Bronx Regional High School in the Fort Apache section of the Bronx. The principal, Mark Weiss, had invited me to observe his school. I have to admit the main enticement he offered was not the school visit but the promise that on the way home he would drive me past the house I grew up in and give me a chance, for the first time in twenty-five years, to see my old Bronx neighborhood.

Mark is one of the most welcoming people imaginable. His face is open, his presence expansive, and his spirit antic. He has a story for everyone, and even if it's often the same story you believe he is telling it for the first time and only for you. This holds for the tales he tells his students as much as for those he tells teachers, other administrators, and visitors to the school. I loved the tales, but something else impressed me more. Coffee, doughnuts, and bagels were set out in the hallway for anyone who wanted them—not just in the teachers' room or the principal's office. The students were treated like adults worthy of comfort and respect. Mark and I waited at the door as the students entered. He greeted each new arrival and embraced at least half of them. Most of these youngsters had troubled school careers and had come back to this school for a last shot at hope. Some had clearly had bad nights, others bad nights and days.

When one young man walked in looking ready to kill, Mark excused himself and put his arm around the student's shoulder—a remarkable feat; very rarely will volatile and enraged youngsters let you touch them. Trust had made it possible for Mark and the student to adjourn to the principal's office for a chilling-out talk. Later that morning I conducted a class and encountered the same student. By that time he had settled down and was articulate, intelligent, and self-disciplined. In many other schools he would have been turned away rather than welcomed.

The human quality of the life at that school—across the street from a crack house, around the corner from burnt-out though partially inhabited buildings and empty lots shared by garbage, rats, and children at play—spoke of hope, of a belief that no matter what the students' past school experiences or their current lives were like, education could have a redemptive value and learning was still possible. As in the Neruda poem "To the Foot from Its Child," at Bronx Regional students were free to look at the raw material of their lives and their past failures and to dream, to embrace the possible rather than become resigned to roles other people expected them to play in the future because of their past failures.

After an exhilarating day teaching and observing at Bronx Regional, Mark kept his promise and I did have a chance to see 1696 Grand Avenue again. The numbers my grandfather had embossed on the glass over the front door in 1939, when we moved in, were still there. And the house looked exactly as I remembered it, only smaller and more vulnerable. It was surrounded by a barbed-wire fence and there was a sign posted next to what used to be the living room window, where my grandmother watched over us when we played stickball out on the street. The sign announced that the house had become a Baptist church, a sacred place. Across the street, where most of my friends had lived, was a six-story apartment building, half burnt out and half in the process of being rebuilt.

I could infer a history of despair and an awakening of hope in my neighborhood—fire and reconstruction. I got to speak to some older members of the church that used to be my home and they seemed delighted that I was a teacher, that I cared about children. They, like my grandparents—perhaps everybody's grandparents— dreamed the world through the eyes of the young.

Mark had another agenda, and taking me home was part of it. He knew that, though I have lived in California since 1968, I'm a New Yorker, and he wanted to get me involved with public education in New York City once again. The question was how to craft a useful role in yet another attempt to make public schools work for all children.

This role emerged slowly as I commuted from California, con- necting with old teaching friends and making new ones. Continuity, change, and continuity—as the poster I received from teachers in Paris in 1968, which still hangs on our kitchen wall, says, "La Lutte Continue": "The Struggle Goes On." A number of teachers I had known for years and who now had a bit more power than we had had as teachers in the early 1960s suggested that it was possible to find support for me to spend time back in New York and help people who were creating new secondary schools from scratch within the New York City system. Mark is one of them and is now the principal of the new High School for the Physical City.

I had to invent a role for myself and to think through, once again but in different social and historical circumstances, how to educate children who have been failed by their schools. Over the years my fundamental conviction that all children can learn has been strength- ened by the results I have seen, both in my work and in the work of other teachers. Balancing a return to New York with writing, while still working with children at my home, has not been easy but, just as I did as a child, I want it all. At this stage of my development as an educator I believe that it is possible to play many roles simultaneously and be effective in all of them.

"Playing roles" in the development of good education is one instance of the central theater metaphor that is at the root of much of my thinking on education. If schooling can be thought of as a performance, a drama and a comedy and a historical pageant all at once, then the creation of new schools, new performances, requires a redefinition of the traditional educational roles. We have to figure out new ways to support innovation that acknowledges that, no mat- ter how well thought out, well researched, or well funded a plan is, the test of its effectiveness is within a community and with specific students who have their own ideas about their lives. My experience has led to the conviction that even the most carefully designed and innovative schools, if they are not self-critical and built for self-modification, will fail.

There is a theatrical role that has recently emerged as useful for the success of performances, a role that crosses old boundaries and creates new responsibilities and relationships among all the people involved in a production. This role is that of the dramaturge. A dramaturge assists in any way possible or useful and works with all of the parties involved in the development of a performance. Ideally, she or he works with everyone from the producers, writers, directors, and actors to the set designers, lighting technicians, costumers, and stagehands to enhance their information and knowledge and provide critical feedback about the current state of the production. The goal is not to judge or evaluate the performance but to help things succeed. I am comfortable doing that kind of thing in education, especially with new schools and with new educational ideas. However, in order to play the role of dramaturge you need an open-minded cast, a support infrastructure, and a desire for success on the part of everyone involved, from the district office to the community, the teachers, and (most of all) the students. Making education work is a collaborative enterprise, in which there has to be a shared interest in the success of all the children rather than a sorting system based on adversarial relationships.

I thought it might be possible, in the context of building new public schools in New York and transforming schools elsewhere across the country, to craft a role for myself as an educational dramaturge. That meant being a critic and a resource in the service of improving a school; a researcher at the service of the teachers; a friend and counselor; a provocateur who scares up new and unusual educational ideas; a listener and friendly observer who helps develop resources for the school, focuses on danger points, praises strengths, notes progress and process, and at times teaches as well. That last was essential—being in direct contact with the children and never forgetting that we are there for them.

To my surprise, there were people who felt this idea was worth investing in. So I began another adventure in New York, which is still continuing. My first teaching experience in one of the schools plunged me into the cold deep waters that I love. It must have been ten-thirty in the morning when I was directed into a class to teach, to show my stuff. I knew that I would be observed by the teachers and administrators and that unless I could hold my own with the kids—could be interesting to them and not be intimidated or demoralized by their resistance to anything I might offer—respect for my work as an educator would simply not develop at the school. People who spend every day in the classroom have a healthy suspicion of all experts who try to tell them how to do their jobs but who could not survive a month in the classroom doing what they preach.

As I walked into the room one of the students jumped up and called me almost every name imaginable about being white and an oppressor and told me to get the hell out of his classroom. I had heard such words before and knew they had nothing to do with me; he didn't know a thing about me. I figured he might be a leader, so it would be good to win him over. He looked at the other students while he was carrying on, so I guessed that his confrontation was more theatrical than a matter of out-of-control rage. Admittedly, this was a judgment that I could make only from experience and that involved risks. So I said, loudly at first but then bringing my voice down so that everyone would have to listen:

"What if I were here to deliver a check for a million dollars, like in one of those shows on television? What if you were the one it was for, and you treated me the way you just have? What would you do?"

I waited and after a few seconds he responded, "I wouldn't talk to you. I'd just get out of here."

I said I wasn't going to leave and didn't have a check for a million dollars either. But, I pointed out, he didn't know what gifts I was bringing and it might make sense for him to give me a chance before calling me all kinds of white people. I told him he might be right, but at least he ought to be sure he wasn't making a mistake that might hurt him.

Rather than wait for him to respond and (consequently lose dignity by being forced to back down in front of the class), I reached into my pocket and pulled out the first object I found. It was a barnacle I had taken off the tail of a dead whale that had washed ashore about five miles from Point Arena.

I always stuff my pockets when I go to visit other people's classrooms. That day I had, in addition to the barnacle, a miniature deck of cards, some little plastic action figures, about ten of my favorite poems that I had had made into a tiny booklet, and some wire puzzles. You never know when you'll need an object or a poem to change the focus of attention, illustrate an idea or story, or otherwise provoke learning in some way.

Instead of the check for a million dollars I showed the class the barnacle and asked the students what they thought it might be. Then I handed it to the student who had challenged me and asked him to pass it around the classroom. I also mentioned that it was valuable to me and hoped he would keep an eye out to see that I got it back at the end of class. This was simply a way to get him to be with me and part of the process and get him out of the problem that he had created for himself.

Everyone welcomed the release of tension. As the barnacle was passed around, the students speculated on what it might be and where it could have come from. They figured out that it was a shell, and they had heard that I come from California so they guessed I found it on the beach. I said yes and no, that I had found it on a dead creature that had washed up on shore. One of the young women in the class shouted out that maybe it came from a whale, and everyone laughed. I said she was right, and we took off on a discussion of whales. We had set off from New York and traveled beyond racism and anger into the curious and wonderful things the world has to teach when the students' minds reach out beyond their wounds and their rage. That is the very source of hope—that we can create places where young people can dare to dream without being brought down by the realities of their terrible experiences in schools and by an adult world that dares them to succeed rather than welcoming their energy, love, and contributions.

The last question the class asked me, after inviting me to return, was, "How do whales make love?" I didn't know, and suggested that from both scientific and poetic perspectives we might all benefit from the answer. Our parting arrangement was that we share our information about the love life of whales during our next meeting. The original question may have been facetious, but, as in all teaching, it's what you make of the question, not its specifics or its original intent, that leads to the learning.

I did return to that school, and still visit as an occasional dramaturge, helping with curriculum development, sitting in on project planning meetings, helping in problem-solving sessions, and whenever possible working directly with students. I also work with other new schools in New York as well as with schools throughout the nation. The schools are not all cut to the same model. Some are academically oriented; others are centered around the arts or based in community partnerships.

In Brooklyn, for example, the El Puente Academy for Peace and Justice involves an N.Y.C. Board of Education collaboration with El Puente, a Brooklyn-based, predominantly Puerto Rican community organization. El Puente is based in an old church building that serves as a community arts, economic development, youth leadership, health, and recreation center. The high school shares space with the health and arts programs, so people of all ages are constantly present at the school.

And some of the high school activities merge seamlessly with community-based activities. For example, there is a toxic dump in the neighborhood of the school, and struggles to clean it up and to document and help people poisoned by the toxins are part of the work of El Puente. The school's environmental education and youth leadership programs are, naturally, part of the effort. What is even more inspiring, El Puente is the only human rights–based high school in the United States, and as such provides a bold model for the reshaping of the curriculum to encompass abiding worldwide issues as well as local ones. Through human rights the school consciously addresses the discipline of hope, which is at the center of teaching.

These are not easy times in which to keep hope alive in poor or even middle-class communities. The most common question I am asked these days is whether the schools are worse now than they were when I began teaching. My answer is no; they are just about as bad. But now there are more local efforts to provide decent schools based on the notion that all children can learn than I have ever seen before. Unfortunately, the world beyond the school is much harsher toward children, much more cynical about the future, and much more indifferent to those children who do not have privilege, support, or special gifts that will enable them to succeed. The ordinary child, my child, your child, our children have a much harder time of it than I have ever seen before, and their needs are not being met by most schools.

And yet I have hope—hope that we will look intelligently at what *is* working, especially for poor children, and learn from those special places how to shape learning for children in the spirit of hope. I hope that we as adults will then make it our business to transform society into the place of hope that we have prepared them for.

A common characteristic of all these schools and educational programs, which I call schools and classrooms of hope, is that staff, parents, and community are in common accord that every child can learn. They all see their role as making the doable possible, and this is reflected in how their students come to believe in themselves as learners. This is in contrast with the majority of schools for the poor, where the staff is demoralized and projects the belief that only a small number of the children can learn. In such schools the community and parents are often considered the enemies; this turns the school into a sad, isolated place that perpetuates failure.

Schools of hope are places where children are honored and well served. They have a number of common characteristics, no matter where they are to be found across the country. They are safe and welcome places, comfortable environments that have a homey feel. They are places where students can work hard without being harassed, but also places where the joy of learning is expressed in the work of the children and in their sense of being part of a convivial learning community. They are places where the teachers and staff are delighted to work and are free to innovate while at the same time they are willing to take responsibility for their students' achievement. If you talk to children in schools like these, they express a pride of place and sense of ownership that are also manifest in how the rest of the community regards the school. Parents feel welcome and often have a role in school governance. Community volunteers are abundant. Hope, projected primarily through the children's learning, is also manifest in how the physical environment of the school is treated with respect.

We do have many schools of hope across the country, and many teachers who try to build classrooms of hope within more hostile and indifferent schools. It is essential to seek out these places, to support them, and to learn from them. Simply acknowledging that there are places where public education works is not a formula for school change. Besides, particular formulas do not work anyway. You have to know the community you serve, know what you want to teach or need to teach. You have to understand the times in which you work and your responsibilities as a citizen to fight for your children. Most of all, you have to love to be there with them, have to be delighted in their presence and feel the awe at their growth that any gardener does in experiencing the unfolding of a beautiful flower or the emergence of a delicious fruit or vegetable. It takes hard, careful, loving work to nurture hope and bring learning into the school—but what a birthing, what a pleasure, what fun despite all the struggles. And because teaching is so full of love, so hope-centered, and so difficult, it is also one of the most painful vocations. Despite the best teaching and the most passionate learning, this society has a way of wasting young talent. To teach well and care about the children has a double edge that keeps one militant as well as romantic, that tempers what you know children can do with worry about what might happen to them after school, on the streets, in the job market, and in their own personal lives.

About four years ago Rick Fine, a student leader at Other Ways and an African American student who walked across all boundaries and commanded respect from all of us, came to visit Judy and me in Point Arena. He arrived with his wife, their baby, several tapes, and a long manuscript. Rick had a story to tell us. He had just escaped from crack, and the voyage was partly due to Other Ways. That's what he wanted us to know: that we provided the kind of strength he could call upon when he had hit bottom and almost forgotten who he was.

The first thing he had to tell us was what the descent was like. Rick had become a computer programmer and was just about to purchase his own home and get married when he encountered crack. It wasn't the crack itself, he explained, but the pain and struggle it relieved, that first took him in. The struggle to get to where he was, to deal with the constant pressure of being considered a "Black" programmer rather than simply a programmer, of always feeling on trial and knowing that even if he succeeded he wasn't respected by his co-workers, made him come home from work every day on edge, feeling that he was where he aspired to be and nowhere at the same time.

Not everyone in Rick's situation descends into despair or imagines that she or he can take a little relief from crack and survive it intact. What is essential to understand, and what Rick helped me understand, was that he only wanted a little space away from the pressure, and instead found himself in the belly of a beast.

Rick escaped crack through music, writing, and meditation, but first he had to leave his community. He explained that he knew too much about the wholesale and retail aspects of the crack trade to be physically safe if he straightened out: as those in the trade saw it, there was always the possibility that he might turn that information over to the police. So when he decided to kick the habit, he moved to another community and used the skills he had acquired from us and in college to get a job and settle into a simple ordinary life. For him, as the Shaker hymn says, " 'Tis a gift to be simple, 'tis a gift to be free."

Rick felt that at Other Ways we had helped him learn how to discipline himself to write on a regular basis in his own voice, to think about the decisions he made and the decisions he had to face, and to use his music as a medium for meditation. It seemed to me that he had learned a little piece of each of those things from different members of the staff. He also knew that our doors were always open to him and that we would not reject him if he got into trouble or tried to hurt himself.

Rick's story about overcoming crack was tempered by other tales he told of successful former students losing jobs, family, and homes to the epidemic. Some of them had died young. I was struck once again by how close to despair and the streets people are when there is no fundamental community coherence, and by how teaching cannot be the only thing. We also have to be advocates for adult decency if we are to truly serve our students.

The vulnerability of Rick's friends is centered around a rage and depression that I believe can only be cured by living in a world without racism. I know it is unfashionable to blame the behavior of African American people on the racism of whites, but my experience is that racism in both personal and institutional forms frames the lives of many of my current and former students. In California, if they look Latino they have to prove that they are not in the country illegally; if they are African American they have to prove that they are not violent. It is always a matter of proving yourself to white people. Even in the college classes I teach, the gap between the students of color and the white students is a problem I have to deal with before I can get us to function as a respectful learning community.

Rick isn't the only Other Ways student I've run into recently. About a year ago, Chris and Julie, now happily married, drove up in their camper. On the top were a kayak, suitcases, and what looked like a picnic table and folding chairs. Julie had been a member of the guerrilla theater troupe and was now a member of Actors Equity. Chris was a nationally ranked nineball player who was on the Professional Pool and Billiard Players Association tour. They traveled together, Julie performing in professional theater productions and Chris playing tournaments. Chris used to bring his pool cue to school every day and take off around eleven in the morning. He convinced me that two and a half hours a day was all he wanted to spend at Other Ways, since his real learning came from the old pros who practiced in the pool halls in the late mornings before the customers came in. Chris developed a personalized vocational education program for himself, and so far it has paid off in his adult life.

I've also run into a number of former students from New York, Berkeley, and Point Arena. Some are doctors and scientists, some political activists, and others lawyers. Some run small businesses and a few work for large corporations. One is an organic farmer. There are a number of actors and musicians, some artists, a few computer scientists. Peter is an independent TV producer. Agnieszka is an opera singer, Jena a painter, Sean a guitar maker, Phil a professional master of theater rigging, Laurie a community organizer, Chiori a journalist. Justin is headed for a career in professional baseball. Many of the young people I have taught are now teachers themselves. And just last summer a young woman came up to me after I gave a speech at a teacher-education college in Tacoma. She told me how excited she was about becoming a teacher, how she was inspired to teach by her own high school English teacher, who gave her a copy of *36 Children* as a graduation present. That caring teacher was Rachael, one of the thirty-six children herself. The young woman concluded by saying that she considered me her educational grandfather. I prefer to think of myself as her child, a new learner who looks to the young as much as to the tradition to engage in the continual renewal of educational ideas and practice.

The hundreds of young people I have taught do dozens of different things, and it is a delight to see many of them embodying the central driving ideas of my life's work as an educator: that everyone can learn; that you can become the person you want to be and do work that you love; that whatever you do with your life, you can also do things for others; and that being thoughtful and possibly controversial and unpopular can be morally more sensible than being passive and conforming.

There are many things I hope to do with children over the next fifteen or twenty years. I still don't know how children learn to read, even though I can teach them to do it, so I hope to learn more about the actual process. I would like to teach calculus to six-year-olds and nonlinear differential equations to eight-year-olds; introduce particle physics and complexity theory into the elementary school curriculum; create and test science and math programs, beginning in kindergarten, that are based on how contemporary scientists work and think —that is, I want to incorporate technology, mathematics, genetics, and the interdisciplinary sciences such as biochemistry and physical biology into children's ways of thinking from the beginning of their formal schooling.

I would also like to create a watershed curriculum based on a study of the history, nature, and future of the places students live in and the dreams they can develop about convivial communities; set up hundreds of poetry and writing groups of the sort I've been doing for years and continue to do; direct a production of *The Tempest* with five young theater troupes, each working on one act, each act set in a different time and place but with color-coded costumes, and each group working independently of the others and then coming together to perform the entire play; and create an extracurricular high school arts and math program that takes up as much time and excites as much passion and commitment as athletics and in which students regularly travel to other schools to participate in the arts.

Those are just a beginning. I would like to work with other teachers to develop a pervasively diverse and excellent literature curriculum that integrates reading, writing, thinking, and discussion and connects them not to critical theory, but to everyday life, personal identity, culture, and community; to set up a school and teacher-education program centered on social justice, the arts, literature, and modern science and mathematics.

Finally, and most centrally, I would like to understand more about how to deal with youth rage and violence and try to use this understanding to make life more nurturing for my students. I would like to create a diverse, compassionate, nonracial community of learners where students honor themselves, respect each other, love what they are learning, are passionate about justice, and prepare themselves for compassionate, connected adult lives. To paraphrase Neruda, I wouldn't mind being a butterfly or an apple—or, even better, a gadfly or a mango.

With these, as with all of the challenges of teaching and learning, I'm looking forward to beginning again. There's no end to the delights and joys of teaching, no limit to the challenges we will continue to face in order to serve children well, and no limit to the creativity and love adults can and should bring to helping children grow through teaching, which is at its heart the discipline of hope.

Acknowledgments

It is impossible for me to list all of the people whose lives have touched mine over the past thirty-six years and whose words and actions have been an inspiration to me. I want to thank all of my students and those educators I've worked with who have committed their time, effort, intelligence, and love to their students. Knowing these wonderful people keeps hope alive in difficult times.

As this manuscript has developed over the past few years I have had the good fortune to have conversations with many educators, community activists, and parents. A number of them have read all or part of the manuscript at different times during its development. Their criticisms and support have been indispensable throughout the long and not always easy process of trying to record my life as an educator. I thank all of the people who have helped me think through these complex issues and whose work has informed my thinking. Rather than risk leaving someone out, I hope they will understand this general statement of gratitude.

I want to specifically acknowledge my agent, Wendy Weil, who has seen me through almost all of my writing adventures and has provided advice, succor, and plain good company. I also want to thank my editor, Alice Mayhew. It has been a pleasure to work with someone whose literary intelligence and editorial wisdom have pushed me to the current limit of my writing ability. Lisa Weisman has also been a gentle though demanding editor, and this book is much the better for it. I believe that the kind of editorial attention

Alice, Lisa, and their colleagues at Simon & Schuster gave to this book is all too rare in the publishing industry these days, and I am grateful for our relationship.

The names of my students have been changed throughout the book in the interest of protecting them. Descriptions of some of the schools and circumstances have also been modified, but everything I've written represents, to the best of my ability and memory, the substance of my educational work. Teaching and learning are at the center of the stories that make up this book.

I want to thank the following for permission to include their work in parts of the book: Ge Vue and Joshua Kohl for their essays; Al Young for "For Poets" (© Al Young, 1971); Victor Hernandez Cruz for "After the Dancing" (© Victor Hernandez Cruz, 1967); the New York Times Corporation for an article dated September 17, 1963 (© New York Times Corporation); William Rukeyser for "Fable" (© Muriel Rukeyser, 1967); Grey Fox Press and Guy Davenport for two lines from *Herakleitos and Diogenes,* translated by Guy Davenport (© Guy Davenport); Curbstone Press for an excerpt from Otto René Castillo's "Before the Scales, Tomorrow" (© Curbstone Press, 1994); and Grove Press and Ben Belitt for two lines from Pablo Neruda's "To the Foot from Its Child," translated by Ben Belitt (© Grove Press, 1974, © Ben Belitt 1974).

Finally, I want to thank my children, Tonia, Erica, and Josh, and Josh's wife, Haruko, for their support and for the examples they provide of what a decent future might look like. They, and of course my wife, Judy, are my primary sources of hope, and I hope I am adequate to the depth and quality of their love.

Index